Sunni → believed any good Muslim could be ¼
the next Khalifa. Sunni's won.
(Both continue to fight ever since.)

Shii (Shia, shiite) → believed the next Khalifa
should be related to Mohummead so
Ali and his sons should rule next.

America + China + India = 3 biggest
oil consumers

The oil will not last forever
which is why Solar power/wind power
are a possible answer to sustainability.

D0392305

ENGAGING THE MUSLIM WORLD

JUAN COLE

palgrave
macmillan

ALSO BY JUAN COLE

AND AVAILABLE FROM PALGRAVE MACMILLAN

Napoleon's Egypt: Invading the Middle East

ENGAGING THE MUSLIM WORLD
Copyright © Juan Cole 2009.
All rights reserved.

First published in 2009 by PALGRAVE MACMILLAN® in the United States—a
division of St. Martin's Press LLC, 175 Fifth Avenue, New York, NY 10010.

Where this book is distributed in the UK, Europe and the rest of the world, this
is by Palgrave Macmillan, a division of Macmillan Publishers Limited,
registered in England, company number 785998, of Houndmills, Basingstoke,
Hampshire RG21 6XS.

Palgrave Macmillan is the global academic imprint of the above companies and
has companies and representatives throughout the world.

Palgrave® and Macmillan® are registered trademarks in the United States, the
United Kingdom, Europe and other countries.

ISBN-13: 978–0–230–60754–5
ISBN-10: 0–230–60754–3

Library of Congress Cataloging-in-Publication Data
Cole, Juan Ricardo.
  Engaging the Muslim world / Juan Cole.
    p. cm.
  ISBN 0–230–60754–3
  1. Islamic countries—Relations—United States. 2. United States—
Relations—Islamic countries. 3. United States—Foreign relations—2001–
I. Title.
DS35.74.U6C65 2009
303.48'21767073—dc22

                                                              2008032388

A catalogue record of the book is available from the British Library.

Design by Letra Libre

First edition: March 2009
10 9 8 7 6 5 4 3 2 1
Printed in the United States of America.

CONTENTS

The Middle East

INTRODUCTION

The Muslim world and the West are at a standoff. Westerners worry about terrorism, intolerance, and immigration. Muslims are anxious about neoimperialism, ridicule, and discrimination. Distrust between North Atlantic societies and the Muslim world has skyrocketed in the twenty-first century. Two-thirds of Americans admit to having at least some prejudice against Muslims. Nearly half doubt the loyalty of American Muslims to their country, and a quarter say they would not want a Muslim as a neighbor. A majority of Britons blame Muslims for not integrating more fully into British society. A slight majority say that Muslims have enriched British culture, but over a third disagree. A fear of terror plots emanating from a handful of radicals, along with apprehensions that Muslims want to impose their mores and religious law on the British, has led to a great increase in the number of Britons who consider themselves "threatened by Islam." That these attitudes and tensions are not inevitable is demonstrated by the difference among Western publics in this regard. The French public, for instance, obviously does not blame Algerian terrorism in France on Islam, but rather on politics and economics. In a 2006 Pew poll, some 65 percent of the French said that they had a very or somewhat favorable view of Muslims, a higher figure than among Americans that year.[1]

Suspicion is rife among Muslims, as well. Majorities in Middle Eastern countries such as Egypt, Turkey, Iran, and Palestine said in a 2007 poll that they believe the West is not committed to better relations with them and that the West disrespects Muslims.[2] Yet both the publics in the West and in the Muslim world emphasize that good relations with one another are important to them.

I have watched with dismay as the rhetoric about Islam and Muslims has become more strident, and as misinformation and disinformation has proliferated. Clerical leaders on both sides have stoked the fire. Pope Benedict XVI held Islam up as an example of religious fanaticism and intolerance, and Ayatollah Ali Khamenei, the Iranian theocrat, calls down imprecations on the West nearly every day. Secular politicians have also poured oil on the fire, whether former New York mayor Rudy Giuliani with his insistence on tying the religion of Islam to "terrorism," or Iranian president Mahmoud Ahmadinejad, complaining endlessly of what he calls Western "decadence" and its allegedly pernicious influence on Iranian youth.[3]

As I've glared at the self-appointed "terrorism experts" who have paraded across my television screen since 2001, I've became more and more alarmed at the dangerous falsehoods many of them purvey. Most of them have no knowledge of the languages or cultures of the Middle East, or any history of residence there. The message of the right-wing pundits and pastors and politicians is that Muslims form a menace to the West unless they are subdued and dominated. In that sense, the military occupation of Iraq that began in 2003 exemplifies the mind-set of American hawks. This policy of confrontation and, frankly, of neocolonialism poses the direst of dangers for the United States and for the world. It is a policy for the most part pushed by the ignorant and the greedy, the ambitious, or the paranoid. It is a policy issuing from the darkest corners of the American and European soul. These militant attitudes and the constant demonization of others—mirrored against the West in radical states in the Middle East—have ratcheted up conflict between the West and the Muslim world. When did Americans begin saying again, after the successes of the civil rights movement of the 1960s, that they do not want to live next to other Americans of a different race or faith?[4] Or that some Americans should be singled out with a special form of identification? Those are the sorts of sentiments being voiced against Muslims in many quarters.

This standoff concerns me on a personal as well as an intellectual level. I have been engaging with the Muslim world since 1967, when my father was sent by the U.S. Army to Kagnew Station, a base outside Asmara, in what was then Ethiopia and is now Eritrea. As a teenager, I first got to know Muslims while living in the Horn of Africa, where I heard languages such as Tigre and Arabic spoken. Later, I lived in Muslim societies for nearly ten years, learning several languages widely used in the region. Although my interests were mainly in early modern and modern history, I worked for a newspaper in Beirut in 1978–1979 and all along have had a keen interest in current affairs.

The 1970s and 1980s were formative for many of the Muslim movements still with us. I lived through much of that history in the region, as a student, English teacher, translator, and researcher. I saw some of the early years of the civil war in Lebanon, met and argued with Salafis (Sunni revivalists) in 1976 in Amman while an auditor at the University of Jordan, visited South Tehran with friends and saw a burned-out apartment building alleged to have been bombed by the Mojahedin-e Khalq (MEK) terrorist organization. I lived in Egypt in from 1976 to 1978, when Ayman al-Zawahiri's group, the Egyptian Islamic Jihad, first became notorious. I was translating Arabic articles on the Iranian revolution into English in Beirut in 1978 and 1979, and saw the Lebanese Shiites begin to mobilize (a Shiite demonstration almost made me miss my plane when I left Beirut in the spring of 1979). In the 1980s I was in India and Pakistan off and on, and traveled up to Peshawar to talk with the Afghan mujahideen not knowing at the time about the Arab volunteers, some of whom later became al-Qaeda. I witnessed the massive food riots of 1977 in Cairo and the 1986 riots of the security police (many of whom had been assigned to guard opulent tourist hotels while being paid pennies a day by the government).

I saw with my own eyes the rise of fundamentalist and radical movements in the Muslim world, but living there, I also gained a sense of proportion, understanding the significant differences among them and which ones were important. As an established academic in the United States, I have continued to travel extensively in the region and am struck by how rooted contemporary crises are in developments I saw firsthand in those earlier decades. Through my studies of classical Islamic civilization, I gained a profound appreciation for its beauty and grandeur. But I developed a deep personal dislike of Middle Eastern[5] fundamentalisms (meaning scriptural literalists, who are not necessarily violent), and was more than once inconvenienced or even menaced by them. That I should now be urging understanding of and engagement with a wide range of Middle Eastern political forces, including fundamentalists, signals not an agreement with them but a pragmatic conviction that as citizens of a single globe, we have to settle our conflicts through dialogue.

The momentous events since September 11 brought me into national prominence as a commentator on Middle Eastern affairs. In addition to giving television and radio interviews, since spring of 2002, I have kept an Internet political diary, or Web log, on current events in the Muslim world, in which I parse and interpret news from the region, often translating from the regional press published on the Internet. "Informed Comment," my Web log, made a breach in the Ivory Tower and has allowed me to interact with a canny public interested in my perspective. This book only rarely incorporates material from that political diary or from my fortnightly columns at Salon.com. Rather, it has been written afresh, as a coherent work in its own right. Inescapably, it sometimes treats at greater length and with more reflection themes first broached in the Web log.

In this book, I examine the myths and realities that provoke Islam Anxiety in the West, and the grounds, legitimate and illegitimate, for America Anxiety in the Muslim world (and often in the rest of the world, as well). The substantive sources of this rising Islam Anxiety are not difficult to find. As you will see, there is a feeling that Muslim states have a stranglehold on the petroleum and gas essential to the lifestyle in industrialized democracies. Furthermore, many intellectuals and politicians have confused political Islam with radical extremism. The Wahhabism of Saudi Arabia and its influence on Muslims outside the kingdom has seemed increasingly ominous to some observers given that Usamah Bin Laden hailed from that country. The calamitous Iraq

War, with its proliferation of Muslim resistance movements and massive violence, has inspired fear and despair in Western nations. The resurgence of the Taliban and even of al-Qaeda in southern Afghanistan and the tribal northwest of Pakistan is of special concern to NATO countries, which have committed nearly 70,000 troops to the task of defeating them. And the Shiite Iran of the ayatollahs, with its extravagant and threatening rhetoric, its alleged ties to terrorism, and its determination to close the nuclear fuel cycle, inspires consternation in Europe and the United States.

I believe that the pressing conflicts between the North Atlantic nations and the Muslim-majority ones can in most instances be resolved more successfully by engagement than by dirty wars and covert operations. By "engagement," I do not mean surrender or accommodation. I mean critique as well as dialogue, pressure as well as basic human respect, sticks such as sanctions as well as carrots such as better diplomatic and economic relations. I mean the demotion of military response from favored tool to last resort. I do not underestimate the challenge of radical Muslim fundamentalism but simply note that guerrilla wars have almost never been won by simple force of arms. Rather, they are generally resolved by negotiation and political compromise. And finally, I believe that the Muslim world, and its significance to the rest of the globe, is so vast and complex that reducing engagement of it to a myopic focus on a small set of ephemeral guerrilla movements is shortsighted and counter-productive. And so it is that this book explores not only security issues in the relationship between North Atlantic and Muslim-majority states (as represented by NATO and the Organization of the Islamic Conference), but other dimensions as well—energy, climate change, the media, and the implications of Muslim and Western public perceptions of one another.

In fact, the rationale for analyzing these two worlds separately can itself be questioned—they permeate one another and cannot be thought of as necessarily in opposition, although obviously there are major issues that divide their politics and public opinion. The historic 2008 American presidential election underlined the way in which the North Atlantic and Muslim worlds are intertwined. The new president of the United States, Barack Obama, unites within himself American and African Muslim heritages. The day before he was elected to the highest office in the land, his maternal grandmother, Madelyn Lee Payne Dunham, who had cheered his campaign from her sickbed, died in Hawaii. A Methodist of English, Irish, and German heritage, she was born and raised in Kansas. On the day that Obama became president elect, his paternal grandmother, Habiba Akuma Obama, held a celebration in her village. A Muslim woman of the Luo tribe, she was born and raised in Kenya. Political commentators regularly portray Obama's mixed heritage as unusual, and in his first news conference as president elect, he referred to himself as a "mutt." In fact, we all live in the same world as Obama, a globalized world of multiple influences and heritages. We are all "mutts," both genetically and culturally. Recognizing the degree to which we are intertwined and depend on one another, across cultural and geographical divides, for our future prosperity and even survival is the key task of the coming decades.

CHAPTER I

THE STRUGGLE FOR ISLAMIC OIL

THE TRUTH ABOUT ENERGY INDEPENDENCE

Among the major drivers of Islam Anxiety is the dependence of the United States and its major allies on petroleum and gas produced in the Persian Gulf. As the twenty-first century unfolds, and as oil producers with shallow reserves exhaust them, and as those producers with growing economies export less and less, the world will increasingly depend on Islamic oil. The United States' status as a global superpower was built on the basis of cheap energy, including coal, petroleum, and natural gas. Petroleum underpins America's entire transportation system, and hence our way of life. America is a nation on the move. Entire social formations such as suburbs make no sense without cheap fuel. Petroleum is historically and still by far the least expensive and most efficient way to move a vehicle forward at seventy miles an hour. All this is not to mention the nearly 60 million domestic and international passengers carried every month by American airliners powered by jet fuel made from petroleum. Hotel, restaurant, and other tourism and travel businesses depend on the money these passengers spend.

The U.S. military depends heavily on petroleum, too, whether in fighter jets flying over Taliban strongholds in Afghanistan or in tanks and armored vehicles on patrol in Baghdad. The U.S. combat missions in southwest Asia are estimated to consume 1.3 billion barrels of petroleum every year, more than the consumption of the entire country of Bangladesh (population 150 million).[1] Without access to this essential fuel, the United States could not remain a superpower, and its allies in the North Atlantic Treaty Organization (NATO) and elsewhere would also be much weakened. We are in some sense dancing through life immersed in petroleum: It fuels our vehicles, transports our goods, grows our food and brings it to us, and provides the raw material for our plastics and even our synthetic clothing.

Despite its indispensability, petroleum is currently unpopular with the public. More and more consumers now realize that using petroleum products contributes to global warming and pollutes the air, and that the need for this fuel makes us beholden to foreign—especially Middle Eastern—suppliers. For this reason, many policies made by politicians to ensure that the United States and its allies have access to oil and gas are dressed up for the public as being about vague ideals such as patriotism, democracy, or deterring allegedly threatening regimes. In short, our leaders have figured out that we despise our bondage to black gold and so they go out of their way not to mention it as a cause of action. Alan Greenspan, former head of the Federal Reserve, told the *Washington Post* in 2007 that he had made a case to Washington insiders in 2002 that removing Saddam Hussein from power was essential to U.S. petroleum security. He was told, he said, by one official, "Well, unfortunately, we can't talk about oil."[2]

The fact is that we are likely to become more dependent on Islamic oil in the coming decades, not less. Eleven of the top fifteen oil exporters in the world are states with Muslim majorities, and five of the most important are in the Gulf. In fact, the Persian Gulf has nearly two-thirds of the world's proven petroleum reserves. Saudi Arabia has the world's largest proven reserves and is the biggest exporter of petroleum. Another vital Muslim-majority petroleum player, Kazakhstan, abuts the Caspian Sea, the world's other big oil slick. Muslims are big in the gas business as well—the tiny Gulf peninsula of Qatar, the home of the Al-Jazeera satellite television channel, has 15 percent of the world's proven natural gas reserves and may be the wealthiest country per capita in the world. Turkmenistan, in Central Asia, has another big chunk of the world's natural gas, and Iran's gas reserves are estimated to be extensive.

It would be irrational to resent our dependence on foreign petroleum only because we dislike being reliant on imports. Journalist Robert Bryce points out that the United States is dependent on imports for 91 percent of its platinum, 72 percent of its chromium, 76 percent of its cobalt, and 88 percent of its tin.[3] Several of these commodities are important to defense industries, so our need for foreign sources is a security issue. Yet there is no clamor for chromium independence. Also, few Americans can remember a time when we imported relatively little petroleum, so the explanation probably does not lie in nostalgia for a bygone time. And yet our energy dependence on the Muslim world generates a good deal of Islam Anxiety. It is possible that petroleum is wrought up with gender and race in the American imagination in a way that cobalt and tin are not. Gasoline fuels automobiles and motorcycles, and American men view these vehicles as symbols of freedom and of masculinity. Being reliant on foreign lands for gasoline, and having its price determined by faraway events, is galling and even perhaps felt as castrating. The foreigners who control the sources of American manhood and liberty of movement are largely Arabs and Iranians, among the more disliked ethnicities in the United States.

Some of the causes of September 11 can be found in the competition for petroleum resources. In the late 1990s, Usamah Bin Laden wrote a letter (which was subsequently intercepted and published by the U.S. government) to Taliban leader Mullah Omar outlining the importance of overthrowing the Saudi ruling family and taking Arabia for al-Qaeda. He said that, first of all, the Muslim holy places at Mecca and Medina are located on the Saudi peninsula, which is thereby a pivotal source of Islamic prestige. But that was not all. "Likewise," he added, "75 percent of the petroleum in the world is found in the Gulf region, and whoever has dominion over the oil has dominion over the economies of the world."[4] Bin Laden pointed to petroleum as the reason the Americans had sought to station troops in Saudi Arabia and why they were happy not to have been forced out of the kingdom when the Gulf War ended in 1991.

Bin Laden was obsessed with the idea that the United States had strong-armed Muslim oil producers such as Saudi Arabia into pumping enough oil to keep the price low. Moreover, the American-sponsored order in the Gulf allowed princely families to usurp the lion's share of profits. The al-Qaeda declaration of war on America was intended to draw the U.S. military into an unwinnable guerrilla war against the Muslim mujahideen who had already defeated the Soviet Union. Bin Laden told British-Arab journalist Abdel Bari Atwan during the latter's visit to Afghanistan in 1996, "I can't fight the Americans on the American mainland. It is too far. But if I succeed in bringing the Americans where I can find them, where I can fight them on my own terms, on my turf, this will be the greatest success."[5] Bin Laden thought that in the aftermath of its inevitable defeat, the United States would be forced from the region, and Muslim radicals could then overthrow what he considered American puppet regimes and consolidate the Middle East into a new Islamic Empire, with all the oil riches of the Gulf and all the human capital of countries such as Egypt.

The United States was not always so dependent on fossil fuels from the Middle East or so focused on the Muslim world as a policy issue. During the cold war, Washington concentrated on countering the Soviet Union and its allies, and put its major resources into NATO and shoring up allies in East Asia. In the Middle East, the United States was mainly concerned that Gulf petroleum should continue to flow freely to its allies—Japan and Western Europe—and that the Soviet Union should not become influential in the area. America itself imported relatively little petroleum from the region.

Although the United States avoided heavy military involvement in the Middle East during the first three decades of the cold war, concern for the energy security of its allies impelled the United States to mount a series of covert operations, including the fomenting of coups that led to a destabilization of the region over time. The Truman administration overthrew the elected government of Shukri Quwatli in Syria in

1949, installing military dictator Husni Za'im, because Quwatli opposed the Trans-Arabian Pipeline, or Tapline, that would take oil from Saudi Arabia to the Lebanese Mediterranean port of Sidon.[6] Following the regime change, the oil flowed freely across those deserts until 1983 (when the development of the supertanker and turmoil in Lebanon killed it). Syria's politics did not soon recover from the intervention. Za'im was overthrown after four and a half months, and Syria spiraled into constant instability and further military coups.

U.S. petroleum security and the interests of U.S. oil majors were also implicated in the Central Intelligence Agency–sponsored coup against Prime Minister Mohammad Mosaddegh of Iran in 1953. Mosaddegh had made the error of trying to nationalize Iran's petroleum, foolishly arguing that it belonged to his country rather than to the Anglo-Iranian Oil Company (AIOC, which later became British Petroleum and then BP). The American oil majors were afraid that Iran's action would set a precedent, threatening their assets throughout the world. Mosaddegh and his fellow Iranian nationalists complained that Iran received only a small royalty on its own oil, pursuant to an outdated agreement made in the early 1930s. In fact, by the time Mosaddegh became prime minister nearly two decades later, the British government received more in taxes on the AIOC than Iran received in royalties.[7] After the 1953 coup, the United States installed dictator Mohammad Reza Pahlevi as shah, and U.S. corporations received a favorable position in the Iranian petroleum industry. The shah's police state enraged the Iranian public, which overthrew him in 1979, initiating decades of bad relations between that country and the United States.[8]

In 1958 the Iraqi military staged a coup, deposing the young king Faisal II and his wily old pro-British prime minister, Nuri al-Sa'id. The king and his entourage were expelled from the palace and then shot. The next day al-Sa'id was captured attempting to escape in women's clothing. He was shot and buried, but furious nationalist mobs, charging that the old regime had sold them into subservience to the West, dug him back up and dragged his corpse through the streets. One of the first inquiries Washington cabled to its embassy in Baghdad concerned the future of the Iraq Petroleum Company under the new regime.

In 1957 the term as president of pro-American Lebanese leader Camille Chamoun was coming to an end. If his party did well in the parliamentary elections that year, however, he could hope to extend his term of office. Chamoun, a Christian, had opposed Arab nationalist Gamal Abdel Nasser during the 1956 Suez War and was considered a pillar of opposition to pan-Arabism and potential Soviet influence in the Levant. Part of Lebanon's importance lay in the aforementioned Tapline. The CIA helped buy votes in the Lebanese 1957 parliamentary election for the benefit of Chamoun. The fraudulent elections were recognized as such, however, by Muslim activists, who revolted against Chamoun in the northern city of Tripoli and elsewhere in 1958.

When Syria joined Abdel Nasser's Egypt in the United Arab Republic (UAR), Lebanese Muslims and leftists demanded that Lebanon also become part of the UAR. In July 1958, a day after Colonel Abdul Karim Qasim overthrew the pro-Western monarchy in Iraq, President Dwight D. Eisenhower sent fourteen thousand marines to invade Lebanon in support of the beleaguered Chamoun, in large part as a way of underlining that the Iraq crisis would not be allowed to impede the export of petroleum to the West through Lebanon. Secretary of State John Foster Dulles had warned that if Washington did not react to the fall of the Iraqi monarchy, the Soviets would be emboldened and the Middle Eastern countries near to it would acquiesce in its leadership. Eisenhower had told his cabinet after the coup in Baghdad, "We have to act or get out of the Middle East."[9]

A few days after the marines landed at Beirut, CIA director Allen Dulles wrote Eisenhower to tell him that "there are three million barrels of oil stored at Sidon. The Secretary [of State, John Foster Dulles] thought perhaps we should move up to guard this oil (although this will have bad connotations)."[10] As it happened, no marines were sent there (the Tapline outlet had its own security arrangements, being well guarded by the Lebanese army), but this passage reveals the United States's oil-based motives behind the invasion. It also shows U.S. politicians' reluctance to allow the public to see that motivation.

Eisenhower concluded in the aftermath of the 1958 crisis that Western Europe was dependent on Middle East petroleum because it was cheap and nearby, and that market forces would ensure that that dependence continued, so it would just have to be accepted. A memo of a National Security Council meeting noted of the president, "He was not aware of any practicable thing we could do we were not already doing in connection with Western European dependence on Middle East oil."[11]

After the 1958 revolution that brought him to power, General Qasim in Iraq became a thorn in the side of the United States and the United Kingdom because he opposed the Iraq Petroleum Company's monopoly on Iraqi development and production and was willing to deal with the Iraqi Communist Party and the Soviets. He put communist "sympathizers" on his cabinet. Current public discourse would lead us to think that Islam has always been a central issue in American relations with the Middle East. But although Iraq was a Muslim-majority country at the time, "Islam" as an issue played no part in U.S. policy toward it at all in the 1950s and 1960s. The question was rather how likely it was to go communist or become a secular, leftist, pro-Soviet stronghold. Qasim headed the only major oil country with a left-nationalist orientation, which made him seem especially menacing to the United States and Western Europe. A CIA unit colorfully called the "Health Alteration Committee" attempted to eliminate Qasim in 1960 by having a poisoned monogrammed handkerchief delivered to him.[12]

Royal Dutch Shell, the French Petroleum Company (later Total), the Anglo-Iranian Oil Company, and a consortium of American companies (including Standard Oil of New Jersey and Socony Mobil) had each received 23.75 percent of the shares when the Iraq Petroleum Company (IPC) was formed in the 1920s.[13] In late 1961 Qasim issued a decree that may have sealed his fate. He demanded that IPC give the Iraqi government 55 percent of its profits and grant it a 20 percent share of ownership of the petroleum company. When IPC rejected these demands, Qasim issued Law 80 setting February 1963 as the date on which the IPC consortium would lose its undeveloped concessions and be left with only the northern fields that were already pumping. It would also be subject to high taxes and face competition within Iraq from the new Iraqi National Oil Company.[14] In response, the oil majors in the IPC kept Iraqi production down, compared to what the consortium partners were willing to do for friendly regimes such as Iran and Saudi Arabia, thereby making the government poorer and weaker than it would otherwise have been.

At the same time, Qasim was making claims on oil-rich Kuwait, which became independent from the British Empire on June 19, 1961. Kuwait had been part of the Ottoman Empire in the nineteenth century and was administered indirectly through the governor of Basra Province, in what is now Iraq. Qasim claimed that Iraq was the successor state of the Ottomans in that region and so had a claim on Kuwait, but his argument was rejected both by the Arab League and by the international community. He angrily withdrew from the Arab League over its stance on this matter.

In late December 1961 National Security Council staffer Robert Komer wrote a memo about the Qasim problem to President John F. Kennedy's special assistant for national security affairs, McGeorge Bundy. Komer had previously served in the CIA. (He later became known as "Blowtorch Bob" for his role in the Phoenix "pacification" campaign in Vietnam.) He concurred with the view that the initiative on policy making should not be left to Qasim. He gloated that "Kassim is increasingly isolated" and that "rumors of a nationalist coup are recurrent, and best guesses around town are that one might occur at any time."[15] Although this assertion is not proof that the CIA was already trying to overthrow Qasim, it is proof that the U.S. government was in touch with dissident officers from whom they heard the rumors of an imminent coup. Komer was especially worried that if Qasim "can add Kuwait production (largest in ME [Middle East]) to that of the IPC, he'll have stranglehold on ME oil. Sovs [the Soviets] would have much to gain." He suspected that Qasim was coordinating with the Soviets and that the dictator had released "Commies" from jail as part of the deal. The National Security staffer disliked the tendency in Washington to defer to the United Kingdom on Kuwait and Iraq issues. "But we own 23.75% of IPC and Gulf has 50% of Kuwait Oil Company." The "we" he was referring to was the American consortium. Gulf Oil was another of the American "Seven Sisters" and, at the time, the eighth-largest manufacturing company in the United States; its assets in Kuwait were being menaced by Qasim.

In the meantime, the Arab socialist, nationalist Baath Party (its name means "resurrection") had infiltrated the officer corps, and in February 1963 its leadership overthrew Qasim and promptly executed him. Komer revealed that he had foreknowledge of the coup, and he was ebullient about the opportunities for cooperation. He sent a memo over to Kennedy: "While it's still early, [the] Iraqi revolution seems to have succeeded. It is almost certainly a net gain for our side."[16] The United States characterized the new government as anticommunist, as not in Nasser's pan-Arab orbit, and as "Baath-Nationalist." Komer was sure that the IPC could be persuaded to extend the Baathists a loan. While the Baathists were willing to play ball with the United States in other ways, however, they insisted that Qasim's Law 80, which took away the IPC monopoly over Iraq's petroleum while leaving it with its already-developed fields, was not subject to negotiation.

A lively controversy swirls about whether the CIA made the 1963 coup through its agents in the Iraqi military. The full truth may never be known, but the allegation is at least plausible. Ali Salih Sa'adi, who served as the Baath interior minister, later told a journalist, "We came to power on a CIA train."[17] Given the way the United States dealt with Iranian prime minister Mohammad Mosaddegh after he took on the Anglo-Iranian Petroleum Company, it would be strange if Qasim's February 1963 deadline for expropriating so many of IPC's perquisites was allowed to pass without reaction.

The new regime lasted for only eight months before another faction of officers, led by the 'Arif brothers, overthrew it. In 1968 the Baath came back into power in another coup, also alleged to have been sponsored by the United States. While the U.S. alliance with the Baath destroyed the Iraqi Communist Party, which had become increasingly important before 1963, in the 1970s Baathist Iraq gravitated toward the Soviet Union and France as sources of weapons and support. The IPC never regained its monopoly position, and from 1972 to 1975 the government of Brigadier General Ahmad Hasan al-Bakr nationalized all of Iraqi petroleum.

In the late 1960s and early 1970s, the North Atlantic community faced three crises from the Middle East petroleum producers. The first was the oil boycotts by Middle Eastern producers in 1967 and 1973. The second was the wave of nationalizations by the Organization of Petroleum Exporting Countries (OPEC) in the early 1970s. The third was the British withdrawal from the Gulf, the last stage in the process of decolonization that began in earnest in 1947 with the independence of India and Pakistan, and which by the 1970s had left that crucial region without a credible guarantor of security.

In important ways, the energy crises of the twenty-first century have some of their roots in the significant changes to the West–Middle East relationship in the late 1960s and 1970s. A canny observer at that time, energy expert John McCone, saw that the relationship of the North Atlantic states to Islamic oil reached a momentous turning point when Arab oil exporters boycotted the United States and the Netherlands in June and July of 1967, in support of Egypt, Jordan, and Syria in their war with Israel.[18] McCone, an engineer and industrialist from California, had been chairman, from 1958 to 1961, of the U.S. Atomic Energy Commission, then served as director of the CIA until 1965. He had extensive contacts with American petroleum companies and with the Gulf producers. Richard Helms, director of the CIA in the late 1960s, urgently sought a briefing from McCone after the Six-Day War of 1967.

Helms's notes show that McCone emphasized that U.S. petroleum corporations active in the Middle East were central to U.S. diplomacy in the region (he barely remembered to give a nod to the State Department). He also reminded the administration that the oil countries of the region bought many more goods from the United States than America bought from them, thus contributing "substantially to the U.S. balance of payments." Middle East oil, then, was not just a matter of private corporate profits, but rather was a "national interest." McCone further emphasized the geostrategic importance of Saudi black gold, saying that that the United States was "getting two or three hundred thousand barrels of petroleum products daily from the Middle East for the war effort in South Vietnam."[19]

McCone saw the Johnson administration's unreserved support for Israel and Israeli expansionism as a profound threat to the position of the United States and its petroleum corporations in the Arab world. He rejected the argument that the Western oil companies had survived the wave of anti-Western sentiment after the 1956 Suez War and would easily survive the resentments stirred by the Six-Day War. He pointed out that President Eisenhower had forced Israel, Britain, and France to give up the territory they took from Abdel Nasser in 1956, essentially siding with the Arabs. (Eisenhower worried that the 1956 aggression on Egypt might push Arab nationalists into the arms of the Soviet Union and that it would undermine the United Nations charter forbidding the acquisition of territory by conquest.)

In contrast, in 1967, the United States wholeheartedly backed Israel. McCone concluded in his briefing that the United States faced the danger, because of President Lyndon Johnson's unwillingness to take an "unequivocal" stand on the territorial issues between Israel and its Arab neighbors (i.e., on Israel's occupation after the war of vast amounts of Arab territory), "of the expropriation, expulsion, and nationalization of American [petroleum] interests." The increasing resentments in the Arab world of knee-jerk U.S. support for Israel, which included its running interference at the U.N. Security Council for continued Israeli occupation and colonization of the West Bank and Gaza, made it difficult for Arab governments to continue to be seen as allowing U.S. corporations to get the lion's share of the benefits from Arab oil. Not only did Iraq proceed with the nationalization of its petroleum in the early 1970s, but also, with the exception of the United Arab Emirates, most other supplying countries did as well. In 1971 Algeria took a 51 percent share of its petroleum from French companies. In the 1970s Libya nationalized most of the concessions owned by foreign oil companies. Kuwait took 100 percent ownership of its petroleum in 1975, paying BP and Gulf Oil a small compensation. Saudi Arabia took 100 percent of the Arabian American Oil Company, known as Aramco, in 1980.

The nationalizations did not leave the great American petroleum companies unscathed. Gulf Oil, a part of the Mellon fortune, with its headquarters in Pittsburgh, had once been a top-ten U.S. industrial company. After losing its Kuwait concessions, it merged in the 1980s with Standard Oil of California, later known as Chevron, losing its independent corporate identity. Other U.S. oil majors survived because they possessed or developed concessions elsewhere, for example in Alaska or Nigeria, or turned to refining and distribution. Eventually some turned to the Caspian fields near Afghanistan when those opened up to Western investment after the fall of the Soviet Union.

At the height of the 1970s oil crisis, only about 12 percent of America's oil imports came from the Middle East. Washington was primarily worried about the impact of the region's supplies on Western Europe and Japan, which might be destabilized and become vulnerable to communism if there was an energy famine. In the 1970s some 80 percent of Western Europe's petroleum came from the Middle East, as did 90 percent of Japan's. Western Europe reacted to the crisis by increasing its energy efficiency—for instance, putting insulation into buildings and improving automobile mileage. France and Japan turned to nuclear energy.

The final British withdrawal from the Gulf in the late 1960s and early 1970s left the region without a Great Power guarantor of security for the first time in centuries—and security was a real concern. The United Arab Emirates, Qatar, Bahrain, and Kuwait were becoming economic powerhouses, but, as tiny principalities, they had all the military potential of Lichtenstein. Even Saudi Arabia, though it was a larger country than the others with regard to both people and territory, had a small population and army relative to Iran, Turkey, and Egypt. The oil monarchies were like big, shining, beautiful, wealthy banks plopped down in the middle of a violent slum. They felt threatened by radical secular ideologies. The communists had taken South Yemen. The Baath Party, socialist and republican in emphasis, ruled Syria and Iraq. Who would protect the small, opulent oil principalities now that the British were gone?

The United States, bogged down in Southeast Asia and focused on the Soviet front in Central Europe, was eager for some proxy power to fill the security vacuum. The Nixon administration fixed on the shah's Iran as the successor to the British. The shah had been put back on his throne in 1953 by the CIA intervention and was a relatively loyal client of the United States. Building Iran up as policeman of the Gulf also had the advantage that it would require Iran to buy large amounts of weaponry and import technical know-how from the United States, thus recycling the huge stock of petrodollars that Tehran was accumulating as a result of the 1970s oil price run-up. The U.S. quest to fill the security vacuum in the Gulf through proxies proved to be a failure. The Iran gambit crashed and burned in 1979, when the shah had to flee a populist revolution and the country was taken over by radical ayatollahs.

When Saddam Hussein invaded Iran in September 1980, he caught the Carter administration by surprise, and policy drifted until late 1983. The Reagan administration had time to consider a new set of policies, since petroleum prices declined in the 1980s. New fields came online, and world petroleum production capacity increased. Oil fell from $40 a barrel in 1980 dollars, at the height of the Iran crisis, to less than $10 a barrel in 1986. Despite fluctuations, petroleum prices did not increase as much in the next fifteen years as did most other staple commodities. Still, the Gulf remained crucial to North Atlantic and Japanese energy security in the face of the Soviet and Iranian threats, and President Ronald Reagan soon developed a new, aggressive policy aimed at ensuring U.S. interests. Reagan sent Donald Rumsfeld, the CEO of Searle & Co. pharmaceuticals and a former secretary of defense under Gerald Ford, to Baghdad to explore an American alliance. The deal for this cooperation between Washington and Baghdad was struck despite tensions over the State Department's denunciations of Iraq for deploying chemical weapons against the Iranians at the front.

From 1984 through 1990, in an attempt to contain radical Iran, the United States backed Iraq as its proxy in the Gulf. Then Saddam, deeply in debt and profoundly ambitious, invaded Kuwait and attempted to annex it and its vast oil wealth. The invasion resurrected the old concerns expressed by "Blowtorch Bob" Komer in the Kennedy era—that possession of both Iraqi and Kuwaiti oil reserves would make a regional government into a superpower and put its fingers on the jugular of the West. The administration of George H. W. Bush turned on Iraq, fearful that Saddam was seeking to control so much of the world's petroleum supply that he could blackmail the industrialized democracies.

After the Gulf War pushed Saddam's armies back to the Iraqi border, in 1991, the United States was in the difficult position of having both Iran and Iraq as enemies in the region. Martin Indyk, an Australian close to Israeli policy circles, had in the 1980s and early 1990s served as the founding executive director of the Washington Institute for Near East Policy, the think tank of the American Israel Public Affairs Committee (AIPAC), a major lobbying organization. With that background, Indyk became influential in the Clinton administration and successfully advocated "dual containment" of both Iraq and Iran. This policy depended on economic boycotts and the deployment of U.S. military might in the Gulf, mainly American overflights of Iraq from Prince Sultan Air Base in Saudi Arabia. Obviously, Israeli security was on Indyk's mind as he pressed this unrealistic idea on Washington.

The attempt to keep the two largest Gulf countries in a box left the United States with the problem of where to find a proxy guarantor of security to the oil monarchies. Over time, the commitment of European allies to dual containment waned because of humanitarian concerns and European corporations' interest in doing business with the two countries, and there was a danger that international sanctions on Iraq might ultimately be lifted. It was an impossible situation for Washington.

Only after equivocating and trying to find proxies for three decades did the United States itself finally step into the security vacuum left behind when the two-centuries-long British imperial stewardship of the Gulf ended. In 2003, the administration of George W. Bush finally decided to replace the British as the major military power in the Gulf. Hundreds of thousands of U.S. troops were brought into the region and major bases were planted there, and Washington, as London once did, shaped local polities for its own purposes.

The United States is far more dependent on Islamic oil today than it was thirty years ago. In 2007 the United States was consuming over 20 million barrels per day of petroleum and other liquid fuels, mainly in its transportation sector, but producing only a little over 5 million barrels of petroleum per day. It was producing 3 million barrels per day of other liquefied fuels, including ethanol. American oil reserves are limited, so the conclusion is simple mathematics. The United States needs about 12 million barrels a day of petroleum or other liquefied fuels from somewhere else if it is to maintain its present way of life. In March 2008 nearly 90 percent of that "somewhere else" was spread over just fifteen countries. The list looks like this:

MAJOR SUPPLIERS OF OIL TO THE UNITED STATES AS OF MARCH 2008 (IN THOUSANDS OF BARRELS PER DAY)

Canada	2,303
Saudi Arabia	1,542
Mexico	1,351
Nigeria	1,158
Venezuela	1,015
Iraq	773
Algeria	427
Russia	394
Angola	379
Virgin Islands	290
Ecuador	238
United Kingdom	218
Brazil	191
Kuwait	178
Colombia	150

Source: Energy Information Administration, "March 2008 Import Highlights," May 12, 2008, at http://www.eia.doe.gov/pub/oil_gas/petroleum/data_publications/company_level _imports/current/import.html

Western Europe and Japan are extremely dependent on middle eastern oil.

Five of these fifteen suppliers—four of which are in the top seven—are Muslim-majority countries. These five countries supply a fifth of all U.S. petroleum imports.

Since oil is traded in a single global market, the list of countries that supply the United States is somewhat arbitrary. The Saudi Arabian government deliberately seeks to be the second or third largest supplier to the United States, just to make a political point about the close relations between the two countries. The world now produces on the order of 86 million barrels of petroleum a day, with some fluctuations. So the United States, with 5 percent of the world's population, consumes nearly a fourth of the world's oil supply, and is therefore the six-hundred-pound gorilla of energy use. The flip side of that predominance is that the United States is deeply dependent on what happens in world energy markets. If any major producer were taken off-line, by violence or a prolonged strike, that interruption would raise the price for everyone and would limit world supply in a way that would affect U.S. consumers directly, whether the United States imports from that country or not.

To show how this works, imagine you are sitting with some friends in one of those portable swimming pools that people put out in their yards in the summer. And let's say that you and your neighbors each have a hose bringing water to the pool and that the pool has a small hole in it draining water from the pool at the same rate that the two hoses fill it. If your neighbors in the pool take their hose away, the waterline inside the pool will start going down, even if your water hose is still delivering water. Petroleum supply is like that. We are all in the same pool together.

Now let us consider another list, not of countries that directly supply the United States but of countries that have large reserves of petroleum. This list is of the utmost importance when we think about the future. The countries at the top of the list are those to which the United States will increasingly be beholden as time goes on and shallow fields are exhausted.

Eleven of the top nineteen countries are Muslim-majority states, and they have half of the world's proven petroleum reserves. OPEC estimates that of the roughly 1.3 trillion barrels of proven petroleum re-

WORLD OIL RESERVES BY COUNTRY AS OF JANUARY 1, 2007
(IN BILLIONS OF BARRELS)

Saudi Arabia	262.3
Canada	179.2
Iran	136.3
Iraq	115.0
Kuwait	101.5
United Arab Emirates	97.8
Venezuela	80.0
Russia	60.0
Libya	41.5
Nigeria	36.2
Kazakhstan	30.0
United States	21.8
China	16.0
Qatar	15.2
Mexico	12.4
Algeria	12.3
Brazil	11.8
Angola	8.0
Norway	7.8
Azerbaijan	7.0
Rest of world	65.5
World Total	**1,317.4**

Source: "Worldwide Look at Reserves and Production," *Oil and Gas Journal* 104, no. 47 (December 18, 2006), pp. 24–25.

serves in the world, their twenty-two members have 900 billion barrels of it, more than two-thirds. Most of the reserves are in the Middle East, with Saudi Arabia, Iran, and Iraq accounting for 56 percent of the OPEC total.[20] These are the countries with the extensive reserves that the world will tap into as shallower reserves run dry. If depending on Islamic oil makes the American public as nervous as a long-tailed cat in a room full of rocking chairs, it is likely to get more nervous yet.

The world is now capable of producing approximately 15 terawatts of power. A terawatt is a trillion watts. An electric light bulb might put out 100 watts of power. An electric heater might produce 1,000 watts, or one kilowatt. A train engine might put out 2,000 kilowatts. Add up all the devices human beings use throughout the world and we are producing 15 trillion watts, or terawatts, to power them. By 2050, when the world's population is expected to level off at about 9 billion, we may well need 30 terawatts just to sustain current standards of living and accommodate the rapidly developing countries moving to our urban, industrialized style of life. So where could we get another 15 terawatts? The short answer is that, given current technology, we cannot. It isn't there to be had.

There is a looming crisis.[21] Regardless of how well exploration goes, the world is as unlikely to double its petroleum and gas stocks as giraffes are to grow wings and fly. New finds of oil reserves have been declining in each decade.[22] Known fields, such as those in Siberia, will be tapped in the near future, but they are not capacious enough to resolve by themselves the problem of global energy scarcity.

The biggest rumored oil find in recent years has been off the coast of Brazil. This news is not as momentous as it might seem at first glance. The two fields identified as likely big petroleum repositories are estimated to have about 40 billion barrels of recoverable petroleum. Such estimates should be treated with caution, since the finders have a strong motivation to exaggerate in order to raise investment capital for developing the fields. But let us assume that the oil is really there and can be accessed (it will be relatively expensive to extract). At current rates of use, the United States alone could gobble up all of Brazil's new hoped-for reserves in about five or six years.

Not only is demand for petroleum rapidly rising, but even in the relatively near future some current producers will witness steep declines in their remaining reserves. In addition, former petroleum exporters are being turned into importers as their own populations start using oil themselves at ever greater rates. Indonesia, an OPEC member that produces about a million barrels of petroleum per day, has been consuming it domestically since 2004, and has now become a net importer. Mexico, the United States's third largest petroleum supplier, is facing declining production and increasing domestic demand. Some analysts think that in a few years it will no longer be a significant source of oil exports.[23] China earned a fifth of its export income from petroleum in the mid-1980s and is still the world's fifth-largest producer, but it now uses all its petroleum domestically and then some.

The era of cheap petroleum lasted until the late 1990s, when the rapid development of China and other Asian economies changed the equation.[24] China's domestic economy began growing some 10 percent a year in 1980 and has continued at similar high rates of growth to the present. It began with such a low base that initially this annual increase had little effect on energy markets, but in the past decade that situation has changed.

At a time when the annual increase in U.S. and European petroleum demand is in the 1.0 percent to 1.5 percent range, China's demand for oil is increasing dramatically. In 2007, its crude oil imports were up 12 percent over the previous year, and oil was China's biggest single import item.[25] In recent years China has become the world's second-largest importer of oil, though it imports only a little over half what the United States does. At current rates of growth, China will have to find an additional half-million barrels a day of petroleum every year for the next ten years. Since supply is unlikely to expand with that rapidity, that task is impossible unless Beijing manages to elbow other users out of some markets. Aware of the anxiety that its energy consumption is producing, Beijing issued a white paper on its energy sector in 2007, declaring "China did not, does not, and will not pose any threat to the world's energy security."[26]

It is instructive to consider where China is looking for increased supplies. Beijing has increased its imports from Saudi Arabia and is partnering with the kingdom in the building of a new refinery. That is not as controversial a move as its other initiative. China's leading petroleum refiner, Sinopec, estimated that it would import 400,000 barrels a day of crude oil from Iran in 2008, making Iran the third-largest source for Beijing after Saudi Arabia and Angola. Further, Sinopec agreed in late 2007 to invest $2 billion in Iran's Yadavaran oil field. In doing so, the Chinese petroleum giant was bucking pressure from Washington, which had threatened to impose economic boycotts on firms that invested in development projects in Iran. Since the United States has a $13 trillion-a-year economy in which most global corporations would like to play, the prospect of being excluded is highly unpleasant.

In May 2008, six years after Royal Dutch Shell signed a memorandum of agreement with Iran, the threat of U.S. sanctions caused the company to withdraw from plans to develop the giant South Pars gas field. Russia's Gazprom, the Indian Oil Company, and Chinese companies are considered the only concerns that might be able to resist U.S. pressure, though none of them has Shell's experience in processing liquefied natural gas (cooling it so as to transport it more efficiently).[27]

A powerful new competitor with the United States for Islamic oil and influence in the Muslim world has emerged in recent years: India. With a population of over a billion, some 13 percent of them Muslims, India has the potential to be a regional player of great importance in coming years. The Indian economy grew only a little over 3 percent a year for four decades after its independence in 1947. Since its population grew at about the same rate, the per capita increase was close to nothing, and the subcontinent remained predominantly rural. Economists grimly joked that it was the "Hindu rate of growth." I lived in India's largely rural Hindi belt in the early 1980s and saw its dire poverty with my own eyes. Population growth was clearly putting pressure on the infrastructure, which was deteriorating rapidly. Lucknow, where I was doing research, still had bicycle rickshaws powered by human beings. Uneasy with the idea of being pulled by a fellow man, I walked when I could and sought out motorized transportation when I could not. But after a few days, the rickshaw cyclists sent a delegation to me. They said, "Sahib, we know you think you are doing us a favor by not using us. You aren't." I got to talking in Hindi to one of them, and he said he was a small farmer and only pulled a rickshaw in the off season. I was even more shocked that persons of property were doing this kind of job in their spare time. Those cycle rickshaws were an indicator of the cheapness of labor in India, and they did not exist in Pakistan to the north, which at that time had twice India's per capita income.

After about 1980, India began shaking off those decades of economic lethargy and flexing its muscles. A forest of unhelpful regulations regarding imports and exports was felled and a more business-friendly atmosphere created. In 2006 India grew at a phenomenal rate of 9.6 percent, decelerating to a still-impressive 8.7 percent in 2007.[28] India possesses limited proven oil and gas reserves, and therefore imports more than 70 percent of the petroleum products it needs, a percentage that is likely to grow. It is now the sixth-largest importer of petroleum, bringing in 2.4 million barrels a day in 2007. Its energy needs had been forecast to grow roughly 5 percent a year for the next twenty years, but in 2007–2008 alone its energy use jumped 8 percent.

Most Indian factories are not powered by petroleum, so industrial growth does not directly cause increased oil use. But rising incomes associated with moving from a rural to an urban, industrial economy give consumers the wherewithal to purchase automobiles, and factory goods are moved by truck and rail. If every family in India (and the rest of Asia) decides it needs an automobile, the resultant pressure on petroleum prices will be explosive. At the moment, the world supports close to 700 million automobiles, but that number is expected to more than double to 1.5 billion in the next decade or two. Some 70 percent of world petroleum output is used to fuel automobiles.[29]

The fate of U.S. attempts to isolate Iran may depend heavily on policies formulated in New Delhi. India is clearly tempted by the Iran option as a way to fill its petroleum and gas needs. Indian state energy companies are planning to develop Iran's Farsi block, which geologists think holds 12.8 trillion cubic feet of recoverable natural gas.[30] The Indian Oil Corporation, the state-run Oil and Natural Gas Corporation, and Oil India Ltd. jointly hold options on developing the field, into which they have invested $90 million to date. They are planning to invest a further $3 billion. The plan is then to transport the gas to India across Pakistan through a 1,724-mile pipeline.

The United States has repeatedly voiced objections to this pipeline plan, which faces numerous technical and political hurdles. The Asian Development Bank, for instance, has firmly rejected any role in providing loans for the financing of the project, given U.S. opposition. Further, the pipeline would run through Pakistan's troubled Baluchistan Province, which has witnessed attacks on existing gas pipelines and is roiled by political demands for more autonomy, more royalties for its natural resources, and generally a better deal from Islamabad.[31] The Pakistani government would have to make a deal with the Baluchis if the project were to have a chance of success.[32] Still, Indian foreign secretary Shiv Shankar Menon averred in June 2008: "Frankly, from our point of view, the more engagement there is, the more Iran becomes a factor of stability in the region, the better it is for us all."[33] If India successfully defies the U.S. boycott of Iran, Washington's entire sanctions regime could effectively collapse.

One tantalizing development for U.S. policy makers and the oil majors in the 1990s was the dissolution of the Soviet Union and the emergence of post-Soviet hydrocarbon states such as Turkmenistan and Kazakhstan.[34] The Unocal and Delta oil and gas companies and figures in the first Bush administration such as Dick Cheney and Zalmay Khalilzad (then working in the corporate sector) began dreaming of a gas pipeline from Turkmenistan down through Afghanistan to Pakistan and India.[35] The United States and its allies have not given up on this pipeline known as TAPI. Although Afghanistan, Pakistan, and India signed a framework agreement in April 2008 to purchase natural gas from Turkmenistan,[36] the pipeline faces perhaps insurmountable obstacles in the short to medium term.[37] The estimated cost of the pipeline has risen to $7.6 billion. And the increasing violence in the parts of Afghanistan through which the pipeline would run, such as Qandahar Province, raises real questions about its viability. Worst of all for the pipeline's prospects, Turkmenistan, tired of waiting, appears likely instead to pipe the gas via Russia, which enjoys the advantages of security and an already-existing pipeline infrastructure. In late July 2008 Russian gas giant Gazprom signed long-term agreements in Ashgebot that seemed likely to lock in Russian control of Turkmenistani gas in the medium term.[38]

When petroleum was a buyer's market, before the late 1990s, the major industrialized consumers did not have to compete for supplies and could be assured of cheap energy, barring political actions such as the 1973 OPEC embargo. It was often said that the producers were stuck, since they could hardly benefit from leaving their petroleum in the ground, and so had to put it on the market. The market favored the consumers, so that the price sometimes collapsed on the producers, and they had to work hard to avoid an unpleasant roller-coaster ride when it came to their revenues over a decade. One purpose OPEC filled in the last decades of the twentieth century was to work against that boom-and-bust cycle. That is, its members did not seek the highest possible price for their commodity, as one might expect were it merely a predatory cartel, but rather attempted to keep the price at about $25 per barrel, which the Saudis in particular considered a sweet spot. That price was considered low enough to discourage big investments in alternative energy that might undermine the value of petroleum and gas, but great enough to pay for the immense task of moving the oil-producing countries toward rapid economic development.

The old target price for petroleum of just a few years ago has gone the way of the five-cent cup of coffee and the fifty-cent pulp paperback. While some of that substantial price increase in the first decade of the twenty-first century has been caused by speculation and the decline of the dollar (because of large American budget deficits), a great deal of the price increase is due to new demand and the failure, in the previous two decades, to discover enough big new fields to meet it. Petroleum, as a seller's market, resembles a game of musical chairs. There are more players than chairs, and some consumers could end up without the supply they want for maximal growth—or even for just maintaining their current style of life, at an affordable price. The United

States could end up being the country without a chair, and would thereby lose its status as a superpower.

The current energy crisis is exacerbated many times over by the global climate crisis. This crisis is propelled in part by the burning of gas and oil that is extracted from beneath the sands of the major producing nations of the Middle East and Caspian regions. American and Chinese coal are also major contributors to the problem of global warming.[39] Consuming fossil fuels raises the amount of carbon dioxide in the atmosphere. Carbon dioxide traps the heat coming to the earth from the sun, making it more difficult for it to radiate away into outer space—the so-called greenhouse effect. The average temperature of the earth's surface has been rising since the Industrial Revolution and will go on rising as long as increased carbon dioxide is being released into the air. The more carbon dioxide in the atmosphere, the more the earth's weather will change. Global warming is only one possible effect of this carbon dioxide accumulation. Some regions may become cooler, at least in the short term. Catastrophic climactic events may also occur, including more frequent and more powerful hurricanes.

James Hansen, now director of the Goddard Institute of Space Sciences, first testified to Congress in 1988 on the dangers of climate change deriving from the vast increase of carbon dioxide and other chemicals being dumped into the atmosphere by industrial society. At that time, there were 350 parts per million (ppm) of carbon dioxide in the atmosphere, up from 275 ppm before the Industrial Revolution. Hansen testified again in the summer of 2008, and warned that the situation had worsened greatly. The atmosphere now has 387 ppm of carbon dioxide. Climate scientists had earlier speculated that more than 450 ppm of carbon dioxide might provoke truly cataclysmic changes. Hansen has concluded that, given current evidence on climate change, we have to get back to 350 ppm in order to avoid a series of calamities such as mass extinctions of animal and plant species, ecosystem collapse, and dangerous rises in sea level. He acknowledged that it was likely that the world would continue to exploit existing petroleum supplies, but urged that the burning of coal should be banned.

He also suggested that the CEOs of the oil majors be prosecuted for perpetrating the fraud that climate change through increased atmospheric carbon is a myth.[40] ExxonMobil, for example, funds a far-right Washington think tank, the American Enterprise Institute (AEI), which has been offering cash to scientists who cast doubts on the existence of climate change, and cite the minority among climate scientists who still express doubts on carbon's role.[41]

Meanwhile, as a result of the higher temperatures caused by the carbon dioxide spewed by coal-fired power plants and seven hundred million automobiles, the ice sheets at the poles and the world's glaciers are melting much faster than scientists originally predicted. Obviously, when land ice melts and runs into the oceans, the water level rises. Even the melting of glaciers already in the ocean can raise sea level, because freshwater melt is less dense than salty sea water and thus takes up more space. In the summer of 2007, more than a million square kilometers of ice melted in the Arctic; the summer of 2008 was just as bad. Climate scientists now expect that soon there could be no ice cover at all in the Arctic in the late summer each year[42] and that, during the twenty-first century, the seas could rise as much as three feet, with devastating consequences for coastal areas as well as islands and low-lying countries, such as Bangladesh.

Global warming's effect on the oceans will have similarly disastrous results, as warmer ocean waters will likely produce more and stronger hurricanes. The great Burmese cyclone of 2008 is estimated to have killed between 100,000 and 200,000 people, and things will get worse if ocean temperatures continue to rise. Everyone wants to avoid the disasters that will inevitably accompany climate change, but everyone also wants continued economic growth and affluent styles of life, which currently require more and more hydrocarbon fuels that increase carbon emissions.

Desperate to escape dependence on Islamic oil, politicians and energy activists have offered various plans whereby industrialized democracies might become energy independent. Some of these technologies are promising in the medium and long term, but many are impractical, and some exacerbate climate change.

Further drilling for oil is obviously highly unlikely to solve the energy problem. If all the known unexploited offshore fields around the lower forty-eight states in the United States were drilled, for instance, they would yield only 400,000 barrels per day, while the United States uses some 20 to 21 million barrels per day.[43] In other words, it would be a drop in the bucket. The most desirable grade of petroleum, light sweet crude, is becoming harder to find, and "sour" oil, with high sulfur and mineral content, is difficult and expensive to refine. Moreover, more drilling and oil use will just add more carbon dioxide to the atmosphere and thus accelerate climate change.

Liquefying coal or shale to create diesel fuel as a solution does not take into account the significant ecological costs. The coal industry admits that if you count the carbon pollution released in the process of converting coal to liquid, along with what it releases when burned as diesel, the total emissions are twice those of ordinary diesel.[44]

Most alternative energy sources, however, either are not up to the task or are not yet ready for prime time. Even if you put wind turbines everywhere in the world where it is economical to do so, with current technology you probably could not generate more than a terawatt or two. Tidal power could generate a little less than a terawatt. Hydroelectric dams could produce an extra terawatt or two if they were placed on all the rivers in the world not already dammed (with possible severe environmental damage). You could get a lot of energy from biomass sources such as ethanol, maybe seven to ten terawatts. But that would involve using up all the crops in the world, leaving nothing for us to eat; and, besides, it would likely generate at least some extra carbon dioxide. Corn ethanol costs almost as much to produce as the petroleum it replaces. Moreover, Oxfam estimated in the summer of 2008 that "rich country biofuel policies have dragged more than 30 million people into poverty, according to evidence that biofuels have already contributed up to 30 percent to the global rise in food prices."[45]

Nuclear energy is also not a magic solution. The problem of how to store nuclear waste safely has never been satisfactorily resolved. Terrorists could steal it and use it to create dirty bombs (packing radioactive material around a conventional explosive, so as to contaminate the surroundings). But even if the world did pursue nuclear technology as a major source of energy, we'd have to build a new nuclear reactor every two days for the next forty-five years to get even eight terawatts of energy. Even that highly unlikely achievement would not remotely solve the problem.[46] Uranium is not a renewable resource, and as a fuel it would become rare and expensive very quickly if a lot of new reactors were built.

The only realistic hope of resolving the twin energy and climate crises of the twenty-first century lies in solar energy. But first two big problems need to be solved. One problem is storage. Better storage would also be important if we were going to move to electric cars, with solar-generated electricity to run them. The second problem is that the cost of alternative energy needs to be brought down if it is to be competitive. Current solar cells are relatively expensive, and solar energy is still several times as costly as that generated by coal or natural gas (in 2008, solar was typically 15 cents a kilowatt versus coal at 5 cents a kilowatt). Of course, this apparent greater cost of solar energy is artificial, insofar as the environmental impact of carbon-based fuels is not figured into their cost, and carbon-based fuels receive various forms of government subsidies in the United States, estimated to total half a trillion dollars over the past fifty years.[47] All-in-all, alternative energy will not likely stop the growing dependency of the industrialized democracies on Islamic oil in the next three or four decades.

Since reserves are declining and developing countries are using more and more of their own petroleum, energy hogs such as the United States, Japan, China, Germany, South Korea, and India are increasingly dependent on producers that have deep reserves, low extraction costs, and relatively low domestic energy demand. The leading such country in the world is Saudi Arabia. Others include Iran, Iraq, Kuwait, and the United Arab Emirates. Petroleum makes the world go round, which means that, increasingly, Muslims will make the world go round. This maxim will probably remain true at least in the medium term, but very possibly even through 2050.

Enormous dangers lurk for the industrialized democracies in their increasingly central relations with the Muslim oil states. One, as discussed, is the temptation to meddle. The United States and Britain have a long history of fomenting coups or manipulating elections to get the government they want in key energy-producing states. Another temptation is neomercantilism, throwing the power of the state behind corporations and other economic interests so as to give those businesses an advantage in global competition. The U.S. invasion of Iraq finally reopened that country to investments by the oil majors, which had lost out in 1972. At the same time, however, the invasion destabilized Iraq, which now may be politically and socially fragile for some time. It also destabilized the neighborhood, strengthening Iran, provoking new Turkish-Kurdish conflicts of some ferocity, and burdening Syria and Jordan with hundreds of thousands of refugees. This outcome hardly created a promising business environment for investments by North American and European firms.

Military intervention and even less robust forms of neomercantilism are far too blunt and risky as tools to achieve assured positive outcomes for the corporate sector, and the societies of the region are too complex to be easily stage-managed. Capitalist democracies have preached the virtues of the market to the rest of the world for a very long time and should have the courage of their convictions to allow their energy corporations to compete on a level playing field.

Harsh rhetoric, demonization, signals of enmity, and attempts to intervene in local politics can all damage relations between producers and consumers. The United States and its allies increasingly need friendly relations with oil-producing states, including Muslim ones. An informed and fair-minded approach to Islam is a key element in Western public diplomacy toward the Middle East and Central Asia. In a highly competitive world in which oil states have a choice of patrons, they may seek out those that are less domineering. For instance, the Bush administration at the very least had foreknowledge of, and may well have been complicit in, a failed 2002 attempt by right-wing military elements to overthrow President Hugo Chavez of oil-rich Venezuela.[48] Now Caracas is building a pipeline to the Pacific in hopes of selling its petroleum to China. Because of high transportation costs, Caracas will realize fewer profits than could be gained from selling to the United States, but the regime is seeking security through diversification of its customer base, fearful that keeping the United States as its primary market will make it too subservient to Washington.[49]

Likewise, many oil and gas producers in the Muslim world are eager to cultivate China as a market in order to counterbalance American dominance. When American politicians make bigoted and hostile statements about Islam and Muslims, they alienate the leaders and publics of Muslim oil states and thus harm U.S. political and economic interests.

Leaders of the United States may think that a militarily weak government like that of Saudi Arabia, which is nevertheless fabulously wealthy, has few options but to seek the shelter of a U.S. security umbrella. They may take such oil states for granted and conclude that they don't need to pay any attention to the Saudi regime's policy advice or accommodate its need for popular legitimacy. The cheerleader quality of U.S. support for Israel in the 1967 and 1973 wars displayed such a heedlessness toward U.S. Arab allies such as King Faisal of Saudi Arabia. While the U.S. relationship with Riyadh survived, that lack of even-handedness harmed U.S. petroleum corporations when the Arab regimes, responding in part to popular anger, nationalized their oil assets in the 1970s.

The United States, despite the loss of prestige it has suffered in recent years, still has the ability to broker difficult agreements, but has not exercised that moral authority for positive purposes in a systematic way in the opening years of the new century. The Saudi royal family, for instance, suffers opprobrium from its own and other Arab publics because of its close alliance with Washington, given that the United States acquiesces in Israeli policies that harm Palestinians. Another push to resolve the conflict between the Israelis and the Palestinians in ways that would benefit both would contribute mightily to U.S. energy security and regional stability. Israel does not actually benefit from the colonization of the West Bank or the permanent siege of the Gaza Strip but would benefit from a stable Palestinian state and better economic and political relations with the Arab League. Likewise, a studied and careful drawdown of U.S. forces in Iraq would greatly improve the U.S. image in the region and aid in energy diplomacy.

The truth is, the great powers find it difficult to exert any control or influence on states that produce pricey primary commodities. In the post–cold war era, the industrialized democracies have often excoriated such wealthy mavericks as "rogue states." The independence of the latter allows them to run authoritarian regimes and to defy the global powers. Legislatures in the West are frequently tempted to deal with such black sheep in the family of nations through economic sanctions. It is unclear that such sanctions have had much success in overthrowing governments, as opposed to making the lives of ordinary folk harder. It is certain that they have harmed innocent civilians, sometimes fatally and in the hundreds of thousands.

The United Nations' and American sanctions on Iraq in the 1990s, for example, are said to have led to the deaths of half a million children: chlorine—needed for water purification—was at times interdicted (children are especially vulnerable to water-borne diseases); key medicines were kept out or made unaffordable; and the sanctions did not even provide for enough food to sustain the populace. Although the Baath regime manipulated the sanctions for political reasons, and thus bears some responsibility for the humanitarian disaster, such self-protective regime behavior surely could have been anticipated as a likely consequence of any sanctions. Heartless policies that punish the population but tend to leave the ruling elite untouched are a public relations nightmare. Usamah Bin Laden cited the Iraq sanctions and their devastation of ordinary Iraqis as one of his reasons for attacking the United States.[50]

The great powers, having now become rivals in the quest for gas and petroleum, face another ruinous temptation, that of going to war to secure the fuel they need. In a context of severe competition for limited energy resources, strong countries such as the United States and China could be tempted to monopolize what fuel there is and deny development opportunities to others. As the centers of deep petroleum and natural gas reserves, the Persian Gulf and the Caspian Sea are among the most likely regions to be caught up in such conflicts. Washington and Beijing, for instance, need an energy hotline, so as to avoid inadvertently falling into conflict as gas and petroleum become more expensive and harder to get in the quantities they desire.

Although alternative energy sources such as wind and solar are unlikely to resolve the energy crisis in the short term, they can make a contribution in the medium term and are absolutely essential in the long term. If Hansen is right and even current levels of 387 parts per million of carbon dioxide in the atmosphere is an unsustainable level, then the prospect of 450 ppm, which is where the world is heading, could be apocalyptic in its consequences. The world needs to invest massively in solar energy so as to resolve the dire problems of climate change and insufficient energy supply. Industrialized states need to harness private sector investment and research by ceasing their hidden subsidies to fossil fuels, and, further, they need to enact legislation to make consumers pay for the full cost of hydrocarbon fuels, including the environmental and security costs.[51] The success that the Green Party has had in making solar energy more profitable in Germany, by using legislation to level the energy playing field, is an example that should be widely emulated. Further, pressure should be exerted on China and India to develop better mass transportation facilities rather than going down the dead end of the automobile culture, and the United States needs more cities with convenient subways and trains so as to cut back on its gasoline addiction.

Ironically, even though the gas- and oil-producing countries of the Gulf have among the world's largest carbon footprints, and so are major contributors to the crisis, rising seas and other effects of carbon-driven climate change could prove disastrous for the Gulf countries themselves. If the Gulf waters rose, dense populations along the littoral would be forced inland. Nor would the quality of life be improved in that region if it were even hotter. (As it is, you need oven mittens to open your automobile door in the summer if it has been sitting in the sun.) In response, Abu Dhabi in the United Arab Emirates is building the first zero-carbon town, Masdar. The town will be fueled by solar and wind power, will bar automobiles, and will use traditional Arabian housing designs suited to a hot, arid climate. The UAE is also building a city with very low carbon emissions in Jordan, but it is much bigger, expected to grow to a million inhabitants.[52]

Most Muslim states are and have long been firm U.S. allies. The steps suggested here are not given their urgency by an absolute need for energy independence, which is in any case unrealizable in the foreseeable future. Rather, consumers and producers have common interests in preventing resource wars and the dislocations of climate change. If the United States joined with other consumers, such as China and Japan, as well as with oil- and gas-producing countries threatened by climate change and rising seas, to form an energy alliance aimed at making crucial breakthroughs in fuel cells and solar panel technology, they could achieve important progress. As demonstrated by the UAE funding of low-carbon cities in the Middle East, some innovative green energy initiatives may well be pioneered by Muslim states flush with oil and gas income, and from whom the United States and its allies may well find much to learn.

A clash of civilizations between North Atlantic consumers and Muslim producers would prove ruinous for both, while greater cultural understanding and cooperation might get us all past the greatest challenge the world has faced: massive climate change that will fatefully alter humankind's only habitat. In the medium term, Western consumers need to accept the inevitability of a close partnership with Muslim producers. In the long term, both must cooperate to foster new technologies and adapt the energy infrastructure to fashion a post-carbon world of alternative energy that will benefit all. Creating that world will also require a new set of policies toward the security challenges emanating from the Middle East.

CHAPTER II

MUSLIM ACTIVISM, MUSLIM RADICALISM

TELLING THE TWO APART

A string of horrific images, including the collapse of the World Trade towers, the mangled wreckage of Madrid trains, the smoke pouring out of the London Underground, and the infernos at the Marriott Hotel in Islamabad and the Oberoi Hotel in Mumbai, has affected the image of political Islam in ways that are often unfair.

By political Islam I mean peaceful movements, such as the contemporary Muslim Brotherhood in Egypt, which engage in parliamentary politics. Such movements are often dismissed by Western politicians as "Islamic fascists" or, worse, "Islamofascists." Quite apart from the inappropriateness of the term "fascist" for parties that actively campaign for seats in an elected legislature, these epithets are offensive insofar as they defame the religion of Islam in general. The word "Islamic," like "Judaic," refers to the ideals of the religion. Thus, there can logically speaking be no "Islamic terrorism" or "Islamic burglary." There can, of course, be Muslim criminals and Muslim terrorists. Members of fringe cults attempting to hijack Islam may call their

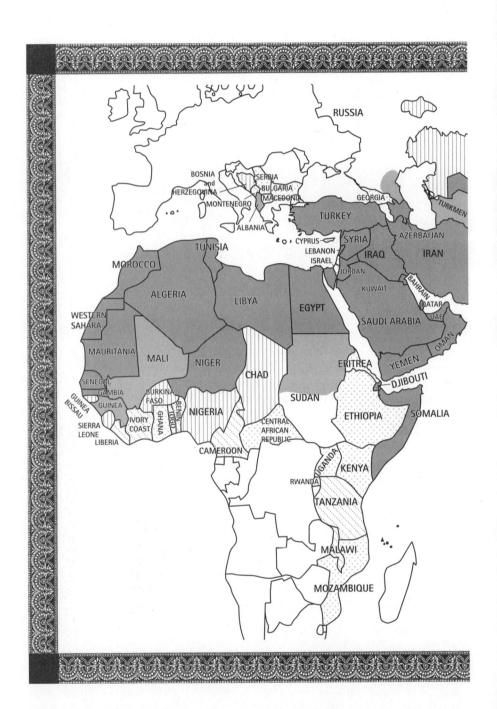

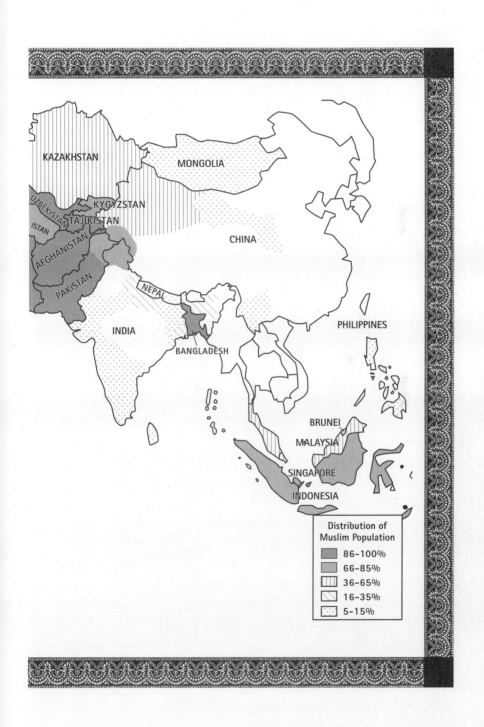

KAZAKHSTAN

MONGOLIA

UZBEKISTAN

KYGYZSTAN

ISTAN

TAJIKISTAN

AFGHANISTAN

CHINA

PAKISTAN

NEPAL

INDIA

PHILIPPINES

BANGLADESH

BRUNEI

MALAYSIA

SINGAPORE

INDONESIA

Distribution of
Muslim Population

86–100%

66–85%

36–65%

16–35%

5–15%

groups "Islamic," but that claim that should be challenged. Likewise, we would not speak of "Judaic terrorists" or "Christofascists." In any case, since the Muslim Brotherhood is the leading fundamentalist political force in the Sunni world, understanding it better is crucial for putting aside the West's Islam Anxiety in favor of practical policymaking.

How misunderstood the Muslim Brotherhood is was demonstrated in the last Republican Party primary. Former Massachusetts governor Mitt Romney remarked that he did not accept the Democratic Party's notion that "this" (that is, the threat of terrorism) "is all about one person [Usamah Bin Laden]." He asserted, "This is about Shi'a and Sunni. This is about Hizbullah and Hamas and al-Qaeda and the Muslim Brotherhood. This is the worldwide jihadist effort to try and cause the collapse of all moderate Islamic governments and replace them with a caliphate."[1] It was odd for Romney to group the Muslim Brotherhood, which has renounced violence and maintains no paramilitary forces, with Hizbullah and Hamas, which do engage in violence and have men under arms, though neither group targets the United States. (It is true that Hamas began as the Gaza branch of the Muslim Brotherhood, but it is now an independent organization.) Further, Shiites actually do not want a caliphate, which is a Sunni notion. Most odd was that Romney accused the Muslim Brotherhood of aiming to undermine "moderate Islamic governments" when, actually, its main political struggles are against secular governments, such as the one in Egypt. At least in its public statements, the current Brotherhood says it wants to *establish* a moderate Muslim government in Egypt.

The Egyptian Muslim Brotherhood raises conundrums for politicians concerned with Muslim radicalism. It is not now involved in violence but was in the relatively distant past. Indeed, its turn to moderation in the 1970s impelled some young people in its orbit to break with the Brotherhood and form small terror groups. The rhetoric of its leaders is anti-American and promotes a puritan morality and the breaking down of any separation between religion and state. It would very much like to supplant the pro-American soft military dictatorship of Hosni Mubarak. It has committed itself to doing so peacefully and politically, however. The largest dissident party in Egypt, the Brotherhood now has 88 seats in the lower house of parliament (out of 454).

Visiting U.S. congressmen who meet with Egyptian parliamentarians therefore meet with representatives of the party, which has caused controversy both in Cairo and in Washington.

Some authors have attempted to depict the Brotherhood as somehow akin to the fascist mass movements of the 1930s in Europe, but such allegations seldom rest on a close reading of primary sources.[2] The idea that the Muslim Brotherhood is, in its origins or essence, somehow imbued with a basic fascism on the European model is just ignorant. So, too, is the even more ridiculous idea that it resembles socialist parties. (The Brotherhood is nothing if not deeply committed to private property; it came out against land reform in Egypt.)

The Brotherhood has never been big enough to count as a mass movement, and it has been inconsistent on issues such as violence and democracy. The most reliable estimate for membership at its height, in 1948, is 500,000, which was 2.5 percent of the 19.5 million population of Egypt at that time. Those who liken it to European fascism have the burden of explaining why that analogy makes any sense, given the Brotherhood's tiny size, how it failed to become a truly mass movement, how its attitude to militancy has fluctuated, and how dissimilar its ideology is to those of Mussolini and Franco. In fact, it is a lower-middle-class urban nativist movement that arose initially at a time when Egyptian politics was dominated by big landlords who had an unspoken alliance with the British. From the 1970s, its leadership has shown a willingness to contest elections where they have been permitted to do so.

One irony in the attempt to depict the Brotherhood and its offshoots as a threat not only analogous but actually kindred to 1930s and 1940s mass political movements in Europe such as fascism and communism is that some of these offshoots have been America's best friends in recent years. The Iraqi Muslim Brotherhood, originally founded in the 1930s in Mosul, is now the Iraqi Islamic Party. That party has closely cooperated with Washington and participated in elections, and its leader, Vice President Tariq al-Hashimi, has been praised by American politicians. The ruling Afghan Jami'at-i Islami likewise is an offshoot of the Muslim Brotherhood. It organized many of the Tajiks who fought the Taliban and formed a key element in the

Northern Alliance. The United States helped install it in power in Kabul in late 2001. Political parties with the Muslim Brotherhood in their genealogy can at times wear white hats from Washington's point of view, despite their continued commitment to implementing Islamic canon law and moving their societies toward a more puritan vision. Understanding the checkered history of this movement, its place in Middle Eastern societies, and its relationship to its fringe offshoots is essential to addressing the sort of ignorance and Islam Anxiety expressed in Romney's remarks.

With the opening in 1869 of the Suez Canal, through which a significant portion of the world's sea trade moves, Egypt's importance to Western policy increased. If worries about petroleum drove post–World War II U.S. policy toward the Gulf, concerns about the freedom of shipping (including of petroleum) through the Suez Canal drove some of Washington's policies toward Egypt in the mid-1900s. A further reason for increased American interest was that Egypt, with a third of the Arab world's population, has been a major arena for the contest among competing ideologies for Arab Muslims—a trend-setter for Arab politics. Because its military government cooperates closely with the United States and its European allies, Egypt typically is not itself a cause of Islam Anxiety for Western publics. While many Americans appear to have unfairly blamed Saudi Arabia for Usamah Bin Laden, they seem not to have blamed Egypt for Muhammad Atta.

Some steps the Egyptian state has taken may help explain this anomaly. Its government made peace with Israel in 1978 and has functioned as a reliable U.S. geopolitical and military ally ever since, offering overflight facilities and engaging in joint military exercises. Its ancient Pharaonic culture and its beaches make it a favorite tourist destination. In recent years the annual number of tourists visiting Egypt has risen to over 11 million, and two-thirds of them are Europeans, including a growing contingent of Russians.[3] The government hopes to increase the number of visitors even more in coming years, and its policies therefore punish Muslim hotel owners who, for instance, decline to sell alcohol in their establishments, by downgrading them to two stars even if they are otherwise luxurious.[4] Whatever the Qur'an says about drinking alcohol, Egypt is arranged for the convenience of Western tourists. Egypt may be the Muslim-majority country with which Westerners are most familiar, and that intimacy may help account for its relatively positive image.

Americans on the whole like Egypt, giving it a 62 percent favorability rating in one recent poll. Younger Americans like Egypt even more, with those aged eighteen to thirty-four being 69 percent favorable toward it.[5] That figure is slightly higher than the ones for South Korea and Mexico, but lower than the favorability rating of France and India. Egypt is far and away the most popular Muslim country among Americans, with Saudi Arabia, Pakistan, Afghanistan, and Iraq—all also U.S. allies—receiving favorability ratings of only 20 to 31 percent. (The Palestine Authority and Iran are palpably disliked, garnering only 14 percent and 8 percent favorable views respectively.[6])

In contrast, the Egyptian public gives the United States among the lowest favorability ratings in the world. In one 2007 opinion poll, 4 percent of Egyptians said they had a favorable view of the United States, while 93 percent were unfavorable.[7] Egyptians, far more than Moroccans, Pakistanis, and Indonesians, saw the world's sole superpower as a major shaper of world events. Some 57 percent of Egyptians said that "nearly everything" that happens in the world is controlled by the United States. Egyptians overwhelmingly believe that Washington's goal is to weaken Islam (so said 92 percent of respondents), significantly more than in other countries. Less than one in ten Egyptians believed that the United States was waging a war on terror primarily in order to protect itself from attacks, believing instead that the war was a pretext for dividing and weakening Muslims, and for dominating them.

Egyptians are more determined to see U.S. troops leave the Muslim world than other publics are. All but a small minority of Egyptians supported attacks on U.S. troops as a way of forcing them out of Iraq, Afghanistan, and the Gulf. They differed in this regard from Indonesians, of whom only 19 percent supported such attacks, and even from

Pakistanis, of whom only a plurality did. Egyptians strongly identify with Sunni Iraqis on Arab nationalist grounds and often view the American occupation of Iraq as deeply affecting them.[8]

A couple of years ago I was talking to an American Fulbright scholar who taught for a year at an Egyptian university. She said that all of her students, however much they liked her as a person, were rabidly against the American presence in Iraq. At the end of the year, they staged a play on the campus square about a brave Iraqi guerrilla band taking on U.S. troops, all of whom they managed to kill at the end, with the students playing American soldiers in khaki sprawling on the steps of the library, covered in ketchup stains. She said that the students abjectly apologized afterward for any hurt feelings and assured her that the theme of the play was not directed against her personally. They just did not like U.S. policy. As the tourism figures given above underline, the Egyptian public does not for the most part dislike Westerners as individuals. Its passions run to the geopolitical.

On the other hand, in the poll mentioned above, 88 percent of Egyptians said that groups such as al-Qaeda that attack civilians are violating the precepts of Islam. Only 7 percent disagreed. At 91 percent, a larger proportion of Egyptians strongly opposed attacks on Americans in the United States than did Pakistanis, Indonesians, and Moroccans, though in all four countries only between 4 and 7 percent outright approved of such strikes.[9] What these responses tell us is that the vast majority of Egyptians has nothing against Americans who stay in the United States, but they deeply resent the American imperial troop presence in the Middle East.

Some Egyptian attitudes seem contradictory. Eighty percent of Egyptians agreed with the goal of keeping Western culture out of their society, but 88 percent said that globalization is a good thing. Based on my own experience, however, I do not think they are actually very interested in keeping Western culture out of their country. Instead, they seem crazy for it. Two decades ago, during one of my stays there for research, I remember Egyptian state television buying rights to American prime-time soap operas of the steamy *Dynasty* sort and running the episodes every weeknight at 9:00 P.M. until the season ended. My neighborhood in Cairo fell quiet during that period as fans were glued to their television screens.

Once, in an Egyptian newspaper, I saw the results of a poll the government had done on the type of television programming people wanted. They said they wanted more American action dramas. Nowadays the Arabsat satellite broadcasting system offers five channels of American programming, and programs such as *Desperate Housewives* are lively subjects of conversation in coffee klatches in the Arab world.[10]

What Egyptians probably mean by "keeping 'Western culture' out of Egypt" is preventing libertinism—casual sex, drugs, and violence—from invading their neighborhoods. They may gossip about what is on the television screen, but living with it is a different proposition, especially in a culture that cares so much about personal and sexual reputation. Of course, most Americans would not want that sort of libertinism in their neighborhoods, either. When Americans complain about Hollywood, they are complaining about a U.S. subculture. When Muslims complain about Hollywood, they often see it as representative of American or Western values.

In contrast to the vague unease expressed by many Muslims about the loose Western morals that seem to them to undermine their societies, there are more irrational and more violent critics of the West. The seventy-year-old father of lead hijacker Muhammad al-Amir Awad al-Sayyid Atta, who lived in the upper-middle-class district of Giza near the Pyramids in Cairo, initially denied that his son had been involved in the September 11 attacks. Four years later, he finally came clean. In 2005, he expressed delight at the July 7 bombing by four Muslim radicals of the London Underground.[11] The elder Muhammad Atta, an attorney and consultant, proclaimed that his son's attack on the World Trade Towers, using American Airlines Flight 11 as a gigantic bomb, had kicked off a fifty-year religious war. He predicted that many young Muslim men like his son, whose photo hung prominently on a wall of his residence, would follow in the hijacker's footsteps. The radical cells around the globe, he told CNN, were akin to a "nuclear bomb that has now been activated and is ticking." He decried the expressions of sympathy issued by Arab and Muslim leaders for the victims of the London Underground bombings as treason and a sign that they were not really Muslims. There was, he said, a double standard, for Muslim victims received no such sympathy. He said he would do anything he could to encourage more attacks on the West.

The elder Atta's diatribe contains clues to the fringe religious ideology in which he raised his son. His positions came from the margins of mainstream political Islam in Egypt. When the elder Atta was born, in the 1930s, many urban Egyptians joined the newly founded Muslim Brotherhood, led by the schoolteacher Hasan al-Banna, the son of a watchmaker and amateur theologian. Al-Banna promised a revitalized Muslim society that would slough off the remnants of British colonial rule and institute a just, Islamic social order.

Most Americans and Europeans will find it hard to imagine the grievances generated among Egyptians by the British conquest and colonial occupation of Egypt that began in 1882.[12] The Egyptians' resentment at having their national identity forcibly reshaped in what they viewed as a kind of large-scale cultural rape and impregnation led to the formation of movements such as the Muslim Brotherhood.

Although Egypt became nominally independent in 1922, after mass protests and a major uprising at Alexandria, British control of the Egyptian military and strong British influence on Egyptian politics lasted well beyond that date. Egyptian Muslims chafed at the laws and administrative rules arbitrarily imposed on them by British Christians. An annual spring festival vilifying Lord Edmund Allenby, the British general who repressed Egyptian nationalism, was held in Port Suez from 1919 until the Egyptian government finally suppressed it in 2008.

Until the 1970s, a majority of Egyptians were illiterate villagers, however, and were not deeply involved in party politics. There were occasional periods of enthusiasm, as between 1919 and 1921, when the nascent Wafd Party united peasants and city dwellers, Muslims and Coptic Christians, women and men, to demonstrate repeatedly against British colonial rule, forcing London to grant Egypt at least nominal independence. The Wafd Party evolved over the decades after 1922 from a broad-based nationalist movement (which all along had a significant Christian element) into a big landlord party mainly representing the owners of haciendas.

With the support of the more politically active urban populations of the 1920s through 1940s, the Wafd and other relatively secular and modern parties dominated parliament. Disputes raged over exactly what were the prerogatives of the king versus those of the prime minister, but the system looked a bit like that of eighteenth-century Great Britain. Most people were Muslim, but those who wanted to make Islam political were a minority.

In spite of the aforementioned recent claims that Egyptian intellectuals were influenced by the European mass movements of the 1930s, the evidence is that most major Egyptian thinkers denounced fascism in newspaper columns and political journals of the day. In 1938, the founder of the Muslim Brotherhood, Hasan al-Banna, condemned fascism, writing, "In Germany Hitler preaches Aryan nationalism, in Italy Mussolini calls for Latin nationalism . . . and other racist slogans. . . ."[13] A small far-right "Young Egypt" party was founded, and the Muslim Brotherhood appropriated some anti-Semitic European discourse as a way of critiquing the Zionist colonization of Palestine. But both were small, lacked representation in parliament or the councils of state, and were ignored by most mainstream intellectuals and politicians.

Al-Banna founded the Brotherhood in the port town of Ismailia in 1928. It moved to Cairo not long thereafter and engaged in social service activities, such as establishing mosques, schools, and hospitals and holding prayer meetings. It had a certain appeal for the urban lower middle class, which in that generation had gained some modern education in Arabic (as opposed to the elite who educated their children in French). Although the Brotherhood periodicals fulminated about continued British neocolonial influence and the legacy of the colonial era in Egyptian law and administration, it was not initially a violent or radical organization.

In the late 1930s and throughout the 1940s, two big issues pushed elements of the Brotherhood toward radicalism. One was the Zionist colonization of the British Mandate of Palestine and the damage it was doing to the interests of the native Palestinians. As a way of getting the international Jewish community on their side during World War I, in 1917 the British promised to establish a homeland for the Jewish people in Palestine. The British conquered the region during the war, and gained it as a League of Nations Mandate at the Paris Peace Conference. They never consulted the hundreds of thousands of Palestinians over whom they ruled about this project and made glib promises that the new homeland would not disadvantage them.

As romantic, nineteenth-century-style nationalists who attached an ancient history to modern groups striving to acquire a nation-state, Zionists argued on the basis of the Hebrew Bible that it was "natural" for Jews to live in what is now Israel. In fact, most European or Ashkenazi Jews are largely European in their heritage, and it would be perfectly natural for them to live in Europe. In the early twentieth century, the British promise to allow free immigration into Palestine by Jews had a relatively small impact, because relatively few wanted to go there. The rise of fascism, however, sparked a big migration of Jews to the Mandate in the 1930s, bringing the Jewish population to about 460,000, alongside roughly 1.5 million Palestinians by 1940.

In 1936, Palestinians in the Mandate, believing that rising Jewish immigration and aggressive land purchases by the Jewish National Fund would displace them, launched a general strike. The Palestinians demanded a general election and an end to unrestricted Jewish immigration. Violence ensued, and eighty-five Jews were killed early on. The British brutally put down the revolt from its inception, killing 1,000 Palestinians, and by 1939 it had petered out. They did, however, restrict further Jewish immigration and announced that they would establish a Palestinian state within ten years. The Zionist movement vehemently rejected the 1939 British white paper outlining this policy, and devoted itself to undoing it and working to establish a Jewish state in Palestine.

In Egypt, al-Banna took up the Palestine cause with vigor, staging a series of impressive rallies in the late 1930s.[14] The Brotherhood launched heated criticisms of the Egyptian government for its alliance with the British government, which in turn was crushing the protesting Palestinians. Ultimately, the Brotherhood put up its own candidates for parliament. In 1941 the British military authorities ordered al-Banna out of Cairo, and he was arrested briefly a few months later.

If al-Banna was exercised by the deleterious effects of British colonialism in Palestine and by the vestiges of British rule in his country, he found the virtual recolonization of Egypt by Winston Churchill during World War II completely insupportable. From the empire came a flood of Australian and other troops struggling to prevent Italy (and later the German army under Field Marshall Erwin Rommel) from taking over the country by way of its colony next door in Libya. Al-Banna, more worried about an actual British occupation than a theoretical German one, continually submitted reform programs and anti-British screeds to the prime minister. The British installed a pliant Wafd Party government in 1942. In response, the Brotherhood founded a "secret apparatus" that turned to terrorist activities.[15]

The Muslim Brotherhood of the 1940s in Egypt was an extremely hierarchical organization. The rank and file could not criticize al-Banna, the "supreme leader," without risking being shunned, and they were forbidden to belong to other political parties. The Brotherhood quite self-consciously divided itself into an outer layer of sympathizers, an inner layer of the committed and knowledgeable, a core of completely devoted cadres, and a still more secret inner sanctum of operatives willing to use violence. The local groups were organized as federated branches in Egypt's provinces, a mechanism that allowed them to survive attacks on the central leadership. The Brotherhood fought foreign influence and sought to impose strict puritanism on society, attacking drinking, gambling, and prostitution. Although most members and perhaps even branch leaders concerned themselves mainly with freeing Egypt of British dominance and working for the provision of social services, the top leadership aimed at abolishing secular law in favor of Islamic canon law and imposing an Islamic leadership that would consult with the ruled but not be constrained by them.

In keeping with its anti-imperial emphases, in 1946 the secret apparatus began targeting British and Egyptian government facilities. According to Egyptian government documents, the Brotherhood used threats to extort money from shopkeepers. Gun battles between members of the Muslim Brotherhood and the police became common. In the summer of 1948, as war raged in Palestine between the Israeli army and Egyptian troops, some brothers firebombed shops in the Jewish quarter in Cairo. Others volunteered to fight as auxiliaries to the Egyptian army in Palestine, gaining valuable military experience combating the nascent Israeli army.[16]

In 1948, the British Mandate of Palestine was partitioned in the midst of communal violence that turned into conventional warfare. The Zionist settler community from Europe created an army that defeated Palestinian militias and engaged in massacres and expulsions of Palestinian villagers. The Israeli forces also defeated a small invading force of demoralized and poorly trained and equipped Egyptian troops. The Jordanian military, having come to an understanding with the Zionist leaders, largely confined itself to taking the West Bank of the Jordan River, which was almost entirely Palestinian and had not been a site of Zionist settlement. In the actual fighting, the Israelis and their Arab foes were just about equally matched with regard to troop strength, but the Israelis had better esprit de corps and experience—some had fought as partisans in Eastern Europe or as soldiers in the British military. Some 82 percent of Palestinians living in what became Israel were expelled from their homes by the Zionists or fled their advancing forces, likely amounting to over 700,000 refugees. They poured, penniless, into the West Bank, Jordan, and Lebanon, with smaller numbers going to Syria and Egypt.[17]

Victorious Israeli leader David Ben-Gurion announced that these displaced persons would never be allowed to return to their homes in what was now Israel, which expropriated their land and property with no compensation. This *nakbah,* or "catastrophe," has roiled Middle Eastern politics ever since, leading to six Arab-Israeli wars, civil wars in Jordan and Lebanon, and constant violence between Palestinians and Israelis. Rage over the British giveaway of Palestine to what they saw as European colonists serving British imperial interests in the Middle East drove many Egyptians, including the Muslim Brotherhood, to become more politically active.

In part because of the poor performance of the Egyptian government and military in the 1948 war, the Brotherhood became even more intent on destabilizing the Egyptian monarchy. Their terrorist activities were discovered by the government of Prime Minister Mahmud al-Nuqrashi in the fall of 1948, and he banned the organization. On December 28, 1948, a budding veterinarian named Abdul Majid Ahmad Hasan, a member of the Brotherhood, assassinated al-Nuqrashi. Although al-Banna denounced the assassination, it is hard to believe that a major section of his organization was acting without his knowledge or blessing. In February 1949, al-Banna was himself killed, probably by Egyptian secret police seeking revenge for the killing of al-Nuqrashi. The police arrested 4,000 members of the organization.

The remaining Brotherhood members went underground. Most of them had not been violent, and most probably had not even known about the secret apparatus. The leadership began coming out of the shadows again in 1951, and directed its paramilitary to begin attacking the British bases in the Canal Zone.[18]

It is striking how the Muslim Brotherhood changed over time and how its fortunes rose and fell. It was a peaceful community organization in the 1930s but developed a terror wing in the 1940s. It tried to run candidates for office in 1941 but turned to assassination in 1948 and 1954. It was radicalized by British imperialism in the 1930s and 1940s and should be seen as more akin to anticolonial organizations in the third world at that time than to any European movements.

The turn of some Muslim Brotherhood elements to political violence in the late 1940s marked a long-term but not permanent or intrinsic development. In 1952 young officers staged a military coup against the corrupt Wafd Party. The new Revolutionary Command Council of the "Free Officers" movement dissolved all mainstream political parties and searched around for allies in civil society. It fixed on the Muslim Brotherhood as a possible source of support, even though the officers were for the most part secular Arab nationalists and even socialists. The Brotherhood took advantage of its renewed legality to organize and grow, adding students, military cadets, and factory workers to its ranks.

The Brotherhood called stridently for an Islamic state, protested the Free Officers' announced plans to carry out extensive land reform, and increasingly demanded "a commanding voice in the affairs of state."[19] Alarmed, the young officers briefly cracked down on the Brotherhood in early 1954, but the rising star within the junta, Colonel Gamal Abdel Nasser, restored their permission to operate as a nonpolitical society that spring. The Muslim Brothers, however, were especially close to the figurehead leader of the Revolutionary Command Council, General Muhammad Naguib, Nasser's main rival. Some of the organization's members saw their new freedom as an opportunity to come to power. Abdel Nasser gave a speech in the Mediterranean port city of Alexandria in October 1954. While he was addressing the crowd at Manshia Square, shots rang out. The attempted assassination failed, but the would-be assassin, a tinsmith who was a member of the Muslim Brotherhood, was arrested.

Nearly a thousand other Muslim Brothers were also arrested, and hundreds were convicted and imprisoned. Some were tortured. Six were executed. The organization was again banned and driven underground. The elder Muhammad Atta was nineteen when the arrests were made. Many devotees of political Islam saw the arrests and torture as the unprovoked actions of a grasping, tyrannical military dictatorship. Nasser moved against Naguib around the same time and became president for life.

Because it was organized by local branches, the Brotherhood always withstood regime attempts to crush it. Unlike the small, upper-middle-class, centralized Communist Party of Egypt, which the Abdel Nasser regime managed virtually to wipe out, the Brotherhood could keep itself going behind closed doors in the popular quarters of Cairo and in the provinces. It often received help from friendly preachers in the mosques. It could be argued that the biggest challenge that the organization faced in the 1950s and 1960s was not the secret police but rather Abdel Nasser's enormous popularity. A powerful, fiery orator and political visionary, the Egyptian president rallied the masses behind a vision of Arab society as progressive, socialist, independent, and relatively secular. He ridiculed the typical Muslim clergyman as obsessed with eating well and being "no more than a stooge of reaction, feudalism and capitalism."[20] In the 1960s his state-led industrialization and extension of education initially produced significant economic growth; real incomes rose in a way they had not in previous decades. Abdel Nasser's land reform, which the right-wing Brotherhood had opposed as too extensive, created a stable rural middle class that was deeply loyal to the regime and that largely resisted the Brotherhood's missionary work.

The Brotherhood was a minority taste in Egyptian politics in the late 1950s, and the radicals within it were a fringe. Most Egyptians, hardly puritans, loved listening to the romantic music of Umm Kulthum, Abdel Halim Hafez, and Farid al-Atrach. They loved going to the movies to see stars like the vivacious, fashionable Faten Hamama and her dashing husband, Omar Sharif, and enjoyed the obligatory lascivious belly dance in most local films. They loved listening to their hero, Abdel Nasser, on the radio, lambasting the arrogant, imperialist West. The men might go to mosque for Friday prayers, but for most of them religion was not ideological. The brooding, nerdy Brotherhood types, who hated secularist liberals like Hamama and Sharif and despised Abdel Nasser, were the odd men out.

A thinker came out of the movement in the 1950s and 1960s whose ideas went on to inspire generations of outright terrorists, even though he was repudiated by the Brotherhood itself. Sayyid Qutb had been a literary critic who had studied in the United States and then moved toward Muslim fundamentalism and was one of those arrested in Egypt by Abdel Nasser's secular Arab nationalist state in 1954. Around 1951, he left his job in the ministry of education and joined the Muslim Brotherhood. After his arrest, he was tortured and suffered during his first three years in prison. Thereafter his conditions improved somewhat, and he was able to write. He veered sharply away from the ideas of Hasan al-Banna.

In his manifesto, *Milestones,* Sayyid Qutb declared that liberal democracy and socialism had both revealed themselves to be dead ends.[21] It was now, he maintained, Islam's turn. He lamented that nothing was left of Islam in the contemporary world but mere belief and doctrine. Qutb's conviction that Islam had to be incarnated in a practical organization if it was to be effective is similar to Karl Marx's assertion that "the philosophers have only interpreted the world in various ways; the point however is to change it." But the last time Islam had been a concrete political community *(ummah)*, Qutb said, was several centuries before. By the 1960s, he maintained, Islam had long since vanished, and the world had reverted to the "age of ignorance," the phrase early Muslims had used to describe the pre-Islamic era of paganism in Mecca. Qutb interpreted the age of ignorance as a revolt against God's sovereignty as embodied in his revealed law. Thus, for parliaments or soviets to claim to be sovereign and to legislate on merely humanist or materialist grounds was to usurp divine authority.

Qutb said that it would be desirable if Muslims could compete against Europeans in the scientific and technological fields but that "European genius" had outstripped others so far that it would now take a very long time to catch up. Qutb concluded that Islam as a powerful political regime could only be restored to the world by cadres or vanguards of armed men willing to wage what he called holy war, or jihad. Qutb urged a struggle on all fronts, combating secular or pagan political doctrines with Muslim polemics as well as "with force and holy war in order to wipe out the organizations and authorities based on them."[22] Qutb's conception of a "vanguard" is at least indirectly derived from the ideas of Vladimir I. Lenin, who argued that the failure of workers to rise up against owners indicated that a front line of intellectuals would have to do it for them. An even more apt comparison would be with the American far right, which invested its hopes for a restoration of liberty and the Constitution in clear-sighted armed militias.

As part of his overall radical program in *Milestones,* Sayyid Qutb not only more or less declared war on both the capitalist democracies and the socialist bloc, but configured most Muslim states as mere toadies to these outside powers and as therefore not truly Muslim. Implicit in Qutb's thought was the idea that to oppose these so-called Muslim regimes was to effectively undermine Western interests. This tactic became known among later radicals as the strategy of taking on the "near enemy" before turning to the "far enemy." As part of this strategy, Sayyid Qutb was willing to declare leaders such as Abdel Nasser "not Muslims."

The Qur'an's word for a militant pagan unbeliever is *kafir*, and to declare another Muslim an infidel is known as *takfir*. This practice is sometimes called "excommunication," but that translation does not capture the full impact of the original, since, after all, most Christians would say that one can be a Christian even if one is denied communion with the church. A better translation is "faith denial." Moreover, many Muslim fundamentalists view apostasy—leaving Islam after having been a member of the religion—as a capital offense. Thus, the implication of Qutb's declaration that officials in the Abdel Nasser government had become non-Muslims was that they could be killed with impunity.

The Sunni Muslim tradition, which is the orthodoxy in Egypt, frowns on the practice of denying someone else's faith. Islam is a big-tent tradition and in some ways developed over centuries in reaction against more narrow sectarian understandings of Islam. The seventh-century Kharijite movement had maintained that Muslims who misbehaved in public, getting drunk or acting immorally, forfeited their faith and were not actually Muslims, but Sunni authorities rejected such a narrow, puritanical understanding of faith. Sunni authorities have sometimes wielded the tool of excommunication against what they saw as heresy, but it was used sparingly inside Sunni society. A blanket declaration like Qutb's, implying that almost all Muslims have departed into paganism, would never have been countenanced by the great Sunni jurists.

Qutb was briefly released from prison in 1964, and promptly became involved with radical Muslim Brothers who held discussions about how to assassinate Abdel Nasser. The plotting was discovered, and it led to Qutb's renewed imprisonment and eventual execution in 1966. Of those arrested at this time, Nasserist judges sentenced three leaders to death (including Sayyid Qutb), twenty-five to life at hard labor, eleven to ten to fifteen years at hard labor, and close to two hundred more to various shorter terms.[23]

Qutb, the ideological godfather of al-Qaeda and kindred small terror groups in our day, became a martyr for Muslim extremists not only in Egypt but, over time, throughout the Muslim world. The following year, 1967, the Israelis inflicted a stupendous defeat on Abdel Nasser, discrediting secular Arab nationalism and sending the new generation seeking for a politics of authenticity that would allow them to restore pride in themselves. Political Islam attracted many of them, and a small number of those turned to Qutb.

As the senior Muhammad Atta's CNN interview after the London Underground bombings demonstrates, he clearly believes in negating the faith of other Muslims, and ties it in to his cultlike vision of an oppressive West leaguing with supposedly Muslim states to crush the tiny band of true Muslims. The image he conveyed to CNN of a whole cadre of Muslim holy warriors who, like his son, were willing to wage a fifty-year struggle against the West recalls Sayyid Qutb's own ideas about the militant vanguard.

The elder Atta, thirty-one when Qutb was executed, was probably even then a member of the radical fringe. It is no surprise that he raised an extremist son who went on to become one of history's most infamous mass murderers. The rage he displayed to CNN at how Muslim lives were shed with no one in the West noticing or caring communicates his sectarian mind-set. He may have been thinking of the Palestinian civilians killed in Israeli military operations. He may have been thinking of the hanging of Sayyid Qutb, the "real Muslim."

Sayyid Qutb's doctrine of faith denial was roundly rejected by the mainstream Sunni Muslim authorities, such as the grand imam (rector) of the prestigious al-Azhar Seminary in Cairo, as well as by the then leader of the Muslim Brotherhood, Hasan al-Hudaybi, and his successors. Those Western observers who believe Qutb to be the most influential thinker for Islamists are just wrong on this score.[24] Mainstream political Islam roundly rejected him. The al-Azhar grand imam Jad al-Haqq, a leading authority for the world's Sunnis, wrote a refutation of Qutb's notion of faith denial in 1982 as a formal fatwa, or legal ruling. He argued that one becomes a Muslim by sincerely reciting the witness to faith: there is no deity but God and Muhammad is his Prophet. Subsequently, no sin short of lapsing into unbelief or hypocrisy (only pretending to believe when one does not) can make a person a non-Muslim. That is, merely breaking Islamic laws, as, for instance, drinking alcohol or committing adultery, does not equal departing from Islam as a faith. If a Muslim breaks the law, that person is a bad Muslim. But that conclusion is very different from declaring that he or she is not a Muslim at all. From Jad al-Haqq's point of view, a doctrine-of-faith denial made its holders like the seventh-century Kharijites.[25] Western journalists and pundits have never appreciated the authority held by the grand imam of al-Azhar Seminary in the Sunni community.[26]

Qutb called parliamentary democracy a "failure" in the Islamic world. But in major Muslim societies, poll respondents say, by a clear majority, that they believe democracy can work in their country.[27] In a 2007 poll in Egypt, for example, 82 percent of respondents said that democracy is a good or very good system of government, while only 14 percent said it was bad or very bad.[28] Between 82 and 99 percent of Muslims overall say that if they were crafting a constitution, they would enshrine in it the principle of freedom of speech.[29] In contrast, a 1999 poll found that 28 percent of Americans thought that the First Amendment to the Constitution went too far, and 53 percent said that the press has too much freedom.[30] Qutb, in any case, certainly is not the theorist of the vast majority of Muslims interested in politics. In

Indonesia and in the recent elections in Pakistan, secular-leaning parliamentary parties got the most votes.

Qutbism represents a tiny, far-right fringe in Muslim societies. No major political party in the Muslim world that actually wins elections and seats members in parliament accepts Qutbist ideas. Qutbists are not a mass movement, they are a small group of activists, some of whom have turned to terrorist violence. They hold no territory, and outside occupied war zones such as Palestine, Iraq, and Afghanistan, they have virtually no political significance.

Abdel Nasser died in 1970 and was succeeded by his vice president, Anwar El Sadat, one of the coup makers of 1952. Sadat was as much a man of the right, however, as Abdel Nasser had been of the left. He despised the Soviet Union (which he saw as an overly controlling patron) and he admired the United States. He thought Arab socialism was keeping Egypt backward, and he was eager to create a class of super-wealthy Egyptian entrepreneurs (he even married his daughter off to a big construction contractor). Sadat faced enormous opposition from the socialists in the government, and he felt that he needed an ally on the right to offset them. He therefore legalized the Muslim Brotherhood, allowing it to publish and organize once again. This bargain with the organization generally worked in Sadat's favor. Unfortunately for him, the wave of Muslim political activism he unleashed against the Arab socialists threw off splinter groups far more radical than the Brotherhood itself. Sadat encouraged the formation at universities of so-called Islamic Groups to offset the power of the leftists on campus, and several of these unexpectedly turned radical, forming the national Islamic Group organization.

I would argue that the radical Muslim fundamentalist movements of the 1970s and after were cults. I mean the term as more than just an insult. I define a cult as a religious group characterized by values that put it in severe tension with the outside society, and organized so as to demand very high levels of obedience and conformity to the cult leader. The tension between the cult's norms and those of most outsiders reinforces group solidarity and isolates members from the mainstream. Both of these effects in turn help the cult leadership make heavy demands on the rank and file; leaders insist that their followers give their private time and wealth to the cult. All religious groups make some demands on their adherents, but we all know of churches in which members are allowed to waltz in three times a year for holy days if that is all the commitment they want to make. For example, in the United States, Moonies and Krishna Consciousness adherents clearly have some values that starkly differentiate them from the surrounding society; most Methodists and Episcopalians do not. In my definition, cults are not necessarily small or unpopular.

The religious ferment of the 1970s in Egypt produced several significant political cults, the most important of which for our purposes are the Egyptian Islamic Jihad and the Islamic Group (al-Gama'ah al-Islamiyah). These radical movements did not recruit primarily from among Egypt's poor and rural populations but from its middle-class and lower-middle-class urbanites.[31]

The most notorious member of the Egyptian Islamic Jihad is Dr. Ayman al-Zawahiri, who went on to become Usamah Bin Laden's number two. The Jihad Organization began as a loose set of small cells in Cairo in 1966, as a direct result of the Nasser regime's execution of Sayyid Qutb, according to al-Zawahiri (then just graduating from high school). Al-Zawhiri, born June 19, 1951, descended from an elite Egyptian family. His grandfather on his mother's side was Egypt's ambassador to Yemen, Saudi Arabia, and Pakistan. His great-uncle, Abdul Razzaq Azzam, was secretary-general of the Arab League and author of a widely read liberal interpretation of the life of the prophet Muhammad. Al-Zawahiri, having trained as a physician, lived and maintained a clinic in the upscale neighborhood of Ma'adi. Although I did not meet the doctor of death, I visited Ma'adi in the 1970s to attend dinner parties thrown by professors at the American University in Cairo, at a time when he was living there. It is a surreal setting of suburban homes and lawns in the midst of an otherwise densely crowded city of skyscrapers. Al-Zawahiri appears to have been radicalized while attending the Ansar al-Sunnah Mosque in Abdeen as a teenager.[32]

In a memoir published after September 11, 2001, al-Zawahiri praised Sayyid Qutb for refusing to ask a pardon of the "tyrant," Abdel Nasser. He exulted in Israel's defeat of the Egyptian regime in the 1967 Six-Day War, saying that it demonstrated that the worm "had begun to eat the idol until he became weak."[33] Al-Zawahiri appears to have shed no tears for the thousands of Egyptian troops killed, rather delighting that the secular military regime was humiliated and its weakness demonstrated. Having joined a cell of the loosely affiliated Jihad Organization, al-Zawahiri became leader of his local group in 1970.

The Israeli occupation of Gaza and the West Bank, including Jerusalem, in 1967 took the Muslim fundamentalists to new heights of rage against Israel. Unlike secular Arab nationalists, the fundamentalists did not see the occupation as a challenge to territorial Arab nationalism. Rather, they perceived the Israelis to be dominating a part of the Muslim political community *(ummah)*, and they wholly rejected Israeli occupation of Jerusalem, the third holiest city for Muslims. (Muslim lore associates Jerusalem with the miraculous Night Journey of the Prophet Muhammad, during which he is said to have stopped there before ascending to heaven—the stone on which the Prophet is believed to have stepped is housed within the Dome of the Rock shrine.) For Muslim fundamentalists, it is insupportable to have this holy Muslim site under non-Muslim control, just as they find unbearable the idea of non-Muslim domination, brutalization, and expropriation of Palestinian Muslims in the Occupied Territories.

Secular Arab nationalists put less emphasis on the violation of the sanctity of Jerusalem and more on the struggle for human dignity and national liberation. The nationalists in the Arab world saw Israel as analogous to French colonial Algeria, and the Palestinian resistance movement that grew up in response to this further Israeli territorial acquisition as a secular national liberation organization. Many Palestinian refugees were educated by the United Nations Works and Relief Agency and had imbibed a modernist perspective. The guerrilla group Fateh, led by Yasser Arafat, had middle-class supporters drawn from shopkeepers and professionals. Other constituent groups of the Palestine Liberation Organization to the left of Fateh embraced socialism or communism. For decades, the Palestinians were excoriated by Westerners, Israelis, and conservative Arab monarchies as leftist radicals allied with the Soviet Union. Although the Egyptian radical fundamentalist groups disapproved of the politics of most of the Palestinians, they were enamored of the idea of rescuing Palestine and driving away the Israelis.

Fundamentalist fury over the Israeli occupation of more Palestinian territory in 1967 and Sayyid Qutb's heretical doctrine of faith denial were two ingredients in the toxic brew that would eventually result in al-Qaeda. A further ingredient was the idea of vigilante violence. Another major theorist of the Egyptian Islamic Jihad was Abd al-Salam Farag, who circulated a poorly written pamphlet, "The Neglected Duty," which became foundational for later Muslim terrorism, even in today's Iraq. Orthodox Islam counts five major pillars of Islam, the key responsibilities of the believer—recognizing God and the Prophet Muhammad, praying five times a day, giving alms to the poor, fasting during daytime in the month of Ramadan, and going on pilgrimage to Mecca once in a lifetime if one can afford it. Farag argued that struggling for the faith, including violence if necessary, was another such key individual duty.

The Arabic word for struggle is *jihad*. It is not used in the Qur'an with the precise meaning of "holy war," a doctrine that developed later in Muslim history. Medieval Muslim jurists considered warring for the faith, whether defensively or offensively, to be a collective duty of the community, not an individual duty. They believed that only the duly constituted authorities could declare war, and only a portion of the community had a responsibility to fight it. Farag, in contrast, wanted to make the waging of holy war an everyday obligation of individuals, who apparently could in his view act in vigilante fashion, without needing the authorization of a Muslim government. For this reason, I will refer to followers of this tendency as fundamentalist vigilantes. Some scholars call them Salafi Jihadis. But "Salafi" refers to reformists who want to go back to early Islamic practice, and jihad is a formal legal doctrine, whereas the followers of Qutb and Farag violate both of these normative traditions.

In 1980, the Egyptian Islamic Jihad formed a joint executive board with the al-Gama'ah al-Islamiya, the spiritual leader of which was Omar Abdel Rahman, a blind country cleric. They decided to have President Anwar El Sadat assassinated. In part, they wanted to exact revenge on him for his peace treaty with Israel, which had left the Palestinians at the mercy of the Israelis. They also hoped to provoke a popular revolution analogous to that occurring in Iran at the time. They had managed to acquire some covert assets among junior officers, and in September 1981, Lieutenant Khalid Islambuli jumped out of the back of a troop transport truck during a military review and sprayed the presidential reviewing stand with machine-gun fire, killing the president. Contrary to the expectation of the small corps of cultists who planned and executed the assassination, the Egyptian public showed no interest in making a popular Islamic revolution. Sadat's vice president, Hosni Mubarak, an air force general trained in Moscow, was quickly anointed by his fellow officers as the new president. He launched a roundup of suspected plotters, arresting hundreds.[34]

Back in America, the idea of depending on Islam and on Saudi Arabia's supposed leadership of the religion to fight Soviet influence, first proposed by Dwight Eisenhower, resurfaced during the Ronald Reagan administration. After the Soviet Union sent troops to Afghanistan in late 1979, in order to shore up a shaky communist military regime, the United States turned to Pakistan for help in expelling the Red Army. Politicians in the United States, including Republicans such as Senator John McCain of Arizona, urged more funding for the Muslim holy warriors, or mujahideen, whom Ronald Reagan called "freedom fighters." On October 3, 1985, McCain joined Representative Tom Loeffler, Republican from Texas, in presenting the Freedom Fighter of the Year award to Afghan tribal leader Wali Khan. He was part of the National United Front, which claimed that it had 20,000 irregulars combating the Soviet occupation.[35]

The American-backed groups in Afghanistan included the Hizb-i Islami led by Gulbadin Hikmatyar, who received a disproportionate share of the billions of dollars the U.S. government sent to the Muslim guerrillas. Hikmatyar had joined the Afghanistan youth branch of the Muslim Brotherhood while studying engineering at Kabul University in 1970. A violent young man, he killed another student and was imprisoned for two years on manslaughter charges. He went into exile in Pakistan and founded his Party of Islam in 1975. After the Soviet invasion, his group took on the Red Army, but was so bloody and factional that it is said to have killed more fellow Muslims than Soviets.

The Reagan administration turned over the implementation of its insurgency plans to the Pakistani Inter-Services Intelligence (ISI), which favored the most hard-line and brutal fundamentalists, such as Hikmatyar. The CIA, in cooperation with Pakistani intelligence, opened training camps for the Afghan guerrillas, teaching them how to make bombs, form covert cells, and plan terrorist operations against the Soviets and the Afghan left. Some of the thousands of Arab Muslim volunteers who came to help the Afghan fighters received secondhand benefits from the American training, learning techniques from their Afghan comrades in arms. The Arabs also had their own training camps, presumably funded by Saudi Arabia.

The Afghanistan struggle became a magnet for members of Egypt's vigilante cults, some of whom appear to have been released from prison by the Mubarak regime on condition they leave Egypt and go to Afghanistan. Among those released was al-Zawahiri, who became a physician to those guerrillas wounded by Soviet troops. Also attracted to Afghanistan were some of the more radical Saudi Muslim activists, such as Usamah Bin Laden, a wealthy socialite from a famed business family. The Saudis, mostly from the Wahhabi school of Islam, did not necessarily share the ideas of their Egyptian comrades. The Muslim Brotherhood tradition was less "puritanical" than Wahhabism, in that it accepted more of the medieval Islamic heritage. It was also less wary of technological and intellectual innovation. Yet, as the Egyptian vigilantes interacted with Wahhabi volunteers in Afghanistan, they learned to cooperate with one another.

In the 1980s, the burgeoning religious right in the United States adopted the Afghan holy warriors as their cause célèbre, seeing them as dear allies against the godless, atheist communists. *Christian Voice,* for

instance, issued a "biblical scorecard," a checklist that voters on the religious right were instructed to use to decide whether to support their
senators and representatives in Congress. A key criterion was whether
the politician voted money to support the Muslim freedom fighters in
Afghanistan.[36] Evangelist Pat Robertson, who ran for the Republican
presidential nomination in 1987, campaigned in support of the Muslim guerrillas, pledging: "I would send arms and supplies to the brave,
indigenous freedom fighters that are found in Angola, Mozambique,
Afghanistan and Nicaragua."[37]

By February 1989, the Soviets, unwilling to bear the costs in blood
and treasure of continuing to attempt to occupy Afghanistan in the
face of mujahideen resistance, had withdrawn all their troops. The
guerrillas believed that they had defeated the Soviet Union. Many, like
Bin Laden himself, cast about for further projects in defense of the
Muslim world and with an eye toward making the Muslims themselves
a superpower.

One project on the minds of Bin Laden's circle was the struggle
against Israel. When they met in Qandahar in the late 1980s, Bin
Laden's comrades, angered by the Israeli crackdown in the wake of the
outbreak of the first Intifadah (or Palestinian uprising) in the West
Bank in 1987, obsessively preached sermons on the liberation of
Jerusalem.[38] The uprising itself had been provoked by Israel's colonization of the West Bank and Gaza in the 1970s and 1980s, and its iron-
fisted rule over the stateless Palestinians. Palestinians saw more of their
land expropriated by settlers, and their wells went dry as settlers dug
deeper ones and the aquifers fell. The colonization of Palestinian territory was pursued by Zionists in quest of a "Greater Israel"; they argued
that such expansion would be the only way for the small state to survive in the long term.

Bin Laden returned to Jidda in Saudi Arabia in 1989, and was allowed to preach a sermon in his local mosque in 1990. In the sermon
Bin Laden spoke of the Palestinian Intifadah and the Muslim fundamentalists' enmity and "contempt" for America because of its support
of Israel.[39] An Egyptian journalist in the audience was taken aback at
how quickly Bin Laden had transferred his long-standing hatred of the
Soviet Union to the United States. Bin Laden's dislike of the United

States only grew. He had to leave Saudi Arabia for Sudan after the Gulf War because of his conflict with the ruling family over its hosting of American troops in the Muslim holy land.

In May 1996, the Sudanese government yielded to Egyptian and American pressure to expel Bin Laden, and he returned to Afghanistan. He at first reestablished himself at Jalalabad with war-lords he knew from the old days. He later allied with a new militant Muslim movement, the Taliban—armed seminarians backed by America's former partners, the Pakistani ISI. The Saudi millionaire recognized Mulla Omar of Oruzgan, the Taliban leader, as the "com-mander of the faithful," or caliph, and pledged fealty to him, as did Afghans who joined the movement. (Most Sunni Muslims believe that the medieval caliphate, a sort of Muslim papacy, has lapsed.) Bin Laden summoned his former comrades in arms, now dispersed to places such as Saudi Arabia, Egypt, and Algeria, to form a new fighting force, the 55th Brigade of the Taliban. These Arab fighters would be the Taliban's best. They did not pledge fealty directly to Mulla Omar but rather to Bin Laden. Technically, it is only those who give Bin Laden their formal pledge of loyalty that constitute al-Qaeda (literally, "the base").[40]

In 1998, Bin Laden issued his Declaration of Jihad on "the Jews and Crusaders," that is, Israel and the United States. He gave three reasons for this announcement of war: The first was the presence of American troops in Saudi Arabia, which, Bin Laden argued, could be considered to be an occupation of, and certainly defiled, the two holy cities of Mecca and Medina. The second was the U.S. and UN sanctions imposed on Iraq after the Gulf War, which Bin Laden claimed were responsible for the deaths of a million innocent Iraqis. The third was the commitment of the United States to "serve the Jews' statelet" and "divert attention from its occupation of Jerusalem and murder of Muslims there."[41] Although Bin Laden mentioned Is-rael's occupation of Jerusalem third, he gave America's desire to pro-tect the Zionist state as one of Washington's motives for the first two offenses. It is often alleged that Bin Laden does not care about the Palestine issue, but this reading of him is false. He feels that his money can do the most good if he supports operations in areas not already served by a Muslim insurgency, as Palestine is. In principle, he sees Israel's encroachments on Jerusalem, and actions that make it hard for the Muslim population of East Jerusalem to remain, as a central grievance of his movement.

At the outset, Al-Qaeda, rather like the Red Brigades in Italy, was more than a small terrorist group but less than a mass movement, showing a capacity to motivate thousands of volunteers and hundreds of thousands of sympathizers (before its popularity rapidly declined in the years after September 11). It is important to underline, however, that unlike the Taliban, it had no prospects of coming to power anywhere in its own right as a political force.

The big unnoticed story of the 1990s was the decisive defeat of the radical vigilantes in Egypt. Extremists in Egypt were responsible for an estimated 1,357 killings between 1992 and 1998. An Egyptian Islamic Jihad assassination attempt against Hosni Mubarak failed in 1995, and the Egyptian government imprisoned 20,000 or more members of and even sympathizers with the fringe cults. Worse, the public was turning against the radicals, denying them funding and moral support. A straw in the wind was the popular 1992 film *Terrorism and Barbecue,* starring prominent Egyptian comic Adel al-Imam, about radical Muslims who take hostages in a government building but are persuaded to let them go by the arguments of the protagonist, who underlined that what they were doing was incompatible with the humane principles of true Islam.

A horrific attack in 1997 on Western tourists at the Temple of Hatshepshut in Luxor left seventy-one dead and provoked widespread disgust in the Egyptian public. Although the radicals coded such acts as "jihad," or holy war, they violated the canons of holy war as an Islamic ritual. These canons forbid holy warriors to kill civilian noncombatants. They stipulate that fair warning be given of an attack, that those attacked be given the opportunity to convert first, and that the warriors need authorization from duly constituted Islamic leaders. Terrorism is not jihad, and Egyptians knew very well what had really happened to the innocent tourists. In Luxor, many local Egyptians, stricken with grief by the attack on their guests, ran to the hospital to give blood.[42]

In the face of their increasing unpopularity, the radicals began to run out of money and recruits. Following the government's massive campaign of arrests, most of the leadership of the al-Gama'ah al-Islamiya and the Egyptian Islamic Jihad still in the country were incarcerated at Tura Prison. The imprisoned leadership of the Gama'ah decided to abandon violence at some point after 1998. They authored twenty "recantation books" that reinterpreted the Qur'an as requiring that they use peaceful means to accomplish their goals.[43] Omar Abdel Rahman, imprisoned in the United States for his role in the bombing of the World Trade Center in 1993, castigated his old organization for its turn against radicalism, but to little avail.

Al-Zawahiri and Bin Laden came to the conclusion that the United States was succeeding in propping up "the near enemy." They decided that they therefore had been going about things backward and that they needed to remove the United States from the equation before they could hope to make their revolutions in the Middle East and elsewhere in the Muslim world. The September 11 operation was not the announcement of a growing, popular mass movement with an appealing ideology. It was the flailing about of a dying organization of aging revolutionaries banished to camps in the rugged wastelands of failed states.

To better understand the nature of Muslim terrorism movements, it is worthwhile to think about them comparatively. At 9:02 A.M. on April 19, 1995, an immense conflagration engulfed the Alfred P. Murrah Federal Building in Oklahoma City. A fertilizer bomb incinerated 168 persons and wounded 850 in the vicinity. Of the 194 workers who managed to get out of the building alive, all but a handful needed urgent medical treatment. The building's day care center had just opened, and

19 children fell victim to the raging explosion. The detonation damaged three hundred nearby buildings. In the aftermath, a small army of 12,000 volunteers had to be mobilized to pick through the rubble for burned and mangled bodies.

The bombers, Timothy McVeigh and Terry Nichols, were part of a right-wing, antigovernment gun culture and were closely associated with persons who believed that Jews controlled the Federal Reserve and that racial minorities were in control of the federal government. It is likely that they denied being white supremacists after their arrest only because they knew that if they admitted to being racists, it would cause the public to dismiss them and their message.

The gun culture in which they moved was fed, moreover, by several cultlike religious movements that had split from mainstream Protestantism,[44] and was part of a diverse network of white supremacists and antigovernment conspiracy theorists in the 1980s and 1990s. (White supremacists deeply resented the 1992 victory of Bill Clinton in the presidential elections, since they felt that the Democratic Party represents the interests of African Americans, Jews, Catholics, and other ethnic groups.) McVeigh had joined a branch of the Ku Klux Klan for a year when he was living in upstate New York. He had also attended meetings of the Michigan Militia, an organization of an estimated 12,000 in the early 1990s.

The antigovernment gun movement commemorated with sorrow the federal operation at Ruby Ridge, when agents attempted to arrest Randy Weaver on a firearms charge and inadvertently killed his wife, a believer in the Christian Identity theory that Anglo-Saxons are the true Israelites, not the Jews.[45] They also felt sympathy with the Branch Davidians, a cult in Waco, Texas, that broke off from the Seventh-day Adventist church and followed self-proclaimed prophet David Koresh; seventy-six Branch Davidians died during an ill-fated government operation against them in 1993. McVeigh visited Waco during the government's siege to show sympathy. He and Nichols thought of themselves as avenging what they viewed as atrocities against whites by a tyrannical federal government infiltrated by UN moles. Presumably inspired by the faithful at Waco, McVeigh later tried attending a Seventh-day Adventist church. He was convinced that the federal agents had gassed the people in the compound and set the fire that killed them. His sister, Jennifer, said, "He thought the people were murdered."[46]

Both Randy Weaver and Timothy McVeigh justified the Oklahoma City bombings as no different from the actions of the federal government toward others. McVeigh excused his mass murders by pointing to Hiroshima and the killing of Iraqi civilians in bombing raids, implying that he was just acting as the government routinely does. Asked by an associate about the likely loss of innocent life as he discussed his plans to carry out a bombing in 1994, McVeigh replied, "Think about the people as if they were storm troopers in *Star Wars*. . . . They may be individually innocent, but they are guilty because they work for the Evil Empire."[47]

McVeigh read and recommended the white supremacist novel *The Turner Diaries*, which dramatizes attacks on Jews and racial minorities in order to establish "Aryan nations" and has scenes both of the bombing of a federal building and of an airplane being flown into a building in Washington, D.C. The author of the *Diaries*, William Pierce, talked of being an atheist, as McVeigh and Nichols did occasionally, but they apparently only meant that they rejected a personal God. Pierce held that the life force is evolutionary, with the white race at the pinnacle. The FBI later found Terry Nichols's fingerprints on a copy, at his house, of *Hunter*, another of Pierce's racist novels, which "portrays a senior FBI official motivated by hate for Jews and homosexuals who hires a man to bomb buildings."[48]

As is shown by their adherence to a nonpersonal conception of the divine, part of the crackpot system of belief that Pierce styled "cosmotheism," McVeigh and Nichols operated at the fringe of religious movements inspired by unorthodox theology and drew support from white supremacist networks at the intersection of racism and religious extremism. McVeigh, for example, had come to know Andreas Strassmeir, "Andy the German," on the gun show circuit. Strassmeir was a militia trainer at the Christian Identity commune at Elohim City, Oklahoma. McVeigh called Strassmeir twice in the period before the bombing, seeking a place to hide out in the aftermath.[49]

McVeigh and Nichols bear a number of striking similarities to members of such radical Egyptian groups as the Egyptian Islamic

Jihad and the Islamic Grouping of the Blind Sheikh, as well as, of course, to the September 11 hijackers. McVeigh seriously considered carrying out a suicide bombing, and in any case said he expected to be caught and executed in the aftermath. He chose a tall building that he saw as the center of a U.S. federal government plot against freedom-loving individuals. He and Nichols devoured books that centered on conspiracy theories about Jewish control of the U.S. government. Like McVeigh and Nichols, some of the hijackers, such as Lebanese engineer Ziad Jarrah, had a relatively secular outlook. Al-Qaeda operatives were Muslim nationalists just as McVeigh and Nichols were white national-ists, and religion was only one marker of identity and not always the most important one for them. Al-Qaeda also feared the United Na-tions as a tool of a U.S. government monopoly on world power.

The most important similarity between the Oklahoma City bombers and the September 11 hijackers is that both belonged to fringe, if significant, movements. The networks of gun enthusiasts, right-wing anarchists, Klansmen, other white supremacists, survival-ists, British Israelites, Adventist spin-offs, and UN conspiracy theorists through which McVeigh and Nichols swirled has its analogs in the Middle East. One wonders whether, if McVeigh and Nichols had struck a building in Beijing, the Chinese government would have rounded up Catholics and Adventists as security risks and begun racially profiling whites as a suspicious ethnic group.

If there is an analogy between the Oklahoma City bombing and the Luxor and other attacks in Egypt, what events play the role of Ruby Ridge and Waco for Muslim fundamentalists? What marginal ideas and unorthodox religious traditions underpin the grievances of funda-mentalist vigilantes? Just as American militiamen nurtured a grudge over a whole set of what they saw as federal encroachments backed by a burgeoning international cabal, so their counterparts in Egypt and Saudi Arabia had similar concerns. The secular, Egyptian military gov-ernment had cracked down on radical Muslim fundamentalists on sev-eral occasions, arresting and torturing them and sometimes carrying out executions, creating martyrs to the cause as poignant for the Mus-lim far right as were Randy Weaver's wife or David Koresh for the American.

When the Algerian fundamentalist Islamic Salvation Front (FIS) won the 1991 elections, the military cancelled the results, imposed martial law, and threw the country into a brutal civil war. Some disappointed FIS members turned to violence, and several even formed small terrorist groups, such as the Armed Islamic Group (GIA), which received money from Usamah Bin Laden. Although most American observers view the conflict between Israel and the Palestinians through Israeli eyes, so that the main issue is Palestinian terrorism, most Muslims see the Palestinians as victims of Israeli ethnic cleansing campaigns and of continued occupation and brutality at Israeli hands. Through this latter lens, Palestinian violence is construed as legitimate resistance to occupation, as a national liberation struggle.

In every case just mentioned—Egypt, Algeria, and Israel/Palestine—the United States is strongly allied with the state perceived to be crushing Muslim activists. Even the U.S. defense of Saudi Arabia in the Gulf War led to the stationing of Christian and Jewish European-heritage troops in the Muslim holy land, a matter of profound humiliation and religious blasphemy for hard-line Muslim activists.

It may be objected that the Muslim far right is much larger than the American far right. It could also be argued that the "Patriot" gun movement in the United States declined from the late 1990s. But the same thing is true of Islamic Jihad and the Islamic Grouping in Egypt. My argument does not, in any case, depend on the analogy being exact, or on the numbers being the same. I am simply asserting key similarities between the far right in the United States and the Middle East. That said, Americans probably underestimate how powerful the far right has been in the United States, and overestimate how popular its analog is in the Muslim world. We tend to forget that when Ku Klux Klan Grand Dragon David Duke ran for senator in Louisiana on the Republican Party ticket in 1990, he gained 44 percent of the state's vote and 60 percent of the white vote. Of course, Duke, despite his vicious barbs against Jews and African Americans, did eschew violence, representing himself as a new breed of Klansman. But if we are talking only about violent extremists—the sort of people who would shoot someone down or blow something up—then they are a tiny fringe in most Middle Eastern societies, just as they are in the United States.

A Washington Post/ABC News poll conducted just after the Oklahoma City bombing in 1995 found that 13 percent of Americans then supported private armed militias. Twelve percent of respondents said that they were afraid of the government. Much more alarming, 9 percent admitted that they were angry at the government, and the same percentage agreed that violence against it could be justified. Six percent of those polled characterized the federal government as "their enemy"! That would work out to 11 million adults at that time.[50]

If anger on the far right at the American government for being too left wing subsided in the first years of the twenty-first century, other ultraconservative themes retained their salience. In a 2006 Gallup poll, 9 percent of Americans said they believe that the Bible should be the only source of U.S. law, and 46 percent said that it should be a source of law.[51] Secular journalists and politicians are often taken aback by similar polling results about Islamic law in Muslim countries but are so out of touch with the American grassroots that they are largely unaware of the desire for biblical law shared by nearly half the U.S. population (and, obviously, by more than half of the Christian population).

Nor has homegrown extremism gone away in the United States. The FBI in recent years has reported over 7,000 hate crimes annually, but some experts point out that frightened victims probably take few such crimes to the authorities. These experts estimate, based on household surveys, that there are nearly 200,000 hate crimes in the United States annually.[52] Even in the small FBI sample of attacks that get reported to police, approximately 2,000 Americans are assaulted in this country because of their race and others are attacked because of their religion every year. The number of hate groups in the United States has grown 48 percent since the year 2000, reaching nearly 900 in 2007, according to the Southern Christian Law Center.[53]

The proportion of Muslims in a 2007 Gallup poll who viewed the September 11 attacks as "completely justified" was only 7 percent, smaller than the percentage of Americans in 1995 who said it was justified to attack the U.S. federal government.[54] As for violence in general, Egypt's murder rate is on the order of 0.5 percent per 100,000 per year, compared to over ten times that for the United States.

Bin Laden and al-Zawahiri formally merged their organizations in Afghanistan in 1998, though Egyptians dominated its twelve-man board. Having decided to hit the United States, al-Qaeda had the good fortune of recruiting some high-powered engineers in Hamburg, Germany. One was the son of the radical attorney and consultant Muhammad al-Amir Atta. Atta made his martyrdom will in April 1996 at the beginning of an operation, during which the Israeli military shelled a UN compound at Qana, where eight hundred Lebanese Shiites had taken refuge during fighting between Israel and Hizbullah. The artillery shells killed 106 civilians and wounded 116, including four UN peacekeepers from Fiji. A UN inquiry later concluded that the Israeli attack was unlikely to have been inadvertent. Muslim activists and, indeed, Middle Easterners in general saw the incident as a deliberate Israeli massacre of civilians, a charge Israeli officials denied.

Atta was driven to become a religious warrior in part by newspaper pictures of the mangled bodies of children who emerged from the compound. Atta and his associates came to believe, like McVeigh and Nichols, that the ends justified the means.[55] There are many reports of the September 11 hijackers visiting strip clubs or bars when in America, suggesting that they had become antinomians, believing themselves above mere law because of the sacredness of their mission. Even Usamah Bin Laden admitted that "those youth who conducted the operations did not accept any *fiqh* [Islamic law]."[56] Bin Laden insisted that, ultimately, they were true to the legal principles of the Prophet Muhammad, but this twisted logic would not convince any reasonable observer.

The Egyptian Muslim Brotherhood and the Egyptian Islamic Jihad represent two divergent paths for Muslim activists in Egypt. The

Brotherhood now has eighty-eight members in the Egyptian parliament, though they had to run as independents because Egyptian law bars parties organized on a purely religious basis. Thirty years before, the Brotherhood gave up violence and organized for participation in civil and political society. How dedicated it is to democratic ideals remains in question, since it has never given up the slogan "Islam is the answer." It is for the moment acting, however, as a parliamentary opposition party.

The Brotherhood's current leader, Muhammad Mahdi Akif, has provoked several controversies. He called the Holocaust "exaggerated" and referred to Israel as a "cancer." He said that as part of the government, the Muslim Brotherhood would honor the 1978 Camp David peace accords, but continued to express opposition to those agreements and said that the Brotherhood did not recognize Israel.[57] In 2008, Akif gave an interview in which he called Usamah Bin Laden a *mujahid* or holy warrior, then had to backpedal when an uproar broke out in Egypt. People began calling him "Bin Akif." He quickly gave another interview in which he stressed that the Brotherhood opposed the use of violence against civilians and slammed Bin Laden for creating an ideology that resulted in that sort of crime.[58] He said that the Brotherhood had nothing to do with al-Qaeda. This assertion is correct. Ayman al-Zawahiri has continually attacked the Muslim Brotherhood for its lack of militancy.

A Muslim Brotherhood willing to participate in civil politics and to foreswear violence is an asset, not a danger. It has been convincingly argued that where a country has a significant party dedicated to political Islam, it takes up the space that al-Qaeda might otherwise fill, and so acts as a barrier to radicalism.[59] Despite Akif's crackpot ideas, his bigotry toward Israel, and his willingness to honor Bin Laden's efforts against Soviet troops in the old days, it may be that he and his organization can help to forestall a turn toward something much worse. If this theory is correct, recent U.S. State Department and congressional contacts with Muslim Brotherhood parliamentarians, condemned by the American right and by the Mubarak government alike, may be the healthiest way forward for American policy.

If the United States continues to be committed to democratization in the Middle East, the Brotherhood cannot be denied a role in Egyptian politics, given that it represents a significant if minority constituency. U.S. congressional contacts with Brotherhood members of the Egyptian parliament should continue and increase, without at the same time ignoring or offending other political currents. Given the likelihood that Hosni Mubarak will pass from the scene in the not-so-distant future, and that Egypt may well transition from military rule to civilian politics, formulating a policy toward the major political trends in Egypt will be crucial to the success of the new American president.

Ironically, the U.S. government has had no difficulty dealing directly with, and even promoting, the Iraqi Islamic Party (IIP), which is the direct descendant of the Muslim Brotherhood and which retains many of al-Banna's goals and emphases. Because Sunni fundamentalists were for the most part repressed by Saddam Hussein, the IIP welcomed the Bush administration's overthrow of his regime and was willing to accept a seat on the U.S.-appointed Interim Governing Council of 2003–2004. Even more remarkable, American proconsul in Iraq Paul Bremer was perfectly willing to appoint members of this Muslim Brotherhood branch to high office in an American-ruled colonial state. Yet the IIP wants Islamic law to be the law of the land in Iraq, just as its Egyptian counterpart does. The main difference between the two lies in their differing attitudes to the United States. If that distinction is the basis for Washington to treat them so differently, then one is not speaking of principled U.S. policy but of ad hoc diplomatic maneuvering, which surely is and should be subject to change with altered circumstances.

There is little difference, ideologically or organizationally, between the IIP and the Palestinian Hamas. Both have been involved in terrorism. The Iraqi Islamic Party has in recent years had secret ties to Sunni Arab guerrilla movements. If the IIP has sometimes been cooperative with the United States and the new Iraqi government, so too has Hamas sometimes announced, and observed, long-term truces. The unwise and unfair refusal of Washington to deal with Hamas seems primarily based on an undue deference to Israeli desires to demonize and marginalize their enemy. The Palestine issue, which has provoked so much righteous anger in the Muslim world, cannot be resolved if major players are excluded from the negotiating table—a lesson obvious to American administrators in Iraq but one that those dealing with the Palestinians seem unwilling or unable to acknowledge.

As for Egypt, rather than stigmatizing the Muslim Brotherhood as a form of European fascism, which it obviously is not, or attempting to marginalize it, the next administration needs to work behind the scenes to encourage it in a democratic direction. The framework within which the Brotherhood operates in Egypt is important to its future. Continued military rule or the succession of Mubarak's son to power as a soft dictator could convince Egyptians that democracy is not a realistic hope and cause them to take a more radical direction. It is therefore important that the United States and its allies bring behind-the-scenes pressure, both political and financial, on Mubarak's successor to open up the political system to genuine democratic elections.

Beyond the realm of high politics, the groundwork needs to be laid for the fulfillment of Egyptians' democratic aspirations. Bringing Egyptian attorneys to the United States for training in civil law and holding colloquies with Egyptian legislators on parliamentary procedure would do more good than strident denunciations of authoritarianism. Meetings of congressional representatives and parliamentarians with members of parliament in Egypt can open important channels of political communication. Involving Asian democracies such as Japan and India in these democratization efforts is important, since Egyptians might be more willing to engage with them than with what they perceive as Western imperialists. Funding for academic centers for the study of democracy at Egyptian universities, and for translations into Arabic of works of democratic theory and practice, would help build the cultural capital necessary to democratic transformation. Discussion and debate between Western thinkers and Muslim ones should be encouraged and funded. Christian priests and pastors, rabbis, and Muslim clerics need more venues in which genuine and open dialogue can be promoted, including with Brotherhood thinkers and activists.

In the promotion of democracy, as in life more generally, if you look after the pennies, the dollars will take care of themselves. The Brotherhood could, if the right policies are adopted in Egypt, come to play a role analogous to the Christian Democrat parties in Germany and other nations of Europe.

CHAPTER III

THE WAHHABI
MYTH

FROM RIYADH TO DOHA

With its austere puritanism and harsh regimentation of society, Saudi Arabia has adopted a distinctive form of Islam, Wahhabism, that generates a great deal of concern among outsiders. The kingdom's centrality to world fuel supplies, its wealth and strategic indispensability, only heighten this anxiety. Explaining everything with reference to a single religious tradition, however, reduces Saudi Arabia to a caricature. It is not the only Wahhabi society, and only a minority of Muslim terrorists have come from that branch of Islam.

There is no mystery as to why the term "Wahhabi" has become synonymous with "dangerous radical" in the North Atlantic world. Since 2001, U.S. politicians continually repeat the mantra that thirteen of the nineteen hijackers on September 11 came from Saudi Arabia, and of course that it is Usamah Bin Laden's country of origin. Many of the charges against the kingdom involve illogical arguments, from guilt by association to stereotyping. Bin Laden, a wealthy and much better organized version of Timothy McVeigh, hardly represents Saudi government policy, and, as former Saudi minister of intelligence Prince Turki al-Faisal charged, Bin Laden likely handpicked the young Saudi men for the hijackings precisely in order to sour relations between the United States and its close ally in Riyadh.[1]

The key planners of September 11 were an Egyptian, a Lebanese, and a Baluchi from Pakistan brought up in Kuwait, none of them Wahhabis. Even Usamah Bin Laden's family is from southern Yemen, and although he was raised in Saudi Arabia, it is not clear that he is a Wahhabi; Yemenis tend to the Shafi'i school of Islamic law and to Sufi mysticism, a very different set of traditions. Of the twelve members of the al-Qaeda board of directors, formed in 1998, nine were Egyptians (and thus from a Sunni background, not a Wahhabi one). The Saudi al-Qaeda members chosen as hijackers, in exile in Qandahar, would have been shot on sight if they had shown up in the Saudi capital of Riyadh, since they were part of a terrorist group that had openly called for the overthrow of the royal family, as did Bin Laden himself after he broke with King Fahd in 1990. For Westerners to use his nationality as a propaganda point against the Saudi monarchy is bizarre, and likely a source of pleasure to Bin Laden himself.

Saudi Arabia has more often been timid than militant in world affairs. Although Saudi intelligence coordinated with the Arab volunteers who went to fight the Soviets in Afghanistan in the 1980s, it did so in deference to the Reagan administration's policy of marshalling private militias against leftist governments. Bin Laden turned against the Saudi government at the time of the Gulf War because he opposed King Fahd's decision to host American troops in the fight to get Saddam out of Kuwait (Bin Laden thought Fahd should have launched an independent jihad against the Baathists). Angered by Bin Laden's challenge, the Saudis withdrew his citizenship in 1995.

Some critics of Saudi Arabia point to opinion polls that showed admiration for Bin Laden in the kingdom after the September 11 attacks. Because of his prominent role in fighting the Soviets in the 1980s and his continued championing of Muslim causes in the 1990s, Bin Laden enjoyed esteem among many Saudi notables and clerics, and it took some time after September 11 for them to adjust their image of him to terrorist killer of thousands of innocents. At first many Saudis refused to believe that he and his organization were behind the attacks.

Other critics correctly assert that the Saudi government was not efficient or galvanized in the fight against al-Qaeda in the months after September 11. But that insouciance began to change in May 2003, when al-Qaeda set off bombs in Riyadh. The Saudi state quickly retooled and made fighting al-Qaeda among its highest priorities. The terrorist group continued to attack Saudi targets, including the port of Jidda and oil facilities. Between 2003 and 2006, al-Qaeda terrorists killed some 150 Saudis and foreigners, while Saudi security forces killed 120 militants in firefights.[2] The violence tapered off considerably after 2006, though between 2003 and 2008 the Saudi authorities arrested some 9,000 persons suspected of al-Qaeda ties, and in early 2008 some 3,000 were still in custody.

The Wahhabi branch of Islam that dominates the kingdom began in the eighteenth century. Its founder, Muhammad Ibn Abd al-Wahhab of Najd in Central Arabia, decried what he viewed as pagan survivals among the tribes of central Arabia, such as their veneration of sacred stones and trees. The duty of the individual to fight against polytheism and laxness even gave the individual Muslim the right to decline to obey rulers and clergymen who in any way departed from pure monotheism. Such upright individuals, he argued, should prefer emigration to living under impious authorities.[3] Ibn Abd al-Wahhab conceived of Islam as strict adherence to the minutiae of the divine law as he formulated it and scrupulous avoidance of any form of polytheism (which he held to be the offering of any sort of prayer or sacrifice to anyone but God, or swearing by anyone but God). In Wahhabi thought, what is not explicitly authorized by a literal reading of holy texts and the early Muslim practice of the first two centuries is often viewed with suspicion, rather as the Amish and Mennonites have resisted innovations.

Willingness to cavalierly stigmatize other Muslims as pagans marked a sectarian mind-set, a departure from the relatively tolerant, big-tent attitude of Sunni Islam. Although nowadays Wahhabism is thought of as a Sunni school, in the eighteenth century it condemned most Sunnis as infidels, and Sunnis returned the favor.

In 1744, Ibn Abd al-Wahhab allied with Muhammad Ibn Saud in east-central Arabia. Ibn Saud, the tribal ruler of a small principality, gained powerful ideological support from the reformer, while Ibn Abd al-Wahhab gained protection, patronage, and the support of a tribal army. There have been three Saudi states in history, and only the last, which came together definitively in 1932, has had a continuous history as a territorial nation-state. From 1902, Abd al-Aziz Ibn Saud built up a powerhouse of a state in the thinly populated Arabian Peninsula. He could not have succeeded without an alliance with the British, who were already guarantors of the small Gulf principalities. As the ruler of a state, he also needed to introduce technological innovations, and brought radio to the kingdom. His cosmopolitan entanglements provoked severe protests from conservative Wahhabis known as the Brethren, many of whom worked for farm cooperatives. Between 1928 and 1930, they rose up against him, and he put them down with main strength. Thereafter, the Saudi state increasingly based itself on the small but growing urban population and pro-regime, seminary-trained Wahhabi clergymen.

In May 1933, Ibn Saud granted Standard Oil of California an enormous petroleum concession for less than $200,000, the best bargain struck by Western businessmen since Dutch factors traded those beads for Manhattan. Later, in the early 1940s, the California-Arabian Standard Oil Company (a consortium that became known in 1944 as the Arabian American Oil Company, or Aramco) convinced President Roosevelt to help the king by including the kingdom in the lend-lease aid program. As a longer-term sweetener for the bargain being struck between Standard Oil and Riyadh, the American oil majors committed to building a Trans-Arabian Pipeline (TAPLINE) to boost Saudi exports and revenues.[4]

The branding of Arabia with the dynasty's name in 1932 coincided with an increasing visibility and influence for Wahhabism. As the Saudi state grew wealthy in the 1950s from its petroleum exports, it was able to project Wahhabi influence into the region. The Saudi rulers had a love-hate relationship with Abdel Nasser, admiring his stand for Arab nationalism but disliking his secular, nationalist, and socialist ideas. Egypt's population is approximately four times larger than Saudi Arabia's, so it is easy to see how the small Gulf state would fear its much more populous neighbor. It is widely believed that in the 1960s and 1970s, the ruling family funneled money and support to the Muslim Brotherhood in Egypt, helping it fight off Abdel Nasser's repression.

Ironically, the United States is responsible for significant past efforts to make Wahhabi Saudi Arabia the spiritual leader of the Muslim world. As the 1950s wore on, some in the U.S. foreign policy establishment became increasingly worried that Arab nationalism of the Abdel Nasser sort was in effect a handmaiden of international communism. Arab nationalism tended to be anti-Western, and fostered more or less socialist economies that limited the potential for Western investment. Arab nationalist states were hungry for weaponry and technical assistance, which they were willing to get from the USSR and the Eastern bloc if it was not forthcoming from Western Europe or the United States.

As a result, during the cold war, American politicians and diplomatic and intelligence officials often saw Islam and Muslims as natural allies against the Soviet Union and international communism. This tendency was perhaps visible earliest and most clearly in the eastern reaches of the Muslim world. Pakistan and India emerged from British India in 1947 as independent countries after a bloody partition, with Pakistan a Muslim-majority state. Only Afghanistan lay between it and the Soviet Union, and by the early 1950s, its prime minister was reaching out to the United States for security cooperation.

The romance of Islam for the American right wing during the cold war is exemplified by Republican senator William F. Knowland, Senate majority leader, caustic critic of the Truman administration, and champion of Taiwan's nationalists against Red China. In 1953, Knowland returned from a tour of South and Southeast Asia to state, "Pakistan has the potential of really being like Turkey ultimately in firmly standing against Communism," adding of its relationship to the United States, "Pakistan could become an ally very definitely."[5] In 1954, Pakistan proved Knowland right. Pakistani prime minister Mohammad Ali Bogra took his country into the U.S.-backed, anticommunist Southeast Asian Treaty Organization, which aimed at containing Mao Zedong. Then, in February of 1955, Bogra signed on to the British-led Baghdad Pact, which involved Turkey, Iraq, Iran, and Pakistan in an attempt to limit Soviet influence in the Middle East and the oil-rich Persian Gulf. On February 29, 1956, Pakistan's parliament declared it an Islamic Republic, which did not appear to bother Knowland or the Eisenhower administration at all.

Faced in the Middle East with the rise of secular Arab nationalism and of leftist politics in countries such as Syria, Washington cast about for a counterweight. President Dwight D. Eisenhower wrote in his diary in the spring of 1956 that "Arabia is a country that contains the holy places of the Moslem world, and the Saudi Arabians are considered to be the most deeply religious of all the Arab groups. Consequently, the King could be built up, possibly, as a spiritual leader. Once this were accomplished, we might begin to urge his right to political leadership."[6] Later that year, after the potentially destabilizing Suez War, Eisenhower cabled his secretary of state, John Foster Dulles, in Paris, "I continue to believe, as I think you do, that one of the measures that we must take is to build up an Arab rival of Nasser, and the natural choice would seem to be the man you and I have often talked about." Dulles agreed that King Saud (bin Abdul Aziz, who had succeeded his father in 1953) could in time be "the best counter to Nasser."[7]

In 1957, the U.S. National Security Council set up a working group to compile a list of Muslim organizations and religious groups that could be propagandized by the United States Information Agency. American intellectuals and politicians worried that Islamic institutions had been weakened by the shock of Western impact on their societies, creating an opening for the communists to make inroads in the region. Eisenhower approved $500,000 toward a study of how to revive the Hijaz railway to bring more pilgrims to Mecca and Medina, hoping to spread Saudi influence so as to counteract the appeal of the left. For his part, King Saud enjoyed playing the role of Islamic leader, and commissioned his favorite building contractor, Muhammad Bin Laden (later the father of Usamah), to oversee the reconstruction of the Great Mosque in Mecca.[8] The question of Israeli access to the Gulf of Aqaba after the 1956 war, however, was a stumbling block in the king's relationship with Eisenhower. King Saud felt that breaking the Arab blockade on the Israeli port of Eilat would reward the Israelis for their aggressive war on Egypt. Eisenhower considered the monarch's preoccupation with this issue "childish . . . particularly when he talks about Allah."[9] When he was being inconvenient, the king's religious rhetoric was dismissed.

Taking practical political action proved more difficult for the opulent monarch. Eisenhower urged King Saud in August 1957 to deploy his standing as guardian of Mecca and Medina to impress on the Syrian government the undesirability of its growing ties to the Soviet Union.[10] Eisenhower even wanted Saudi help with installing a pro-Western regime in Syria. King Saud, caught between the nationalism of the Arab League and his growing ties to Washington, defied the president and actually went to Damascus to show his solidarity with the Syrian regime.[11]

Eisenhower's plan to make Wahhabi Saudi Arabia the spiritual leader of the Middle East, as a way of shifting the region to the right and blocking Soviet influence, failed during his own administration, in part because King Saud bin Abdul Aziz lacked spiritual stature or widespread Arab popularity. King Saud, enormously wealthy from the kingdom's petroleum exports and busy with his harem, was no match for Abdel Nasser, who knew how to appeal through powerful oratory to the aspirations of the Arab masses. Furthermore, Eisenhower did not realize that many Sunni Muslims viewed the Saudi's Wahhabism as intolerant and sectarian, an attitude that limited Saudi influence. Finally, King Saud could not in the end shake suspicions in the Arab world and in his own kingdom that he was a creature of Washington.

The Saudi leadership idea did not go away, however, and was resurrected by later American presidents. Washington appeared to think that, just as mainstream Protestants such as theologian Reinhold Niebuhr were bulwarks against communism in the United States, so Wahhabism could underpin a conservative moral order compatible with the sanctity of private property in the Middle East.

After September 11, Washington suddenly rethought its promotion of Saudi Arabia and Wahhabism as buttresses of a conservative, capitalist order in the Middle East. From being the cynosure of North Atlantic hopes for a robust anticommunist ally in the region, Saudi Arabia suddenly became an object of suspicion. Critics of the kingdom maintain that while it has stepped up to the task of defeating al-Qaeda at home, it has lagged in preventing private citizens from sending money to Islamic charities that serve as fronts for terrorism. Some also charge that Riyadh was lax in preventing Saudi volunteers from going off to fight U.S. troops in Iraq. These arguments contain three fallacies: They overestimate the capacities of the Saudi state, they ignore the genuine and significant steps the Saudis have taken, and they do not take into account the royal family's self-interest in stability and security.

Controlling the finances of 22 million Saudis is beyond the talents of the finance and interior ministries. Likewise, preventing a few hundred angry young men from slipping into Iraq would not have been easy, especially since many appear to have been from the Saudi north, near Iraq. In recent years, the U.S. military in Iraq typically has had fewer than 150 foreign fighters in custody at any one time. While Saudis have sometimes formed a significant proportion of them, their absolute numbers have been small. Similar numbers of captured volunteers came from Libya, Morocco, and elsewhere (in other words, from Sunni countries).

Contrary to the popular image of Saudi fighters in Iraq as hardened terrorists, studies have found that for the most part they are in their twenties and were never involved in violence before going to Iraq, which they view as being under oppressive foreign occupation. Incidents such as the revelation of torture of Iraqi prisoners at Abu Ghraib by the U.S. military and the brutal assault on the city of Fallujah in November 2004 led to an increase of Saudi volunteers. They appear to be driven by pan-Islamic nationalism, a feeling of solidarity with Iraqis. Nevertheless, their numbers were smaller than is usually alleged in the U.S. press.[12]

The royals were petrified that the young men who went to fight in Iraq would come back radicalized and threaten the government in Riyadh. A U.S. State Department report on counterterrorism explained, "Saudi Arabia has strengthened its border controls and security and, in particular, its border with Iraq to address travel by Saudis to Iraq to join terrorist groups fighting against Coalition Forces and the travel of non-Saudis through Saudi Arabia."[13]

If we listen to the government in Baghdad instead of think tanks inside the Beltway with axes to grind, the significance of this State Department report is clear. In a 2008 press interview, Iraqi national security adviser Muwaffaq al-Rubaie, a Shiite, called Saudi cooperation with the Iraqi government on counterterrorism "a model" and revealed how the Saudis helped identify dangerous Saudi prisoners captured in Iraq by Americans.[14] Behind the scenes, beginning in January 2005, the Saudi and Saudi-backed pan-Arab press began promoting the idea of using Sunni Iraqi tribal levies to fight the fundamentalist vigilantes. The idea was initially resisted by the Bush administration, which was strongly allied with Iraqi Shiite fundamentalist parties and feared offending them. But the Saudi suggestion was ultimately implemented with some success by U.S. general David Petraeus, who paid "Awakening Councils" to restore law and order in Sunni areas. It is likely that Saudi King Abdullah supported this program behind the scenes. The Saudis have cooperated extensively with the U.S. Federal Bureau of Investigation and the Treasury Department in shutting down so-called Islamic charities that funneled money to unsavory groups. The U.S. State Department reported in 2008 that the Saudi government had arrested more than thirty "terrorist financiers" in

2007 alone. Riyadh has forbidden Saudi charities to send money abroad until an oversight commission can be implemented.[15] The Saudis' demonstrable progress in counterterrorism has been grossly underestimated by critics of the kingdom, though certainly a great deal remains to be done.

The kingdom tends to be vilified and viewed in a one-dimensional way by both the left and the right. In his film *Fahrenheit 9/11,* Michael Moore crudely caricatured the kingdom. Moore complained that dozens of Saudis, including members of the Bin Laden family, departed the United States on September 13 and 14, 2001, after the terror attacks. Unless he is arguing for racial profiling, it is hard to understand why all Saudis should have been sequestered. Plane flights were allowed again on September 13, and many people flew at that time. Some thirty Saudis were interviewed by the FBI before they left, and all their flights were approved by the bureau, according to the 9/11 Commission report. The U.S. authorities allowed the Saudis to leave because—unlike other stranded travelers—their lives were believed to be in danger from mob action. If Moore intended to imply that members of the Saudi elite knew about 9/11 beforehand, he was being ridiculous. Why would a Saudi who was aware of the plot have voluntarily come to the United States beforehand? Surely everyone could have foreseen that they would be in danger from an enraged American public. Moore unwittingly contradicts himself, inasmuch as elsewhere in his film he complains plangently about the extent of Saudi investments in the United States. Moore's exaggerated statistics on the extent of Saudi U.S. holdings raise the question of why these wealthy investors would want to destroy their portfolios—U.S. stocks lost over one trillion in value after the attacks. Nor is there any evidence of Saudi investors selling short before the attacks.

Saudis are often hated simply for being rich—something with which Westerners should be able to empathize, but instead we pillory them for it ourselves. When American politicians look at the United States or Europe, they explain economic phenomena with economics, but the Muslim world is apparently a mystical realm where religion or national character flaws explain everything. For example, in one of former Secretary of Defense Donald Rumsfeld's memos, called "snowflakes" by his weary staff, he wrote that petroleum wealth had detached Muslims "from the reality of the work, effort and investment that leads to wealth for the rest of the world. Too often Muslims are against physical labor, so they bring in Koreans and Pakistanis while their young people remain unemployed. An unemployed population is easy to recruit to radicalism." He added that if radicals "get a hold of" oil-rich Saudi Arabia, the United States will have "an enormous national security problem." Rumsfeld saw Muslims' importation of cheap labor as pathological and attributed it to the lack of a Protestant ethic, on a moral laziness that created idleness, unemployment, and extremism. This indolent road to terrorism, his memo alleged, threatens the United States not only through violent attacks but also because it menaces the stability of Saudi Arabia, the world's largest exporter of petroleum and therefore a key support for America's hydrocarbon economy.[16]

To begin with, few Muslims live in petroleum states. Populous countries such as Morocco and Egypt have little oil. Even in Muslim countries that do have fossil fuels, unemployment is certainly not due to laziness. In reality, income generated from exporting oil (or other high-priced primary commodities) enhances the value of the local currency, which in turn makes other potential exports (such as agricultural goods, handicrafts, and factory-made goods) more expensive for potential buyers, thus limiting their potential market and destroying jobs. This phenomenon was first noticed by economists in the Netherlands in the 1970s, when that country's natural gas production resulted in a stagnation of the rest of the economy. They dubbed this problem the "Dutch disease." Saudi Arabia suffers from it in spades, accounting in part for its high rates of unemployment.

Other roots of unemployment include the kingdom's extremely high population growth rate, which increases demand for jobs, and the insufficiently regulated "sponsorship" (kafil) system, whereby individual Saudis bring foreign workers into the country, taking jobs away from citizens.[17] There are an estimated 7 million guest workers in

Saudi Arabia, on top of a native population of 22 million. However, dependence on guest workers for manual labor is not unique to Saudis—the United States and France both bring in large numbers of foreign workers for manual labor. Presumably Rumsfeld does not blame Christianity for French and American unemployment. The notion that "Muslims" are "against physical labor" is ridiculous, and Rumsfeld himself suggested as much when he said that the Gulf oil states "bring in . . . Pakistanis." Hint: Pakistanis are Muslims. It is true that persons of Bedouin background often dislike manual labor, associating it with peasant work, but such attitudes are common among pastoral nomads throughout the world and have nothing to do with Islam.

The common image of the opulent Saudi style of life is an exaggeration. While the top tier of princes is made up of billionaires, few of them can compete with the salaries of leading American CEOs. As for the Saudis in general, any per capita figures given are artificial in an oil economy, since petroleum income fluctuates a good deal. And, of course, it is not divided equally, contrary to the impression given by a per capita estimate. There is plenty of poverty in Saudi Arabia. Although unemployment is estimated at around 10 percent, it is widely thought to be twice that, and among young men it is probably higher still.[18] An exposé by a Saudi-owned newspaper in early 2008 showed 4,000 families living in a shantytown in Arar, on the northern border with Iraq, in squalid conditions.[19] And, as noted, even high oil prices can hurt middle-class and poor Saudis, because they increase the cost of many imported goods, and Saudis are highly dependent on imports.[20]

Sometimes the critique flips over from the Saudis being rich to their being backward. Egyptian diplomat Taseen Bashir famously remarked that in the Middle East only Egypt and Iran are real countries, and the rest are "tribes with flags."[21] In fact, despite the pastoral nomadic heritage of some Saudis, over 95 percent of the population is now settled, and some 81 percent of the population is urbanized, about the same as in the United States.[22]

While it is easy to criticize the Saudi state for not doing more to ensure that the riches are shared more equally, getting money from a pricey primary commodity owned by the government into the

pockets of citizens is not as easy as it sounds. If the government attempted simply to distribute that much money to individuals, it
could cause enormous inflation that would eat up the money's
value, like a dog chasing its own tail. (Inflation is defined as too
much money chasing too few goods. Pumping money into an economy that is not showing increased productivity just causes prices to
go up.) King Abdullah has responded to this challenge by embarking
on projects such as the building of an entirely new city of 2 million,
aiming to provide a million jobs to Saudis, and by developing industries such as aluminum, steel, fertilizer, and petrochemicals so as to
diversify the economy.[23] No doubt the Saudi government has shown
little interest in working for social equality, though its interest in the
development of economically productive citizens has been greater
than it is generally credited with.

Outside observers often blame Islam or Wahhabism for the abysmal
Saudi human rights record. The kingdom is run as an absolute monarchy. It does not allow freedom of religion or of speech. It discriminates
against religious minorities. It imposes strict gender segregation, called
"gender apartheid" by some critics. It represses political dissidents. Some
of the punishments it imposes for crimes against property and morality,
such as beheading, flogging, and stoning, strike Westerners as being out
of the Dark Ages. Obviously, anyone with a social conscience will critique and work against these Saudi laws and practices. If we are to blame
political and social repression on Islam rather than on the Saudi regime,
however, we must first demonstrate that there is a broad Muslim consensus on the desirability of authoritarianism. Yet 58 percent of Saudi Muslims say that democracy is the best form of government, thereby rejecting authoritarian values.[24] Moreover, since many Muslim countries,
including Lebanon and Senegal, have much better human rights records,
it would be difficult to isolate Islam as the independent variable here.[25]
Some distinctive Saudi ruling-class practices and ideas may be rooted in
the traditions of Central Arabia (Najdi) or the political culture of the
Saud dynasty, affecting their interpretation of Islam. Since Wahhabi

Qatar is not nearly as repressive, it is not evident that the human rights shortcomings lay with that branch of Islam per se.

It is unclear, moreover, that these issues in governance and religious custom should be determinative for U.S. diplomacy. It is natural that the American government and civil society organizations should protest political repression and cruel and unusual punishments and pressure the kingdom to abandon them. But dislike of a reactionary Saudi government and legal policies is hardly a reason for boycotting the kingdom commercially, for which some pundits seem to argue.[26] The United States as a superpower has to deal with many authoritarian governments that are far less friendly to American policy goals than is Riyadh. Washington has in recent years made a concerted attempt to improve relations with Vietnam, an effort in which John McCain played a role despite having been a prisoner of war in the Hanoi Hilton. Yet Vietnam is a communist dictatorship that, if anything, is less tolerant of individual liberties than Saudi Arabia, and has been guilty of concerted discrimination against some minorities and religious groups as well.

Saudi Arabia is often slammed for the influence of its puritan Wahhabi form of Islam on supposedly more tolerant Sunni traditions. Saudi religious norms are more rigid than those of most Sunnis, but there are some Sunnis who also insist on strict gender segregation, puritanism in public morals, and a fundamentalist approach to Islamic law. Many Shiites in Iran and Lebanon share these ideals, and they are the farthest thing from being influenced by Wahhabis, many of whom still excoriate Shiites as idolaters. It is true that Saudi missionaries have used the kingdom's oil riches to promote Wahhabi ideas and practices in societies such as Pakistan and Indonesia, where most people are traditionalists or modernists rather than fundamentalists. Saudis are even doing missionary work as far afield as India and Spain. And yet it is ironic that Americans in particular should fault these missionary enterprises, which are far less extensive than those of American evangelicals who also fish for souls abroad and promote puritanism and scriptural norms, and, sometimes, the repression of women's rights.

It is sometimes implied that the Saudi effort to spread Wahhabism has the effect of spreading terrorism and anti-Americanism. That outcome would be difficult to demonstrate.[27] The two major Wahhabi countries in the world, Saudi Arabia and Qatar, are close allies of the United States. Nor is it just a matter of regime attitudes. In a recent poll of Saudi citizens, 69 percent favored better relations between Riyadh and Washington. Some 40 percent had a favorable opinion of the United States, which is high for a Muslim country, and most say that their view of America would improve dramatically if it withdrew troops from Iraq.[28] Since they want better relations with America, and their view of the United States is dependent on issues such as the Iraq War, the Wahhabi theological tradition is clearly not determinative of their attitudes toward Washington.

Further, it is not at all clear that puritanism or Wahhabism, while it may produce negative attitudes toward consumerism and libertinism, predisposes people to commit terrorism, as some pundits have alleged.[29] Most suicide bombings in the past thirty years have not been carried out by Wahhabis or persons influenced by them, but rather by individuals fighting what they see as the foreign military occupation of their country. Lebanese Shiites under Israeli occupation from 1982 to 2000, Iraqis of various ideologies after 2003, Hindu-background Marxists of the Tamil Tigers in Sri Lanka, and Palestinians, many of them leftist secularists, are more typical suicide bombers.[30]

Connecting a religious tradition to terrorism would require more evidence than a few instances of guilt by association. In Uganda, Western missionaries succeeded in converting Africans to Christianity, but some of those converts and their descendants went on to establish the violent Lord's Resistance Army, which deploys thousands of fighters and terrorism in the quest for a theocratic state.[31] Western Christian missionaries are no more directly implicated in that terrorism than Wahhabi preachers are in some of the small rogue groups that have misused Muslim puritanism.

While it may have been self-serving, Saudi Interior Minister Prince Nayef bin Abdul Aziz argued in an interview about a year after September 11 that Saudi Arabia had been harmed not by Wahhabism, which had a long tradition of political quietism and loyalty to the state, but by the Egyptian Muslim Brotherhood (and its offshoots). He alleged that Brotherhood figures took advantage of the asylum offered in the kingdom and studied at its universities, but showed little gratitude. He said, "Whenever things became difficult for them or they faced execution in their own countries, they came to the kingdom, which safeguarded their lives."[32] He also pointed to the tendency of Brotherhood supporters and similar groups to back Saddam Hussein's 1990 annexation of Kuwait. He accused the organization of making trouble throughout the Arab and even the Muslim world. Prince Nayef underestimated the extremist tendencies of some Wahhabi clerics and too hastily dismissed the existence of al-Qaeda cells inside the kingdom at that time. His broader point, however, that Saudi Wahhabism had been less political than the Brotherhood and less radical than its extremist offshoots, cannot be dismissed so easily.

In short, a distinction must be made between a simple critique of Wahhabi fundamentalism and a concern about militancy or terrorism. Many fundamentalist Muslims are political quietists and leave the affairs of this world in the hands of God.[33] It is not at all clear that Wahhabis in general have in modern history been more militant, or more likely to commit terrorism, than Egyptian Sunnis, for instance, or for that matter Northern Irish Catholics and Protestants. Egypt fought four wars in the second half of the twentieth century. Saudi Arabia could not be said to have fought any, though it played the role of a helpmeet in others' wars (it sent some token forces for the 1973 Arab-Israeli War and was involved in the Reagan administration's covert struggle against the Soviets in Afghanistan).

If religious conservatism, as opposed to violence, were the issue, then many of the objections to Wahhabi Islam voiced by critics—literalism, legalism, suspicion of modernity, insistence on modest dress for women, patriarchy, shunning of individuals for nonconformity, advocating harsh criminal and moral punishments, and so forth—could also be lodged against many other religious or even political groups. They would include non-Muslim ones such as the Haredim of Israel, who have been important in the illegal Israeli colonization of the Palestinian West Bank,[34] or to some extent the Amish of Pennsylvania. Relatively few calls for diplomatic boycotts are launched against those groups. It is not even clear that most Saudis raised in the Wahhabi tradition adhere to the values preached by their more narrow-minded clergymen. In polling, ordinary Saudis overwhelmingly reject harsh punishments for moral infractions such as adultery.[35] One pollster found that only 62 percent of Saudis even describe themselves as "religious," a much lower percentage than Jordanians or Egyptians.[36] Most Wahhabis go through life without killing anyone. Cultural traditions do not commit violence, people do, and they do so for concrete reasons in particular situations.

Beyond myths and history, the big policy question for Westerners is whether the kingdom poses a geopolitical threat or whether its rulership will generally act in a friendly and helpful way. It seems undeniable that the answer is that Saudi Arabia has, since at least 1945, been a close ally of the United States and of the North Atlantic countries (even if there have been ups and downs in the relationship), yet its form of religion and social policies are problematic for those rooted in the Enlightenment tradition.

The major dissenters from this obvious conclusion have been Israeli or pro-Israel authors driven by a desire to bolster that country's influence in Washington against its Saudi rival. Behind the scenes in Washington, high politicians and policy makers are typically engaged in a delicate attempt to balance Saudi and Israeli demands, since both countries are important to U.S. Middle East policy, even though the Israel lobbies ensure that the Zionist state has by far the better public press. It is no accident that when, in July 2007, the Bush administration announced that it would sell $20 billion in arms to Saudi Arabia and other Gulf Cooperation Council states, it simultaneously pledged $30 billion in new arms for Israel over the succeeding decade and pressed Saudi Arabia to commit to keeping its new missiles and weapons storehouses in parts of the kingdom farthest from Israel.[37]

Both Israel and Saudi Arabia have at times opposed U.S. policy initiatives. Judging an ally by how obsequious it is poses real dangers for a superpower. It could be argued that Saudi Arabia has been a better friend to the United States when it dissented from some of Washington's wilder projects rather than joining in. The contrast between King Fahd, who ruled in the 1980s and 1990s, and his successor, the current monarch, King Abdullah, is instructive in this regard.[38]

With the windfall profits that his country reaped from the quadrupling of the price of petroleum after 1973, Fahd, the power behind the throne from 1975 before becoming king in 1982, energetically set about modernizing his society, including initiating substantial advances in women's education. The kingdom had struck it rich, but now its fabulously wealthy rulers had more to lose from threats such as Iranian radicalism or international communism. In 1979, Muslim fundamentalists and millenarians rose up in the holy city of Mecca, and the rebellion was put down only with some difficulty. In the same year, the Soviet Union invaded Afghanistan to prop up a shaky communist military dictatorship that had come to power in a 1978 coup. The Soviet invasion sent tremors through the elite in Riyadh, which was only 1,506 miles from Kabul (about the distance from Washington, D.C., to Denver). Also in 1979, the shah was overthrown in Iran, with the Ayatollah Khomeini coming to power. Khomeini, a Shiite, taught that monarchy is incompatible with Islam. If the ayatollah gained influence among Sunnis, the thrones of the oil monarchies could be toppled just as the shah's had been.

Fahd made the fateful decision to seek the security umbrella of the United States. In exchange for sophisticated U.S. weaponry, such as F–15 fighter jets and AWACS spy planes, he signed on to help create Reagan's anticommunist militias, giving them Saudi money in Nicaragua, Angola, and Ethiopia, and vastly increasing aid to the mujahideen in Afghanistan. Saudi officials deny ever having a formal relationship with Usamah Bin Laden (who was then raising funds from Saudi clerics and entrepreneurs on behalf of the Muslims fighting the Soviets). Saudi intelligence, urged on by the Americans to find resources for the mujahideen, nevertheless probably recruited him for that purpose.

Although the Saudi royal family had long despised the Arab nationalist ideology of Baathism, Fahd joined the Reagan administration after 1983 in supporting Saddam Hussein, whom the Arabian monarch called "my brother" and "my sword," against Khomeinist Iran. But when Saddam invaded Kuwait in 1990, Fahd was presented with a fateful decision. Prince Bandar Bin Sultan, Fahd's man in Washington, argued that he should bring in the American army as a means of gaining a permanent security commitment from the United States. With Saudi Arabia offering its territory, bases, and logistical support, a large United Nations–sanctioned force assembled and pushed the Iraqi military back out of Kuwait. For the first time, the U.S. military, and the militaries of Western Europe, had hundreds of thousands of troops on Saudi soil. After the Gulf War, Fahd gave the United States use of Prince Sultan Air Base. Among those outraged by then was Bin Laden, who declared war on the Saudi dynasty years before he declared war on the United States.

Fahd associated himself closely with Ronald Reagan's Great American Jihad against Soviet-dominated Afghanistan. Together, Reagan and Fahd—one using proxy armies and arms, the other petrodollars—launched a worldwide campaign against what they saw as the radical specters of communism and Khomeinism (radical Shiism). To fight this battle, they gave billions to Sunni Muslim fundamentalists. Arabia came in for little criticism in the United States during this period, but Fahd's partnership with Reagan helped produce the radicalization of the Muslim far-right fringe and made Saddam Hussein into a regional power.[39]

Crown Prince Abdullah became the power behind the throne in 1995, when Fahd suffered a debilitating stroke. In 2005, on Fahd's death, he became king. King Abdullah, who has far worse press in the United States than his predecessor, is a much more cautious man, not given to his half-brother's dangerous adventurism. As America faces the long, daunting task of recovering from George W. Bush's catastrophic foreign-policy blunders, solidifying relations with this key, if problematic, ally should be high on the list of priorities. Tarring this friendly government and its favored tradition of worship with the brush of terrorism is mere propaganda. To the extent that Saudi Arabia is indirectly implicated in the rise of al-Qaeda in the 1980s, its partner in crime was surely the Reagan administration, the U.S. Congress, and the American religious right—who, by encouraging brigades of Muslim volunteers to go to Afghanistan, created the preconditions for al-Qaeda's rise.

Abdullah has reigned during difficult times and has responded with a mixture of caution and flexibility. He allowed popular elections for municipal councils, among the first Saudi steps toward representative institutions. The elections were carefully circumscribed, with only half the seats on the councils filled through the polls, the other half being appointed by the central government. But neither were the elections meaningless. Religious political activists, dubbing themselves the Golden List, used grassroots campaign techniques and networking to win majorities on most urban councils. In Shiite cities such as Qatif, for the first time Shiite Muslims, who had been very much second-class citizens in the Wahhabi kingdom, were elected to office. Once there, they made policies less oppressive toward members of their branch of Islam.[40]

With regard to the problem of al-Qaeda and terrorism within the kingdom, Abdullah has used both better policing and incentives. He has popular support for these measures. In a poll in late 2007, a vast majority of Saudis said that they opposed al-Qaeda, and 88 percent approved of the government security forces pursuing al-Qaeda activists. While 10 percent of the sample said that they had a favorable view of al-Qaeda, it is likely that they are from the same group that tends to deny that the organization was behind September 11. That is, most of the Saudis who express such approval do not think of themselves as supporting terrorism but are remembering Usamah Bin Laden's achievement in helping push the godless Soviets out of Muslim Afghanistan. Evidence for this conclusion is found in the poll itself, since a majority of the small minority that supported al-Qaeda also said that fighting terrorism should be a high priority: if even al-Qaeda supporters are worried about terrorism, the Saudi information campaign must be having some effect.[41]

Since 2003, Abdullah's military and intelligence forces have aggressively moved against militants, killing dozens in pitched battles and arresting hundreds. Abdullah also launched an active program to win over the Saudi public. Saudi television displays gory images of the aftermath of terrorist attacks. Senior clerics of the Wahhabi branch of Islam have been persuaded to fulminate against all acts of terrorism against innocents, including the September 11 attacks. Some 2,000 Saudi clerics, out of 100,000, were temporarily removed from their positions for being too militant, and they were allowed to return only after retraining. Saudi religious officials have engaged in debates with militants on Internet chat sites, drawing arguments from Islamic texts and traditions, a technique that has been shown to have some success. In 2007, the government arrested 400 suspected terrorists and their helpers, including some businessmen.[42] In late May 2008, CIA director Michael Hayden spoke of a "near strategic defeat for al-Qaeda in Saudi Arabia," an achievement that would hardly have been possible unless King Abdullah and his security agencies had wholeheartedly devoted all their resources to it.[43]

Abdullah has also played an important positive role in regional foreign policy. In spring 2002, he sent an envoy to President George W. Bush with some tough words. To avoid a big regional blowup that would endanger the U.S.-Saudi relationship, something would have to be done about the Israeli government's treatment of the Palestinians under then prime minister Ariel Sharon. Abdullah put forward a comprehensive peace plan with Israel that offered it full recognition and relations, a plan adopted by the entire Arab League.[44] Within the context of Arab politics, it was an audacious step. Yet the proposal, which called for Israeli withdrawal to pre-1967 borders and the establishment of a Palestinian state, was never taken seriously by the expansionist government of Ariel Sharon, nor by the stridently pro-Israeli politicians in Washington. After the Israeli-Lebanese War of 2006, in which the Israeli army performed poorly and proved unable to defeat its foe, Hizbullah, decisively, the Israeli government began reconsidering whether the Arab League plan might form the basis for some advance in the peace process.

Abdullah sent word to Bush before the Iraq War that he believed that the Saddam regime was an "arms control" not a "war on terrorism" issue, which should be resolved legally. Note the contrast with

Fahd, who was persuaded to welcome 750,000 foreign troops into his kingdom for the Gulf War of 1990–1991 and who later allowed an unpopular long-term U.S. military presence. Abdullah declined to join in the younger Bush's crusade, though as a loyal ally he did quietly make available Saudi facilities and airspace for the invasion. The hawks in Washington responded by smearing Abdullah as a coddler of terrorism. Then RAND analyst Laurent Murawiec was even invited to give a presentation at the Pentagon, at the invitation of neoconservative strategist Richard Perle (then head of the influential civilian Defense Policy Board), in which he called on the United States to invade Saudi Arabia and seize its oil fields.[45] Hostility to Saudi Arabia was widespread in the highly pro-Israel neoconservative movement exemplified by then Deputy Secretary of Defense Paul Wolfowitz and the head of the Near East and South Asia bureau at the Pentagon, Bill Luti (who is said to have ended every thought with "Fuck the Saudis"[46]). After a diplomatic flap ensued, U.S. officials distanced themselves from the Murawiec presentation.

It might be thought that an Arab leader who risked his prestige on a quest for a comprehensive peace in the Middle East for both Israelis and Palestinians, who opposed the catastrophic Iraq war, and who helps keep the U.S. economy afloat by recycling vast amounts of petrodollars into investments in this country would get at least some positive press in the United States.

For his part, King Abdullah is menaced by the instability in Iraq, which could easily spill over into his kingdom. He faces a challenge for regional hegemony from Iran. His response has not been, as Washington urged, to engage in a cold war with Iran and ally himself with Israel, but rather to seek a détente with the Iranians and to keep lines open to Tehran. He has hosted the Iranian president in Riyadh for that purpose. He is keenly aware that the legitimacy of the Saudi monarchy is damaged by the ongoing failure to achieve a state for the Palestinians. The Arab street lays that failure at the feet of the United States and its one-sided support for the most bellicose policies of the Israeli right, and the kingdom is well known in the region to be best friends with the United States. That perception led Abdullah in 2007 to attempt to resurrect his Arab-Israeli peace plan, and to bring Hamas and representatives of the Palestine Liberation Organization (PLO) to Mecca to resolve their dispute, which had given Iran an opening to bestow patronage on Hamas.

Riyadh's relatively independent and forceful policy initiatives may signal a new assertiveness in the kingdom as it plays a wider-ranging leadership role in the Arab world. The marginalization of Baghdad and Damascus, and Cairo's concern with its own problems of reform and the challenge of the Muslim Brotherhood, have, as Saudi Arabia expert Mamoun Fandy noted, helped propel Saudi Arabia into the forefront of Arab diplomacy.[47] The generally moderate policies the kingdom is pursuing in support of peaceful resolutions to outstanding regional disputes give cause for hope.

Abdullah must find a gradual way to open up Saudi politics to wider participation. The restive educated middle classes are growing rapidly. A wise policy would be to promote smaller families and birth control, since rapidly increasing population and consequent demand for employment is creating challenges that the regime cannot always overcome. Unemployment is growing, and youth vandalism is becoming a real problem.[48] Other Middle Eastern monarchies—in Libya, Iraq, and Iran—faced similar political and demographic challenges and failed. The fate of the kingdom depends on whether it can deal with these difficulties, and the fate of the world depends to a significant extent on the fate of the kingdom. Remember, Saudi Arabia produces on the order of 11 percent of the world's petroleum every day.

Many Americans think of Wahhabi Saudi Arabia when they grumble about their gasoline dollars going into the hands of conservative Muslims. However, Saudi Arabia is only one of a number of oil states in the Gulf. Although it has an image of being insular and hidebound, the Gulf is actually among the more cosmopolitan places in the world. Most Gulf societies have huge guest worker populations, and often their numbers dwarf those of the native citizens. Most of the Gulf monarchies are not Wahhabi. Kuwait, Bahrain, and most of the states in the United Arab Emirates are ruled by Sunni dynasties loyal to the Maliki school of Islamic law (Wahhabis follow the rival Hanbali school). Iraqi Sunnis tend to follow yet another school, and most of them reject the precepts of Wahhabism. Some two-thirds of Bahrainis, a majority of Iraqis, an overwhelming proportion of the traditional population of the Eastern Province of Saudi Arabia, and most Iranians are Shiites. These Shiites, however, differ substantially among one another in their religious and political outlooks.

In order to evaluate the claims made about the Wahhabi tradition—that it foments radicalism—it is worth considering another Wahhabi tradition than that of Saudi Arabia. The world's other Wahhabi state is Qatar. I visited Qatar in 2008 to participate in the Doha Debates, which are supported by the BBC and the Qatar Foundation and are shown on BBC World. They aim at spreading to the Middle East the custom of public political and social debates in the Oxford University tradition. I had previously been to Qatar on a speaking tour in 1988. The changes over those two decades were stupendous. Before, it had been sleepy and self-contained. Now it is anything but. Qatar is a small peninsula jutting into the Gulf, bounded to its south by Saudi Arabia. It is ruled by the Al Thani dynasty, which adopted Wahhabism in the nineteenth century. The current ruler, Sheikh Hamad, took power in a coup against his rather backward-looking father in 1995. Qatar has some petroleum, but its claim to fame is that it has 15 percent of the world's proven natural gas reserves. On a per capita citizen basis, it may be the wealthiest society in the world.

Sheikh Hamad practices a wide-ranging diplomacy, doing deals with China but at the same time giving the U.S. military an air base at al-Udeid, west of the capital. He is said to have played a role in helping the United States capture al-Qaeda operatives Ramzi bin al-Shibh and Khalid Sheikh Muhammad. In the spring of 2008, he successfully stepped in to help negotiate an end to a crisis in Lebanon between the Shiite Hizbullah and the Sunnis and their allies. Qatar's very reputation for quirky independence, underpinned by its vast wealth, allowed Sheikh Hamad to play a role that once would have fallen to the United

States or perhaps Saudi Arabia.[49] Those two, however, were too identified with the majority government in Beirut, and seen as too hostile to the Shiite Hizbullah, to act as honest brokers.

Sheikh Hamad shook up the conservative Gulf by helping establish and fund the Al-Jazeera satellite television channel. It gave employment to professional journalists of Arab heritage who had been working for concerns such as the BBC or Voice of America. The American public has the mistaken impression that Al-Jazeera is connected to al-Qaeda because it shows excerpts from the videos of that organization's leaders. In fact its tone is not Muslim fundamentalist but rather old-style pan-Arab nationalist. The modernism of its journalists can be seen in the way they dress. Al-Jazeera's female anchors mostly wear Western fashions and do not veil. The men for the most part are clean-shaven and wear business suits. I bring up the fashions on Al-Jazeera only because dressing as if you just went on a shopping spree in Paris is generally perceived in the Arab world as a sign that you are opposed to religious fundamentalism. (There is nothing at all unusual or overtly political about veiling or wearing traditional robes, which are much more comfortable than Western clothes in a hot, dusty climate; it is just that such local fashions generally are not worn by the on-screen talent on this station.) While a place is given to Islam in the programming, it is a relatively small place, and the channel seems mainly interested in it as an element in Arab nationalism or anti-imperialism.

Because the director and staff are largely from Cairo, Beirut, or Palestine, Al-Jazeera is much more focused on the politics of the southern Mediterranean, on Lebanon, the Israeli-Palestinian issue, Egypt, and North Africa than on the Gulf itself. Its staff tends to take a critical stance toward the U.S. military presence in Afghanistan and Iraq.[50] Shiite Iraqis have charged that the channel has been biased toward the Sunni Arabs in Iraq, and the Baghdad government banned the channel's bureau in 2004. (Al-Jazeera correspondents still go to Iraq.)

On my trip to the capital, Doha, I interviewed Al-Jazeera Arabic's editor in chief, Ahmad Sheikh, and I asked him about the channel's policy of broadcasting clips from the al-Qaeda leaders.[51] Sheikh replied, "We do not support al-Qaeda's policies. Al-Jazeera tries to cover all sides in the U.S. conflict with al-Qaeda. It attempts to balance stories by giving both points of view." Sheikh pointed out, as well, that Al-Jazeera interviews American figures at length. He said it also gives Israeli officials plenty of air time, much more, he alleged, than Israeli television gives Arab spokesmen. (No other Arab media give Israeli officials a chance to be heard directly, in part because of the Arab League boycott of that country.) This philosophy contrasts with that of corporate media in the United States, which typically take their cues from the White House and single-issue pressure groups about which interview subjects are legitimate to put on the air.[52] Al-Jazeera is backed by an endowed foundation, and while it cannot be critical of the Qatari government or royal family, it can cover virtually everything else in the world without fear that sponsors will drop their spots or consumers will organize for that purpose. Al-Jazeera, however, remains a source of fear in Washington, as demonstrated by the great steganography scandal.[53]

In late 2003, CIA analysts became convinced that Al-Jazeera broadcast signals were carrying secret messages from al-Qaeda about which targets should be hit next. Encrypting messages in images is called steganography. As the analysts looked more deeply into this crackpot notion, however, they discovered that it was not true. The scare, however, produced at least one security alert for the American public (at the cost of how many millions of dollars?). Quite aside from the improbability of the notion, why did these analysts believe that Sheikh Hamad, a pillar of the pro-American Gulf establishment, would allow his prized project to become a tool of a disreputable terrorist group? Qatari fighter pilots had flown alongside the U.S. Air Force against the Iraqi military in Kuwait during the Gulf War, and there has been a long history of friendly relations between the Qatari royal family and the United States. American observers misunderstood Al-Jazeera's philosophy of covering all sides as a form of advocacy for radical Islam. This tragic misunderstanding tells us volumes about American expectations that media will ignore voices outside the Establishment and that giving dissidents or enemies a spot on television is a sign of treason.

I have the sinking feeling that these misunderstandings of Al-Jazeera's commitments led to great miscarriages of justice, including several U.S. attacks on the channel's journalists, one of them fatal. The United States bombed the Kabul office of Al-Jazeera in November 2001. Although the U.S. military said it was an accident, I remain suspicious that it was deliberate, that the Pentagon saw the station as a vehicle for the Taliban and al-Qaeda to get out their messages to the world. (Note that the Voice of America in the United States also interviewed Taliban leader Mullah Omar in that period.) Likewise, the U.S. Air Force bombed the Al-Jazeera office in Baghdad in early April 2003, killing Jordanian cameraman Tarek Ayoub and wounding another journalist. Al-Jazeera maintained that it had informed the United States of the location of its offices, which neighbored those of other international media.[54] A former British government official even alleged that Bush at one point considered bombing the Doha offices of Al-Jazeera, apparently over its critical coverage of the U.S. invasion of the Iraqi city of Fallujah in November of 2004.[55] Bush administration spokesmen denied that charge. U.S. officials had railed at the independent channel for saying that the United States had killed hundreds of civilians at Fallujah, arguing that the charges were false and inflammatory and would get U.S. troops killed. (The U.S. military destroyed two-thirds of the buildings in Fallujah, which it maintained was the center of the Sunni Arab insurgency, and it is likely that the civilian death toll was high.) At the least, Bush pressured Sheikh Hamad to close the channel down, something the emir refused to do. As a result, Sheikh Hamad was not welcomed for a state visit to Washington during the last administration.

If the bombings of Al-Jazeera were deliberate, I very much doubt that the officers who ordered them had ever actually watched Al-Jazeera. It certainly has a bias against the United States, but it is not a propaganda organ for terrorism by any means. The irony has been little noted: The United States attempted to close down a channel sponsored by a Wahhabi sheikhdom that has done marvels for freedom of the press and freedom of speech in the Middle East.

The American and European preoccupation with Wahhabi puritanism and intolerance, so visible in the punditry on Saudi Arabia, could scarcely be so easily justified in Wahhabi Qatar. There have been very few terrorist incidents in Qatar, and none committed by a native Qatari.[56] Shiites are allowed their own personal-status law. The government has licensed a Catholic church for guest workers of that persuasion, mostly Filipinos and South Indians. Five more churches are said to be planned. Note that Saudi Arabia does not allow churches to operate in public (it is the only Muslim-majority country out of more than fifty in the world with such a restrictive policy). A Hindu or Buddhist temple in Qatar might serve more people than a church—I figure about 40 percent of the over one million Qatari residents are South Asians from India, Nepal, Sri Lanka, and so forth. While I was there, I read an article about Indian jewelers in Qatar celebrating a Hindu gold festival—not the sort of thing you expect to find in the newspapers of a Wahhabi state. In the old days, Qatari merchants plied dhows to India and were always more cosmopolitan than their Najdi coreligionists. In Doha's five-star hotels, alcohol is served and there are a few nightclubs. In these ways, Qatar is starting to resemble the United Arab Emirates (UAE) to the south more than it does Riyadh. The UAE, especially Dubai, has a reputation for high living. Wahhabi policy in Qatar is far more laid back and much more tolerant of difference than in Saudi Arabia. A Qatari friend and former student suggested to me that this was simply the difference between Wahhabism of the sea and Wahhabism of the desert.

Bringing Qatar into the discussion helps make it clear that the tensions between the West and Saudi Arabia are not caused only or mainly by the Wahhabi religious tradition. It clearly cannot be Wahhabism that is intolerant of public Christian worship in the Arabian peninsula if one Wahhabi state encourages it even as another prohibits it. The Najdi way of being Wahhabi may have been historically wrought up with vehement puritanism, dislike of technological and theological innovation, and dislike of foreign influence, but such emphases and traditions change over time. Riyadh, a Wahhabi capital, is in some ways hypermodern, and the kingdom now has millions of foreigners. There were no Wahhabi suicide bombers until after the Reagan administration launched its struggle, with the help of the mujahideen, against the Soviets in Afghanistan, and there is no warrant in Wahhabism for suicide, or it would not have taken 150 years for it to occur to a Wahhabi fighter to sacrifice himself in that way. It is wrong to tar all the members of a religious tradition with the brush of terrorism based on the actions of a small number of persons among them.

Saudi Arabia has had a strong security alliance with the United States for decades, despite occasional tensions. Its puritanical domestic politics and its poor civil rights record have not stopped it from playing a positive role in the past five years in combating al-Qaeda. Given its current windfall from high petroleum prices, Saudi Arabia has enormous resources at its disposal for the exercise of various forms of soft power.

Because Saudi Arabia has integrated itself firmly into the international political and economic order, it is more open to pressure over its human rights violations and its authoritarianism than it might seem. The most useful pressure the North Atlantic states can apply to Riyadh in this regard, however, would be behind the scenes and quiet. Saudi notions of honor and face would make it difficult for the government to bow to open strong-arming from the West, and the Saudi public would revolt. The United States, after the torture scandals at Guantánamo and Abu Ghraib, is not in the most favorable position to push for such changes; it needs to clean up its own act so as to regain credibility on this score. Offering training to Saudi judges in human rights law would be a good first step.[57] (The kingdom has signed several UN treaties with implications for domestic human rights law.) Cooperation in fighting al-Qaeda should be reformulated as an effort to guarantee the right of citizens to live in peace and security, without the fear of vigilante violence.

Instead of attempting to enlist Saudi Arabia in vendettas, as the Bush administration did, pitting Saudis and their Sunni allies in Lebanon against the Iran-backed Shiite Hizbullah (which ended badly in May 2008 when Hizbullah militiamen demonstrated that they could take over all of Beirut if they so chose), or attempting to set Saudi Arabia and other Gulf oil monarchies against Iran, the United States should see the Saudis as the ultimate potential peace brokers in the region. Saudi investors have poured hundreds of millions of dollars into tourist hotels in Beirut and have every reason to want Lebanese politics to evolve in a peaceful direction. Saudi pressure on the various players in Lebanon, backed by big-money grants for development of their ethnic communities, could have an important calming effect. Beirut is the eastern Arab world's economic, social, and political window on the Mediterranean, and a peaceful and prosperous Lebanon is important to the human development of the entire region.

To his credit, King Abdullah has shown no interest in pursuing a new cold war with Iran. Instead, he has hosted high-level Iranian delegations in Riyadh. A Saudi and Iranian entente would allow the two to cooperate in pushing for social peace in both Lebanon and Iraq. By keeping their lines open to one another, Saudi Arabia and Iran can avoid inadvertently falling into proxy wars, a development that would irreparably harm the whole region and possibly cause a ruinous further spike in petroleum prices.

Saudi Arabia has likely played an important behind-the-scenes role in Iraq in enlisting tribal levies against the fundamentalist vigilantes. The Saudi royal family has important connections to Sunni tribes in Iraq.[58] It should be asked to go beyond fighting the vigilantes, however, to encouraging Sunni Iraqis to reconcile with the new government in Baghdad. Although Iraq is also an oil country, its many wars have left it without the bureaucratic, financial, or development infrastructure to deliver the oil wealth to its people in ways that would tie them to the elected government. Saudi Arabia has extensive experience in this field and could offer important help to Iraq. The United States should broker better relations between the Saudi government and the elected, Shiite-majority government in Baghdad with this aim in mind. By abandoning the myths created about Saudi Arabia and Wahhabism and by working with the Saudis to achieve shared goals, the West will be in a better position to influence domestic Saudi policy in the direction of greater democracy and human rights.

CHAPTER IV

IRAQ AND ISLAM ANXIETY

HOW FEARMONGERING GOT UP A WAR AND KEPT IT GOING

The American right wing invokes Islam Anxiety to ensure that the United States does not depart Iraq, and have discovered that nothing inspires greater Islamophobia than mentioning al-Qaeda. In the 2008 presidential campaign, John McCain warned, "My friends, if we left, [al-Qaeda] wouldn't be establishing a base. They'd be taking a country, and I'm not going to allow that to happen, my friends. I will not surrender. I will not surrender to al-Qaeda."[1] McCain thus went beyond the argument against withdrawal made by then vice president Dick Cheney in 2008 at Balad Air Force Base in Iraq: "We have no intention of abandoning our friends or allowing this country of 170,000 square kilometers to become a staging ground for further attacks against Americans."[2] (It is unclear how Iraq could be a staging ground for "further attacks" on the United States, given that it had never been a staging ground for any such attack in the past.)

McCain did not envisage a Sunni Arab enclave from which al-Qaeda could plot a strike on the U.S. mainland, but rather an al-Qaeda takeover of all Iraq. Commentators were puzzled as to how McCain

could think a small fringe group of fanatically anti-Shiite Sunni terrorists had the ability to take over a Shiite-majority country. (Although
the Baath regime had a Sunni bias at the top, many generals were Shiite, half the middle- and lower-ranking officials were Shiite, and most
army troops were Shiite—a level of support the fanatically anti-Shiite
Sunni fundamentalists could never hope for.[3]) But during the campaign, such details seemed beyond the Arizona senator. McCain notoriously confused hyper-Sunni al-Qaeda with Shiite groups linked to
Iran. He said in Amman, Jordan, in 2008, "Al Qaeda is going back into
Iran and is receiving training and are coming back into Iraq from
Iran."[4] He had to quickly backtrack, but he made the very same mis-
take at a Senate hearing just a month later, in April 2008. Islam Anxiety
is so powerful that it obliterates the distinctions between secular and
religious, between Sunni and Shiite, and between Iraqi Salafis or Sunni
revivalists and al-Qaeda.

The same Islamophobia that is now used to keep the United
States in Iraq was once deployed in political and media discourse to
enable the United States to begin the Iraq War.[5] Washington's
tremendous echo chamber transformed the secular Arab nationalist
Baath state into a handmaiden of radical Muslim al-Qaeda. Spin-
meisters such as Richard Perle deployed the standard stereotype of
the fanatical, unrestrained, unreasoning Muslim within his warnings
about the dangers of the alleged Iraqi nuclear, biological, and chemical weapons programs. Many of the smears were anonymous, as
when, in late 2002, "two senior administration officials" confirmed to
CNN "that perhaps Iraq passed on the nerve agent, VX, a deadly
nerve agent, to Islamic fundamentalists associated with al Qaeda in
recent weeks."[6] On such implausible nonsense was based a war that
has left a million dead.

After the fall of the secular Baath regime, the Bush administration
presided over the victory of fundamentalist Shiite religious parties
whose leaders had spent over twenty years in exile in Tehran as guests
of the ayatollahs, and which remained close to Tehran even as they be-
friended the Republican Party. Instead of admitting that it had turned
Iraq from an irreligious police state into a Muslim theocracy, the White

House attempted to convince journalists and the public that it had liberated Iraqi women and was combating Islamic extremism.

When the minority Sunni Arab Iraqis launched a disparate and determined guerrilla movement, the Pentagon immediately called it al-Qaeda. In fact, Iraqi Sunni leader Abu Musab al-Zarqawi had been acting through his own organization, Holy War and Monotheism, and had been a rival of Bin Laden's, instructing his followers not to send money to al-Qaeda. Only gradually did al-Zarqawi come to agree with the Pentagon that there might be advantages to rebranding his small group "al-Qaeda in Mesopotamia."

Bush pounced on this development. In a speech at Fort Bragg on July 28, 2005, he said, "The only way our enemies can succeed is if we forget the lessons of September 11 . . . if we abandon the Iraqi people to men like Zarqawi . . . and if we yield the future of the Middle East to men like Bin Laden." The previous week, Bush had said that the United States was in Iraq "because we were attacked." Al-Zarqawi was the perfect plot device for an administration that wanted to perpetuate the falsehood that the Iraq War was directly connected with September 11 and al-Qaeda. The following year, a U.S. general, Rick Lynch, actually alleged that al-Zarqawi "led" 90 percent of the attacks in Iraq.[7] How anyone other than a Marvel Comics supervillain could blow up things in Mosul in the north, Baquba in the east, and Baghdad in the center all on the same day was not clear.

It got so that if any Sunni Arab Iraqis were killed in a firefight with U.S. forces, the corpses were automatically labeled al-Qaeda, and the news media went along with it. It was not a new tactic. In Vietnam, after a firefight, a former Green Beret reminded me, if it was dead and it was Asian, the U.S. military declared it Viet Cong. This "al-Qaeda in Iraq" propaganda allowed the White House and the Pentagon to link Iraq in the public mind with Usamah Bin Laden, even though there was, in fact, almost no connection—the United States has been fighting a collection of Iraqi cells, many of them secular nationalists in orientation. Over time, the United States came to have as many as 26,000 Iraqi nationalist guerrillas in custody, virtually none of them al-Qaeda or linked in any way to that organization, though some proportion of them had adopted a fundamentalist vision of Iraqi Islam.[8]

At the same time that Washington reframed the national liberation struggle waged by Iraqi Sunni Arabs as "international Islamic terrorism," it succeeded in disguising its own dependence on fundamentalist parties. Among the few Sunni Arab allies of the United States was the Iraqi Islamic Party (IIP) of Tariq al-Hashimi, the Iraqi version of the Muslim Brotherhood and Hamas. Merely by being willing to serve in a pro-American government, the IIP avoided the opprobrium of being called a fanatical terrorist group, even though it has had connections to—and it is unclear how its social and political goals differ from—Sunni paramilitaries.

On the Shiite side of the ledger, there was little ideological difference between the Shiite Islamic Supreme Council of Iraq (ISCI), led by pro-Iran cleric Abdul Aziz al-Hakim, and the Sadr movement led by Sayyid Muqtada al-Sadr. Both wanted strong clerical influence in government, and both wanted Islamic law to be the law of the land. The main difference was that the Sadrists wanted U.S. and other foreign troops out of Iraq on a short timetable, whereas ISCI was willing to host U.S. forces for at least the medium term. Washington therefore coded Sadr as a fiery extremist and al-Hakim as a "moderate."[9]

In a spring 2008 poll, 81 percent of Arabs said they believed that Iraqis were worse off in 2008 than they had been under the regime of Saddam Hussein.[10] The sounding was done by the University of Maryland and Zogby International in Egypt, Jordan, Lebanon, Morocco, Saudi Arabia, and the United Arab Emirates. Many Americans will find this attitude baffling. Were there not now elections in Iraq? Were there not now over two hundred newspapers free of censorship? The Washington narrative of the U.S. invasion and subsequent troop presence in the country underlines the themes of liberation and the fostering of democratic institutions in the place of a dictatorship. In essence, the American right saw the invasion as a way of pushing Iraq to do what Poland had done voluntarily in the late 1980s and the 1990s, moving from the darkness of a Stalinist police state into the light of a capitalist democracy. Clearly, Muslim and Arab publics viewed these events rather differently.

In the poll, Arab publics were asked to choose the two consequences of the Iraq War that most troubled them. Nearly 60 percent chose the answer "Iraq will remain unstable and spread instability in the region" as one of their two top concerns. That proportion, up from 40 percent in 2006, demonstrated that public anxiety about how the Iraqi situation would affect them is increasing in the region. Roughly four in ten chose one of the following answers: "Continuing trouble in Iraq will divert attention from other issues such as the Palestinian question," "U.S. will continue to dominate Iraq long after the transfer of power to the Iraqis," and "Iraq may be divided." Although American headlines at the time were dominated by the building tension with Iran, only 8 percent or the Arabs reported anxiety that Iran had become a more powerful state.

What alarmed Arab publics about the Iraq War was the threat that the massive violence, including daily bombings, sniping, and religious and ethnic conflict, would spill over into their countries. They also worried about a breakup of Iraq (probably for similar reasons) and about a loss of autonomy to a neoimperial superpower attempting to implant itself more firmly in their lives. They were concerned that the Iraq issue takes the spotlight off the plight of millions of stateless Palestinians in the West Bank and Gaza, who—as *New York Times* columnist Nicholas Kristof described it in a June 2008 column—are living under "colonial" conditions of Israeli domination.[11]

About a quarter of Arab respondents thought that there had been a genuine reduction in violence in the second half of 2007 and early 2008 and hoped it was a sign that Iraq would now move toward stability, though only a small minority attributed the improvement to the arrival of more U.S. troops beginning in 2007. Two-thirds told the pollsters that they either flatly disbelieved the falling death rates or thought that the violence would likely reemerge. That is, most Muslim

Arabs in this poll thought that the fabled success of the "troop surge" trumpeted by John McCain and others was a publicity stunt at best and a fraud at worst. As for McCain's dire warnings of an al-Qaeda takeover of Iraq if the United States were to leave, that view was not widely shared in the region. Three-fifths of those polled said that in the absence of the Americans, they were sure that Iraqis would find a way to bridge their differences. Another one-sixth thought that things would remain pretty much the same without the U.S. troops. Only a bit more than one-eighth feared that the civil war would expand greatly.

American right-wingers and Muslims on the street came to different conclusions because they start with different assumptions. McCain and others see the United States as a guarantor of stability and democracy. Many Muslims view Americans as grasping carpetbaggers, a twenty-first-century equivalent of the Mongol hordes that sacked Baghdad in 1258. The predominant Muslim experience in the twentieth century was of being ruled and economically exploited by white, Western Christians and of having to mount national liberation movements to attain independence. Nobody in the region believed that Western troops showed up out of the goodness of their hearts, and nobody thought life worth living if it could not be lived in conditions of independence.

Given a choice between an autocratic but autonomous government not bound to the Christian, capitalist North Atlantic world and a democratic state under the sway of foreign governments, the Muslim Arab publics tend to favor the former. During the many years I spent in the Muslim world, I gained the firm impression that part of what Muslims mean by "democracy" is precisely national independence. From this perspective, the government that existed in Iraq in 2005 and in the years that followed was not truly democratic, since it was clearly under the thumb of Washington. This is why the issue of a big U.S. troop presence in Iraq is a major stumbling block in relations between the United States and the Muslim world. As noted earlier, some 85 percent of Saudis polled late in 2007 said that a U.S. withdrawal from Iraq would improve their opinion of America.[12]

One reason that the Middle East, and the Muslim world more generally, sees Iraq differently from Americans is that they have watched two different wars on their television sets. Over two-thirds of Americans turn for their political news to cable television news or their local television stations. Similar percentages resort to their local newspapers and to network television news.[13] Despite the hype about the Internet, television news is still primary in most Americans' lives. In contrast to the Arab satellite news channels, U.S. channels seldom depict wounded Iraqis. They almost never interview Iraqi politicians, and certainly not ones critical of the United States. Many of the stories have been done by journalists embedded with the U.S. military. Many of the military analysts used by the networks and by cable news are retired military officers, often with ongoing but hidden relations to the Pentagon or military contractors.[14]

With the beginning of the presidential campaign as the big news in the spring of 2008, U.S. news programs began to virtually ignore Iraq. The three prime-time networks devoted only 181 minutes to Iraq in the first half of 2008, compared to 1,157 minutes in the whole year of 2007.[15] CBS closed its Baghdad bureau in early 2008 as a cost-cutting measure, and even networks with reporters on the ground were reluctant to put their stories on the air because they felt the presidential campaign and the economy were the more pressing stories for viewers. Yet polls in mid-2008 found that a quarter of Americans named the Iraq War as their number-one concern. You would have thought that 75 million Americans would be enough of a potential audience for producers.

The most-watched satellite news channel in the Arab world is Al-Jazeera; 53 percent of Arabs in a recent poll said that they most often turned to it for news. Various Egyptian channels, such as Nile, came in second place with 17 percent, with Al-Arabiya, based in Dubai, third, favored by 9 percent. Only 2 percent said that they most often watched news on al-Hurra, the U.S.-sponsored television channel for Arab viewers.[16] I watch Al-Jazeera quite a lot, and its Iraq coverage continually shows corpses, including those of children; victims of violence in hospitals with blood on their bandages; burned-out automobiles and shops engulfed in flames after bombings; explicit footage of torture victims; and destitute Iraqis, including refugees, widows, and orphans. Aside from actually displaying the mayhem, Al-Jazeera's anchors and reporters interview Iraqis of all political views, including those who support what the United States calls the insurgency. Al-Jazeera reporters in Baghdad are not embedded or stuck in the Green Zone. They are professionals, and they sometimes have a background in U.S. network television.

The U.S. invasion and military occupation of Iraq undeniably unleashed a tsunami of violence and disorder that has blighted the lives of millions. The displaced Iraqis swelled to a river of humanity, a startling 4 million persons by any conservative estimate. Ironically, during the years of the American troop escalation, 2007–2008, the number of those Iraqis who had fled their homes for another part of Iraq grew markedly. In the summer of 2008, the United Nations High Commissioner on Refugees (UNHCR) estimated the number of internally displaced Iraqis at 2.7 million; before the surge, in January 2007, that number was estimated at 1.8 million.[17] It is large tragedies like this one, unfolding in the midst of the supposedly good news of lower monthly death tolls, that make Muslim publics suspicious of the triumphal U.S. narrative of progress.

In 2006 and 2007, Baghdad, a city of 6 million, witnessed substantial ethnic cleansing of Sunni Arabs, with the city ending up 75 percent Shiite, according to the U.S. military. Many Sunnis were forced abroad, to Syria. Baghdad is estimated to have been half Sunni Arab in 2003, when the United States invaded. This cleansing thus occurred under the nose of the U.S. troops. Of those displaced from Baghdad to other provinces in Iraq, 71 percent said that their property had been seized and claimed by private citizens. The internal refugees "remain particularly vulnerable to the harsh living conditions of squatter settlements, which offer no or little access to medical care, education, drinking water and other basic facilities," according to the intergovernmental International Organization for Migration, which added, "In Anbar Al-Ka'im district, IOM monitors reported that many children were forced into begging and their mothers into collecting garbage for resale in order to survive."[18]

It is likely that there are about 200,000 Iraqis in Jordan (larger figures sometimes appear in the press, but my research indicates that they are exaggerated), and over a million in Syria. There are also 30,000 each in Egypt and Lebanon and about 40,000 in Sweden. About 1 million Iraqis had been displaced before the American invasion, but at least 400,000 of those had gone to Iran, and they returned with the fall of Saddam. We may conclude that approximately 1.5 million Iraqis have been forced abroad by the U.S. invasion and its chaotic aftermath. They are disproportionately well educated (half those in Jordan have had some college) and middle or upper class— by 2008, at least a third of the Iraqi middle class had fled abroad. The total displaced since 2003, internally and externally, equals nearly a sixth of the entire Iraqi population.

In 2008, roughly 50,000 Iraqis in Jordan and most Iraqis in Syria faced dire circumstances, with many of them quickly running out of money.[19] In Syria, few Iraqi children were being schooled, and some were becoming malnourished. Girls and women sometimes were forced to turn to survival sex. From February 2007 through June 2008, only about 10,000 families, or 50,000 persons, had come back to Iraq from abroad. These arrivals invariably generated a rash of wire service articles, especially when journalists were prompted by the Iraqi government, but the scale of returns was dwarfed by the continued outflow. The UNHCR office in Amman told me in August 2008 that it discouraged such returns, considering the situation inside Iraq still too dangerous.

American pundits who praised the "success" of the troop surge were oblivious to the ethnic cleansing, but it was no secret to infuriated Iraqi and regional Sunni Arabs. In 2007, journalist Ghassan al-Imam wrote an impassioned column for the pan-Arab press entitled "The Battle of Baghdad: The Extirpation of Sunnis and of Arabism."[20] As a result of the American conquest, he said, the Shiite militias, especially the Mahdi Army, had been enabled to begin "openly adopting the technique of deliberately, and in a systematic and programmatic fashion, ethnically cleansing Baghdad's Sunnis." Baghdad, the glorious capital of the medieval Abbasid Empire, is dear to the heart of all Muslims, and Sunni Arabs will not lightly relinquish it. They are not pleased about the role of the United States in "preparing the way for" (as al-Imam put it) its transformation into a bastion of Shiism, which the Sunnis (unfairly) associate with the non-Arab Persian culture of Iran.

My research in Jordan in the summer of 2008 helped me understand the reasons for which the Iraqi refugees generally declined to return, despite worsening economic situations for many. Some Sunnis complained to me that their Iraqi neighborhoods had been mixed but were now entirely Shiite, so that they would no longer feel safe there. A fourth of the refugee families who applied for assistance in Jordan had had a child kidnapped. I was told by a CARE official in Amman that many Iraqis in exile had received personal threats from militias warning that they would be killed if they ever showed their faces in their old neighborhoods again.[21] In some instances, refugees had continued to be threatened even in Jordan, and had to move apartments frequently for security reasons. The relative decline of violence from the horrific levels of 2006–2007 had not reversed the ethnic cleansing in Baghdad or removed the militias that issued the personal threats. The Iraqi press reported in summer 2008 that many families had left Iraq because of poor services, including lack of potable water, electricity, and security.[22]

Despite the lowered civilian death tolls in Iraq from September 2007, the problems of militia intimidation, ethnically cleansed neighborhoods, and lack of basic services remained. Fear, unwillingness to suffer further, and hope of being resettled abroad led some 50,000 destitute Iraqis to live furtively in Amman, even when denied work permits or temporary residency visas and constantly looking over their shoulders. Some Iraqi women in exile who were heading their households had run out of money and were baking bread for neighbors, sewing, or running informal beauty salons in their living rooms to eke out a living. Others could not afford a sewing machine or oven, and were seeking aid to get one, but found that nongovernmental organizations were unwilling to risk helping them work illegally. UNHCR could provide them only about $75 a month in refugee aid, which went less and less far as gasoline and food prices rose throughout 2008.

It is true, as apologists for the Bush administration will aver, that much of this human catastrophe was created not directly by U.S. troops but by Sunni and Shiite guerrilla groups who displayed a blood thirst akin to the killing fields of Pol Pot's Cambodia in the 1970s or the genocide in the Democratic Republic of Congo in the late 1990s and beginning of the twenty-first century. Historians have an answer to these excuses. We speak of "proximate causes." The guerrillas may have been the immediate cause of the expulsions, but it was the U.S. invasion that set them off.

In absolute numbers, the Iraqi refugee crisis would be equivalent to a cataclysmic natural disaster forcing the bulk of the population of a small country, such as Israel or Jordan, out of their homes. Since the United States is eleven times more populous than Iraq, 4 million displaced Iraqis would be proportionally equivalent to 44 million Americans. That is, if we mapped the refugee flow in Iraq onto the United States, it would be as though the entire populations of California and Michigan had been put on the road to elsewhere, losing their accumulated property and the comfort of their houses and apartments. Only in Hollywood disaster movies about large meteor strikes or global warming are such scenes even considered by most Americans, but for Iraqis they have become a reality.

The United States, for the most part, sidestepped its responsibility for these Iraqi refugees and offered asylum or refugee status to only a few thousand, thus doing far less for them than Sweden, a country of 9 million that had not even been involved in Iraq. The United States said it would admit 12,000 Iraqis in 2008, while Sweden had long since admitted 40,000. Even Iraqis who endangered their lives by working for the United States in Iraq have been turned away. In contrast, President

Gerald Ford allowed 100,000 Vietnamese into the United States at the end of the war there.

Islam Anxiety comes into this story in two ways. The reluctance of the United States to take large numbers of Iraqi refugees, which its own war helped create, likely derives in part from fear that some of the immigrants might harbor resentment and turn to terrorism once they arrive. As Quang X. Pham, a Vietnamese American and Gulf War veteran, observed in 2007 to journalist Andrew Lam, "Iraqi refugees, unlike Vietnamese refugees, have no champion like President Gerald Ford, and they will find much opposition to their immigration to the United States due to fallout from Sept. 11 and specifically, the Patriot Act." [23]

A general anti-immigration mood on the right also plays a role. Congressman Tom Tancredo (R-Co), notoriously bigoted against Muslims, maintained that there was no need to admit Iraqis to the United States because the 2007 troop escalation had succeeded in reducing violence. [24] He neglected to note that the violence, though reduced, continued and that no significant number of refugees had returned home. This inattention by the United States to the Iraqi refugee calamity signals to potential U.S. allies in the Middle East that America does not take care of its friends. It signals to the international community that the United States makes messes and does not clean them up. It therefore lessens the likelihood of the United States finding friends and supporters for future major foreign policy initiatives.

In addition, this mass of displaced humanity puts political and economic pressure on Jordan, a longtime friend and ally of the United States, and has the potential to push already unstable Syria into an even more parlous crisis. Neither development would likely leave U.S. ally Israel unaffected. The happy-go-lucky inattention to this problem, a characteristic of the Bush administration, must be reversed.

Public health researchers with experience in conflict zones have put the number of excess deaths since the U.S. invasion of Iraq at hundreds of thousands. Les Roberts, now at Columbia University's Mailman School of Public Health, and Gil Burnham, of the Johns Hopkins University Bloomberg School of Public Health, led two studies of Iraqi households, both published in the peer-reviewed medical journal the *Lancet*.[25] In October 2006, they estimated that about 600,000 Iraqis had died violently between March 2003 and June 2006, beyond what would have been expected given the death rates before the war. Only 31 percent of the excess violent deaths were attributed by the families interviewed to Coalition troops (which were in the main American and British, and mostly American). The other excess violent deaths were the product of tribal feuds, criminal gangs, and neighborhood vendettas as well as of guerrilla groups and ethnic cleansing. The vast majority died from gunfire. If the *Lancet* interviewees were telling the truth, at least 200,000 of those deaths are directly attributable to the U.S. military and its allies. Many of the families who blamed a death on the Coalition reported that their loved ones had been killed in an aerial bombardment. The troubling U.S. practice of intensively bombing densely populated Iraqi cities already theoretically under American occupation probably accounts for a good many of the excess deaths.[26] In spring of 2008, the *Washington Post* interviewed a ten-year-old Iraqi girl in Sadr City who took shrapnel in her legs from an American missile strike. She said, "They kill people. . . . They should leave Iraq now."[27]

Even if we granted that violent deaths of civilians have somehow been exaggerated by the *Lancet* and other surveys (the Opinion Research Business poll also projected over a million excess Iraqi deaths by late 2007), violent deaths are only one source of excess mortality in American Iraq.[28] Frederick Burkle, of Harvard University's Department of Public Health and Epidemiology, ran Iraq's Ministry of Health briefly after the war.[29] He noted in an interview that enormous numbers of physicians and nurses fled the violence, and clinics suffered from lack of money, lack of medicines, and even poor provision of electricity. Infants in displaced families also often lacked access to clean water. All of these problems would have contributed to increased Iraqi mortality.

Even if only 300,000 excess Iraqi deaths occurred in the aftermath of the U.S. invasion, which seems to me the lowest estimate that is plausible if we count both violent and nonviolent causes, that would comprise the entire population of cities such as Pittsburgh or Cincinnati. A million dead Iraqis is proportionally like 11 million dead

Americans, as though a death ray had mown down everyone in Ohio. In a conflict situation such as Iraq, the ratio of wounded to those killed would be at the very least three to one. That ratio would suggest that the U.S. invasion of Iraq has resulted in the wounding of as many as 3 million Iraqis. Proportionally that would be equivalent to 33 million Americans wounded, that is, almost the entire population of California crippled or in bandages.

The official death totals for Iraqi civilians announced by the Iraqi government and the U.S. military fell considerably after August 2007, from the almost apocalyptic violence in 2006–2007, when as many as 2,500 civilians were killed every month. The typical tagline of most U.S. news reporting thereafter was that Iraq was now "calm" or "calmer." The improvement was only relative, something difficult to convey in sound bites, and Iraq remained one of the world's crisis areas. By the aforementioned rule of eleven, even 500 Iraqi civilians killed in political violence a month would be the equivalent of 5,500 Americans killed per month or 60,500 per year. (Note that this 60,500 figure would only be political deaths of civilians, since it does not include criminal homicides or activists.) The annual number of murders in the United States is about 16,000, including political violence, what little there is.

Deaths, woundings, and displacements on an almost cosmic scale do not exhaust the charges against the U.S. misadventure in Iraq as seen by Muslims. They have not forgotten the torture at Abu Ghraib or the subsequent torture of Sunni Arabs by the Shiite government's Interior Ministry. Abu Ghraib photographs have been spread around Internet bulletin boards with denunciations of the United States and allegations that the harsh practices reveal something about the warped character of the American soul.

When, in June 2008, the online magazine *Al-Islam al-Yawm* (Islam Today) carried an article on U.S. torture of detainees, one of the readers asked, "Is this an advanced civilization? Is this a civilized nation?" He denounced U.S. tyranny and complained about "what the Muslim women in Iraq have suffered," implying widespread American rape.[30] Such charges were lent plausibility by the sexual character of the humiliation forced on Iraqis at Abu Ghraib.

The image of Iraq purveyed by the White House and the Pentagon during the past few years, as a cauldron of religious radicalism, differs completely from the one projected by Washington in previous decades. How Iraqis went from being coded as potentially dangerous, left-leaning Arab nationalists to being grouped with al-Qaeda as a radical Islamic menace to the United States demonstrates the opportunistic character of Islamophobic discourse.

Back in 1972, the State Department worried about Iraq's Arab nationalism, socialist politics, and growing ties to the Soviet Union. A National Security Council briefing for President Richard M. Nixon prepared in the spring of 1972 blamed Iraq's recent turn to extremism on the defeat that the Israelis, backed by the United States, inflicted on the Arabs in 1967. "The passions of that war unleas[h]ed the most left-ist nationalists and by 1968 the Baathis (who also dominate in Syria) consolidated in power and remain there today."[31] The briefing explained to Nixon that "generally speaking, all good Baathis ascribe [sic] in excess to the Arab nationalist principles of unity, socialism, liberty and revolution and to the theory that the Arab world is an indivisible political, social and economic whole."

Anxiety about Iraq pervaded the U.S. diplomatic corps in that era. Earlier in 1972, the U.S. embassy in Beirut had written back to Foggy Bottom that the "estimate that the Soviets, having established themselves in a position of considerable influence in Baghdad, are working assiduously to assure continued domestic tranquility in Iraq seems to be correct." That is, the cooperation of the small remnants of the Iraqi Communist Party with the Baathist popular councils was being mandated by Moscow. The report continued, "The country is already dependent almost exclusively upon Moscow for arms, and in other respects (economic assistance, for example) the USSR . . . appears intent on identifying itself completely with the Ba'thist regime."[32]

The long tradition of U.S. officials seeing the Baath Party as radical, socialist-leaning Arab nationalists was interrupted for a few years in the 1980s, when the Reagan administration formed an alliance of convenience with Baghdad against Khomeini's Iran during the Iran-Iraq War of 1980 to 1988. But with the Gulf War of 1990–1991 and the subsequent decade of attempts to contain Saddam Hussein's Iraq, the radical Arab socialism rhetoric returned to prominence (it was noticeably redeployed during the first year that the United States ruled its new colonial possession, 2003–2004).

U.S. spokesmen initially characterized the Sunni Arab guerrilla movement that began in 2003 as neo-Baathist or "dead-enders." The Pentagon blamed a spectacular December 2003 bank robbery in Samarra, north of Baghdad, on the "Saddam Fedayeen," or "those who sacrifice themselves for Saddam," a Baath special forces unit. After the capture of Saddam soon thereafter, the United States suddenly stopped talking about dead-enders or the Baath Party, even though it is likely that former Iraqi vice president Izzat Ibrahim Duri ran a neo-Baath guerrilla cell in the Mosul area for years. As late as December 2006, Sunni Arab crowds demonstrating in the provincial capital of Baquba northeast of Baghdad unfurled Baathist and pro-Saddam banners, provoking the largely Shiite police to shoot some of them down. The Arabic press reported that, over time, the Baath had split into four parties. There was an aborted plan for these splinters to reunite at a party congress in Damascus in January 2007, but Duri successfully vetoed the gathering on the grounds that formalizing the resistance might be a first step to negotiations with the American occupiers.[33]

After the execution of Saddam by the Shiite government in late 2006, the interior minister warned that there was a widespread revival of interest in the Baath Party and its successors, such as the shadowy "al-'Awdah," or "the Return," even among Iraqi government employees.[34] At least some part of the guerrilla resistance to the United States and the new Shiite- and Kurdish-dominated government derived from secular Iraqi nationalist cells that saw themselves as successors to the failed Baath Party. A steady stream of Baath communiqués appeared on resistance Web sites claiming credit for attacks on U.S. troops.[35] This secular nationalist element in the resistance was completely ignored in the American press, in large part because White House and Defense Department spokesmen never mentioned it. Occasionally, when the United States accused Baathist Syria of supporting the insurgency, the charge was based on U.S. intelligence suspicions that Damascus was running Baath cells against the United States as a way of maintaining influence in northern Iraq near the Syrian border. Similarly, the Shiite politicians who came to power in Baghdad under American auspices often gave speeches in Arabic denouncing the Baath Party for its continuing terrorist activities.

Sociologist Mansoor Moaddel helped conduct several nationwide polls in Iraq from spring 2004 through summer 2007. The polls were carried out by an Iraqi research firm, the Independent Institute for Administrative and Civil Society Studies, and funded by the National Science Foundation. Over 7,000 respondents were polled, weighted for sect and ethnicity.[36] The polling revealed that in 2004, about a third of Sunni Arabs in Iraq thought it was important to have a government that solely implemented sharia, or Islamic canon law. But by April 2006, that proportion had fallen to 13 percent and fluctuated around that number through the summer of 2007, averaging about 15 percent. Implementing the law of God rather than man is a key demand of Muslim fundamentalist groups, and Moaddel's polling found that fundamentalist attitudes, never characteristic of the majority, had declined steeply over time.

That finding tracks with the political reality that in 2006 and 2007, the Awakening Council movement gained enormous ground against radical Salafi organizations such as the Islamic State of Iraq. Whereas in 2004, Moaddel found that only 22 percent of Sunni Arabs agreed that Iraq would be better off with a separation of religion and state, by July 2007, some 53 percent of Sunni Arab respondents backed a separation of religion and state.

Other indications that over time Sunni Arabs were returning to their secular traditions emerged in the polling. In 2004, only 21 percent of Sunni Arabs said that they were "Iraqis, above all," that their national identity trumped their identities as Muslims. By July 2007, that proportion had risen to 57 percent. This privileging of national identity over the religious one by Sunni Arab Iraqis in 2007 made them remarkable. In contrast, two 2004 polls showed that only about

26 percent of Jordanians considered themselves Jordanians first and Muslims second; a much bigger percentage said that they were Muslims first.[37] U.S. politicians and journalists' concentration on the small religious guerrilla cells operating in the Sunni Arab regions gave the wrong impression, that a majority of Sunni Arabs are fundamentalists and that they might even try to erect an al-Qaeda state that would strike at the U.S. mainland.

On a sweltering August day in 2002, an Iraqi intelligence official penned an urgent circular, stamping it "top secret," about the rumored presence in Iraq of persons "accused of dealings with the al-Qaeda organization led by the Saudi Usamah Bin Laden."[38] He enclosed photographs, likely supplied by the Jordanian secret police, of Ahmad Fadil Nizal al-Khala'ilah, better known as Abu Musab al-Zarqawi, the Jordanian terrorist.

The official instructed that a search should be launched for the suspect in tourist hotels, apartments, and rented homes and among the Jordanian expatriate community in Iraq. "Give it," he intoned, "the very highest importance." The file was followed by a series of notes from other officials maintaining that the suspect was not in their area. The correspondence was enclosed in a file stamped "Republic of Iraq, Office of the Presidency, Intelligence Service." It was numbered 408 and on the other side was written: "On the possibility that persons from al-Qaeda have entered the country." The alarmed tone of the correspondence shows that this file contains an all-points bulletin, in which Saddam's secret police launched a determined attempt to find and arrest al-Zarqawi and his associates. The Iraqis seem to have known little about him, and needed the Jordanian photographs to help identify him. The wily terrorist mastermind, however, eluded them.[39]

In late 2002, in a speech to leaders of the U.S. National Guard in Denver, then vice president Dick Cheney alleged that Saddam Hussein's regime "has had high-level contacts with al-Qaeda going back a decade and has provided training to al-Qaeda terrorists."[40] The Iraqi

Baath had in fact done no such thing. Shadowy contacts between Iraqi intelligence and all sorts of seedy characters took place, as with any intelligence organization, but Cheney was alleging an operational cooperation for which there is no evidence even after the U.S. military combed 6 million captured Baath documents.

In his presentation to the United Nations justifying the U.S. war on Iraq in February 2003, Secretary of State Colin Powell alleged that al-Zarqawi had come to Iraq in May 2002 and received hospital treatment for a leg injury in Baghdad and that thereafter a whole coven of terrorists joined him there. Powell implied that the Baath regime actively allowed the terrorists to operate in Iraq in that period. Over a year later, Cheney was peddling the same narrative, saying

> Senior al Qaeda associate Abu Musab al-Zarqawi took sanctuary in Baghdad after coalition forces drove him out of Afghanistan. From the Iraqi capital in 2002, Zarqawi—along with some two dozen associates, al Qaeda members, and affiliates—ran a poisons camp in northern Iraq, which became a safe haven for Ansar al-Islam as well as al Qaeda terrorists fleeing our coalition in Afghanistan. The Iraqi regime refused to turn over Zarqawi even when twice being provided with detailed information on his presence in Baghdad.[41]

The captured document published by the U.S. military after the invasion demonstrates that Iraqi intelligence only learned that al-Zarqawi might be in Iraq in August 2002 and that throughout that month, they mounted a search for him but could not find him. The story of his arrival months before and receiving government-sponsored hospital treatment was clearly just another of the many falsehoods purveyed by Washington to pave the way for an illegal war of aggression on Iraq. Iraqi intelligence officials would not have reported back to the initiator of the all-points bulletin that they could not find al-Zarqawi if he had been their honored guest. Little details such as the alleged hospital stay were built up into a narrative that was intended to carry the audience along without being able to ask any questions about it. The arguments were made on the basis of contiguity, of one thing being next to another, rather than on the grounds of causality, motive, and proportionality.

Al-Zarqawi was said to have established himself in northeastern Iraq, in an area that Saddam did not even control. Powell alleged that "from Baghdad" he was training members of Ansar al-Islam (a tiny Kurdish organization engaged in a struggle with the Kurdistan Regional Government) to make ricin, a poison. That al-Zarqawi, a high school dropout, was doing sophisticated chemical experiments seems unlikely even if he had been in the Ansar al-Islam compound in that period, which has not been proved. Reporter Borzou Daragahi, who visited the Ansar al-Islam camp before the war, found mud huts, scruffy fundamentalist Kurds, and no chemical workshop. It is typical of the wild allegations made by the Bush administration that they were easily disproved by the visit of a lone journalist. When the United States had the opportunity to hit the Ansar al-Islam camp in the run-up to the invasion of Iraq, it declined to do so, apparently fearful that removing the group would weaken the case for going to war against Baathist Iraq. But Ansar al-Islam was an enemy of the Baath regime, operating outside its area of control, and so could never have justified an American invasion of Baghdad anyway.[42]

Some of the fable of Saddam's operational cooperation with al-Qaeda came from the falsehood factory of corrupt expatriate banker Ahmad Chalabi and his Iraqi National Congress, which fed single-sourced, dubious allegations to gullible Bush administration officials such as Douglas Feith, the undersecretary of defense for planning. Chalabi's group had a prime motive for fraud: they hoped Bush would overthrow Saddam and install them in power. Feith, a key figure in the Israel lobbies such as the Jewish Institute for National Security Affairs. He had pushed for a war with Iraq in a 1996 white paper he coauthored for Israeli prime minister Binyamin Netanyahu, and was overeager to swallow the myths because they fit with his preconception that the Baath regime was involved with al-Qaeda.[43]

Another source of disinformation was al-Qaeda operative Ibn al-Shaikh al-Libi (captured in late 2001), who asserted under torture in January of 2002 that the Iraqi government was training al-Qaeda agents in chemical weapons use.[44] He later recanted, according to Washington officials who spoke to the *New York Times* and other news organs off the record. Even in 2002 and 2003, he was contradicted by other high al-

Qaeda officials, who maintained that Bin Laden had forbidden them to cooperate with the wretched secular atheist, Saddam. It is possible that al-Libi was attempting to entice the United States into Iraq, in accordance with Bin Laden's thesis that if al-Qaeda could get U.S. troops on the ground in the Muslim world, they could do to America what it had done to the Soviet Union. In any case, Dick Cheney and then national security adviser Condoleezza Rice both went public with al-Libi's fabrication in the months before the United States invaded Iraq.

For the American hawks, al-Zarqawi was the gift that kept on giving. Since he was associated with Afghanistan, he could be painted as al-Qaeda. His mere presence in some part of Iraq was invoked as a reason to invade that country. After the overthrow of the Baath government, as Sunni Arab Iraqis mobilized to conduct a guerrilla war against the United States and its Shiite and Kurdish allies, the Pentagon made al-Zarqawi the poster boy of what they called the insurgency. They thus recast a movement of national liberation mainly fought by Iraqis on a variety of ideological grounds, secular and religious, as a mere outgrowth of Bin Laden's al-Qaeda.

The primary goals that drove the United States to war in Iraq in fact had almost nothing to do with Islam. First of all, the U.S. wanted to ensure the flow of petroleum and other hydrocarbons from the Persian Gulf. Second, the Bush administration preferred that U.S. energy companies be in a position to develop Iraqi petroleum and gas fields, rather than to continue to have to boycott that country. Third, the United States wished to prevent rivals such as China and India from locking Iraqi resources into long-term proprietary contracts that would exclude the United States. Fourth, Washington wished to prevent Iraq from emerging as a regional dominant power that could determine the politics and economies of the Persian Gulf and its Levantine hinterland. Fifth, it wished to preserve the leading position of its two major allies, Israel and Saudi Arabia, as regional dominant powers. The rabidly pro-Israel neoconservatives in the administration actually hoped to replace Saudi Arabia with an Iraqi puppet regime, but that was never the goal of Bush and Cheney, both of whom had long and warm ties to Riyadh. In order to accomplish these goals, it would be necessary for key figures in the Bush administration to intimate that all Middle Eastern leaders, even secular ones such as Saddam, were intrinsically allied to fanatic terrorists.

The Bush administration's invasion of Iraq in 2003 was also intended in part to resolve the problems they had with the Clinton-era "dual containment" policy, which aimed at boxing in both Iraq and Iran through a combination of economic sanctions and pressure exerted by the U.S. Air Force, which regularly flew over Iraq and near Iran. The plan had not been entirely successful—in the 1990s, Iran continued to do substantial business with Western Europe and with East Asia, and the commitment of U.S. allies in Europe and elsewhere to the deadly sanctions on Iraq was slipping. At the same time, U.S. petroleum companies and companies servicing that sector, such as Bechtel and Halliburton, were afraid that Congress would increasingly squeeze them out of Iraq and Iran by ratcheting up unilateral sanctions.

As CEO of the oil and energy services company Halliburton in Dallas, Texas, from 1995 to 2000, Dick Cheney deployed his network of contacts—built up when he was secretary of defense in the senior Bush's administration during the Gulf War—in a wide-ranging quest for new petroleum fields. He sank $1 billion into making Halliburton a leader in "smart wells" that employed "computer software and magnetic imaging" to help identify underground reserves. He maintained warm relations with the long-serving Saudi ambassador in Washington, Bandar bin Sultan, attending his wedding anniversary party in 1998. He also expanded Halliburton's reach into the Caspian Basin, seeking deals in post-Soviet Azerbaijan and Kazakhstan. Kazakhstan's president, Nursultan Nazarbayev, appointed Cheney, along with the CEOs of Chevron Corporation and Texaco Inc., as a member of Kazakhstan's Oil Advisory Board.[45]

During this period, Cheney quickly emerged as an opponent of congressional attempts to slap ever more sanctions on countries ruled by regimes its members disliked. The United States imposed unilateral sanctions on Libya, Iran, and Azerbaijan and participated in multilateral sanctions against Libya and Iraq. Cheney, a former congressman, urged the petroleum industry to take a "proactive approach" to battling such sanctions. He complained that legislators multiplied trade sanctions as a painless way to take a stand on policy and to "satisfy their domestic constituencies." The latter phrase referred in part to lobbying by the American Israeli Public Affairs Committee (AIPAC) to sanction states hostile to Israel. Cheney said, "When prices are low, lawmakers feel free to use oil as a sanctions weapon." He pointed out that U.S. oil and gas corporations have no choice but to explore where the reserves might be, which impels them to deal with countries whose policies are anathema to the United States. He explained, "The long-term horizon of the industry is at odds with the short-term nature of politics. The U.S. government needs to extend its horizon and avoid quick, light-switch diplomacy."[46]

On a visit to Malaysia in 1998, Cheney lashed out against Congress for its new, unilateral sanctions on Libya and Iran, which were pushed by AIPAC.[47] He said that such boycott moves were "ineffective, did not provide the desired results and a bad policy." The new sanctions imposed penalties on U.S. companies that invested more than $20 million a year in the targeted countries. Cheney told the Malaysian press, "I have made it clear that [the U.S. unilateral] sanctions policy is wrong." He said he supported the multilateral sanctions imposed by the United Nations on Iraq but rejected these new unilateral moves by the United States against other countries, adding "The U.S. needs to be much more restrained than we have been in terms of pursuing unilateral economic sanctions." One possible reason Cheney did not mind the multilateral sanctions on Iraq was that they provided for a food-for-oil program in which Halliburton was involved, thereby helping the Baath government increase its exports. In another interview from this period, Cheney revealed that he now saw Iran as a key potential ally in countering Baathist Iraq, saying "I think we ought to begin to work to rebuild those relationships with Iran . . . it may take ten years but it's important that we do that."[48]

In making that argument, Cheney was taking on AIPAC, the prime force behind the new congressional sanctions on Iran, and on third parties that dealt with it. AIPAC had begun pushing for stronger Iran sanctions in 1995, just as Cheney went off to Dallas.[49] Even as U.S. corporations were being largely excluded from Iraq and pushed out of Iran by AIPAC, other players, such as the French firm Total and Russia's Gazprom, were exploring investment in Iran.[50]

While the Israel lobbies were successfully defeating the oil majors by imposing further unilateral sanctions on Iran and anyone who invested in its energy sectors, the neoconservative movement began arguing for a war on Iraq. While it is not clear exactly how the confluence came about, by 2001, as Cheney came back into national politics, he had decided to ally with the hawks in the Israel lobbies. It takes a conceptual leap now to remember that Cheney was, in the period after 1992, not a hawk. He had not signed on to Martin Indyk's "dual containment," essentially an AIPAC policy. He favored positive engagement with Iran, and Halliburton was still doing some business with Saddam's Iraq. He had rejected the idea, long championed by the neoconservatives, of simply overthrowing the government in Baghdad.

In a speech after the Gulf War, Cheney had said that if the United States had gone into Baghdad in 1991, "then we'd have had to put another government in its place." He asked a farrago of excellent questions about building such a new state: "What kind of government? Should it be a Sunni government or Shi'ia government or a Kurdish government or Ba'athist regime? Or maybe we want to bring in some of the Islamic fundamentalists?" He further wondered, in fine fettle, "How long would we have had to stay in Baghdad to keep that government in place?" Looking even farther into the future, he demanded to know, "What would happen to the government once U.S. forces withdrew? How many casualties should the United States accept in that effort to try to create clarity and stability in a situation that is inherently unstable?"[51] Cheney in 1991 was sure the cost of an Iraq War was not worth it.

By January 2001, accounts of administration insiders such as Treasury Secretary Paul O'Neill show that Cheney had completely rethought these reservations, either having become convinced that the dilemmas to which he pointed could be avoided or that the risks he had outlined were now worth it. By spring of 2001, O'Neil told journalist Ron Suskind, Cheney and his more hawkish allies on the cabinet, such as Secretary of Defense Donald Rumsfeld and his neo-conservative deputy Paul Wolfowitz, were planning an Iraq war, over the objections of Secretary of State Colin Powell.[52] What likely changed between 1991 and 2001 was that Cheney had spent half a decade leading a major energy corporation and had come to see the absolute necessity for American companies to become involved in developing Iraqi and Iranian fields of gas and petroleum, among the biggest unexplored such reserves in the world, given that there had been few new big finds in the 1990s and projections ten and twenty years out suggested vastly increased demand. Cheney had been in a position to foresee that the petroleum and gas markets were becoming like a game of musical chairs and that the United States might, because of AIPAC's boycott policies, end up the player without a chair. Such a fate would equal the demotion of the United States to a second-rate power.

My conjecture is that Cheney and other petroleum company executives had despaired of ever besting AIPAC on the sanctions issue. Therefore, they believed that they would be locked out of Iraq and Iran and their enormous oil and gas reserves while France, Russia, and China positioned themselves to benefit from developing those fields. Cheney had spent most of the 1990s fighting the Israel lobbies and consorting with Saudi princes and Muslim presidents and prime ministers. Yet when he set up as vice president in 2001, he created a rump national security council of his own that he staffed with figures such as Irv Lewis Libby, John Hannah, and later on David Wurmser—all prominent neoconservatives who were ideologically close to Israel's right-wing Likud Party.[53] This about-face is so stark that it should make our necks snap. Big Oil, with its strong ties to the Arab hydrocarbon monarchies, was cohabiting in the vice presidential mansion with AIPAC and the Project for the New American Century.

The simplest explanation would be that Cheney made a conceptual breakthrough. He may have seen that if he pushed for regime change in Iraq and Iran, he could turn AIPAC and the Israel lobbies into allies of the oil majors' plans for investment in Iraq and Iran. If he committed to removing the governments that threatened Israel and replacing them with pro-Western regimes, then Congress would lift those implacable boycotts and allow Houston and Dallas finally to play in Mesopotamia and Khuzistan. Such a development could well be crucial to maintaining the position of the United States as a super-power into the twenty-first century. Cheney and such cabinet allies as Rumsfeld and Wolfowitz needed to convince Bush to commit major resources to overthrowing the Baath regime in Baghdad.[54] Bush, even as governor of Texas before becoming president, had repeatedly expressed a desire to "take out" Saddam, but was skeptical of foreign interventions and nation-building projects, and so would have had to be convinced that the project could be achieved relatively painlessly.

John Mearsheimer of the University of Chicago and Stephen Walt of Harvard University, prominent political scientists of the realist school, have attempted to explain the Iraq War almost exclusively by reference to the Israel lobbies and neoconservative influence on the Bush administration and Congress.[55] While Zionist organizations and their members, especially right-wing ones, played a prominent role in getting up the war, they could not have done so had not Bush and Cheney, both close to the U.S. petroleum corporations and to the oil monarchies of the Gulf, agreed with them. The Israel lobbies do bear important blame for the war in another way: their insistence on keeping Iraq and Iran under tight sanctions frustrated the U.S. petroleum corporations at a time when discoveries of new fields worldwide had slowed, when it had become clear that successful competition for oil would become more crucial and difficult, and when it was known that Iran and Iraq had enormous untapped reserves.

Rumsfeld initially envisaged some sort of limited covert operation to remove Saddam, according to the memoirs of Paul O'Neill, who described the deliberations of the Bush cabinet and National Security Council in early 2001.[56] That path had the drawback that such an operation would be extremely difficult to pull off successfully. The September 11 attacks resolved that dilemma for Rumsfeld and Cheney. They could now push for all-out war, a much surer proposition. With AIPAC already in Cheney's corner, he had a good chance of getting congressional authorization. The American public was angry about the al-Qaeda attacks and was looking for someone to blame. The quick, inconclusive war in Afghanistan had not satiated much of the public, especially since Bin Laden and some of his high command had eluded U.S. forces.

Reasoning back from Cheney's statements, I conclude that he decided that all that would be needed to overthrow the Baath regime, satisfy AIPAC that a threat to Israel had been removed, and gain U.S. oil majors access to Iraq's vast petroleum reserves would be to convince the public that Saddam was somehow connected to September 11, to al-Qaeda, and to other dire threats to U.S. security. In other words, Iraq would have to be transformed into an object of Islam Anxiety for the American public, however unlikely a candidate the Baath Party, earlier excoriated in Washington as a leftist, pro-Soviet menace, seemed for such a role.

Cheney became the point man in making that case. How much of it he himself believed is still unclear, and historians may dispute the matter for decades to come, given the secretive and taciturn ways of the man. Surely he knew that some of the allegations were based on evidence less certain than he portrayed it. Journalist Ron Suskind gave evidence in the summer of 2008 that Cheney had asked the CIA in the fall of 2003 to provide a forged document shoring up the case for Saddam Hussein's contacts with al-Qaeda.[57] If true, this action would indicate profound dishonesty on the part of Cheney and his staff on this issue. Officials of the Bush administration denied the story. If Cheney was arguing the case for instrumental purposes, however, truth and falsehood mattered little. The important thing was the objective: the opening of Iraq to U.S. energy corporations. Further, there was the prospect, however distant, that after Baghdad, the United States could go on to Iran and open it as well, turning the clock back to 1977.

In June 2008 it was announced that BP, ExxonMobil, Total, and Shell were considering returning to Iraq to carry out repairs and give technical support to Iraqi oil fields, though it is likely that these negotiations will be protracted. These were the Western oil majors that had dominated the Iraq Petroleum Company from the 1920s through the oil nationalization of 1972. However badly things had turned out in other ways in Iraq, Cheney had succeeded in reopening Iraq's fields to U.S. investment.[58] Even if there were a delay of a decade, while Iraqis struggled to find a new modus vivendi, before the U.S. oil majors could do actual development in Iraq, that would still be a win compared to the situation before 2003, when sanctions had largely kept them out. From the vantage point of a former CEO of Halliburton, the Iraq War had permanently changed the energy industry in ways that would ultimately benefit Dallas and Houston. It was a success.

Iraq has been roiled by five great struggles since the overthrow of the Baath government in 2003. There has been a political struggle to erect a new Iraqi government and to control its bureaucracy and security forces. There has been a guerrilla war against the presence of U.S. forces. And there have been three civil wars among Iraqis: One centered on Kurdish struggles with Arabs and Turkmen for the oil province of Kirkuk in the north. Another involved Shiite militias struggling with each other and with the government for control of the oil province of Basra in the south along the Persian Gulf. And in the third, in the center of the country, Shiite Arabs and Sunni Arabs battled for control of the capital, deploying the tools of ethnic cleansing, terror, and mass murder.

Today, any one of these struggles could erupt and cause even more substantial turmoil for the United States in Iraq, especially given the instability of the Iraqi government as it has been fashioned under American military occupation. The U.S.-installed parliamentary regime confronts severe obstacles in establishing a genuine democracy. The relatively weak central government, despite recent improvements, still faces problems in competing with local militias and in getting its bureaucracy to be responsive. It has been overly dependent on the Badr Corps, the Iran-trained militia of the Islamic Supreme Council of Iraq, among Prime Minister al-Maliki's primary backers in parliament. Shiite and Kurdish political dominance has alienated Sunni Arabs, who mounted an insurgency and tied down U.S. forces in a continued containment effort. The conflict between the Kurds and the Arabs over control of Iraqi territory in the north, muted in the first years of the war, has become increasingly contentious and further threatens the stability of Iraq and its neighbors.

Some of Iraq's major problems derive from the form its politics has taken, which does not provide strong guarantees for minority rights. Although Iraq uses a proportional voting system, the parliament functions as a tyranny of the majority. There is, so far, a single chamber of parliament, which takes most decisions by simple majority (that is, a majority of the members of parliament present, when there is a quorum). Of 275 seats, 132 were gained by the Shiite religious parties in December 2005, a slight reduction from January 2005, when they had 140 or so (138 is an absolute majority).[59]

The Shiites have an agreement with the Kurdistan Alliance (58 seats), whereby the two ethnoreligious groups can consistently outvote Sunni Arabs and secularists. This agreement depends on the Shiites respecting Kurdistan's semiautonomy and the Kurds allowing the Shiites to implement Islamic law and their other desiderata in Arab Iraq (that is, outside Kurdistan). The Sunni Arabs have only 58 seats in parliament and have been unable to find allies in important votes. Sunni Arab discontent and their occasional resort to violence continue in part in response to the permanent marginalization promised them by this majoritarian system within the federal parliament. They can be assured of losing every vote in parliament forever, as long as the other groups maintain a majority of 138. Majoritarian systems are more likely to lead to civil war than other systems in which there are large minorities that cannot avoid being continually outvoted.[60]

The United States attempted to address the issue of the majoritarian tendency in the parliament by urging Nuri al-Maliki, when he became prime minister in the spring of 2006, to form a national unity government. This initiative collapsed when several Shiite parties and the Sunni Arab party pulled out of the government in the spring and summer of 2007. In the subsequent year, the United States responded to this crisis by building up the executive headed by al-Maliki, allowing it to run roughshod over parliament and giving its security forces logistical aid and close air support in campaigns against the rival Shiite Sadr movement in Basra and Sadr City. The idea of a national unity government fell by the wayside, replaced by a new image of al-Maliki as a sort of strongman, acting for the most part without parliamentary backing for his initiatives. He maintained this independence even after the Sunni Arab Iraqi Accord Front (a fundamentalist coalition) rejoined his cabinet in summer 2008. (By this time, the Iraqi Accord Front represented only a fraction of the Sunni Arabs.) Al-Maliki the strongman, however, presented new problems for Washington, as he began showing independence, even to the point of broaching a timetable for the withdrawal of U.S. troops. Nor was he actually all that strong, as Iraq's fractious tribes and urban quarters remained beyond his control.

Iraq's problems are not surprising, and few of them have much to do with Islam per se. Political scientists have long pointed to some basic preconditions that make political rebellion more likely. Low-income societies experience more rebellion than high-income ones. Despite its government's petroleum income, Iraq's population is largely destitute, and has been since the UN and U.S. sanctions began in the 1990s. Where a country depends heavily on the export of natural resources, there is typically an increased incidence of political rebellion. Where a quarter of the gross national product derives from a high-priced commodity, violence is five times higher than in states lacking such commodity incomes. Finally, a discourse of group social grievance (based on ethnicity, religion, or class) is important to such rebellions.[61] Iraq suffers from all these predictors of significant social turmoil and was never a good candidate for forced democratization.

The Iraqi federal government erected under American tutelage is extremely weak. Despite recent improvements in the performance of the Iraqi army, the state still lacks a monopoly over the use of force, and its bureaucracies have poor capacity, morale, and responsiveness to the orders of superiors. Tens of thousands of experienced bureaucrats, officers, and noncommissioned officers were fired on suspicion of Baath loyalties by the Shiite fundamentalist parties that came to power after 2003. The new American-formed army still has weaknesses, cannot fight independently of American logistical and close air support, and is ethnically divided. That many Iraqis see their government as an American puppet detracts from the loyalty of some troops.

Given the virtual collapse of the central state, power devolved to neighborhoods, clans, and regions. These have created guerrilla cells or militias that conduct neighborhood protection patrols. But the militias' work usurps government prerogatives, and some cells have even turned to active insurgency. Others are involved in death squad activities against members of a competing sect or ethnic group. The major Shiite militias include the Badr Corps of the Islamic Supreme Council of Iraq (originally trained by the Iranian Revolutionary Guards Corps while in exile in Iran); the Mahdi Army of the Shiite nationalist Muqtada al-Sadr; the paramilitary of the Islamic Virtue Party (Fadila), which predominates in Basra; and the army tribal levies of the Marsh Arabs and other rural Shiite groups, some of whom have now come into cities such as Basra and Amara to compete with the party militias. Members of the Badr Corps and Mahdi Army have infiltrated the local police, the Interior Ministry special police commandos, and even the Iraqi army. The Mahdi Army in particular is implicated in ethnic cleansing of Sunnis from Baghdad.

Sunni-Shiite conflict was not a significant political phenomenon in the twentieth century. In the 1950s the big conflicts were between the monarchy and the left. In the 1960s, they were between mass parties such as the Baath and the communists, neither religious in character. It is mainly since 2003 that political entrepreneurs have emerged, seeing a benefit to engaging in a religious form of exclusionary politics and seeking to enrich their sectarian group by crushing another.

The Sunni Arab guerrillas have a large number of cells and local organizations. They consist of Baathists, ex-Baathist nationalists, Salafi fundamentalists, radical Muslim vigilantes, and the self-styled al-Qaeda in Mesopotamia. The Sunni Arab guerrillas are among the more formidable fighters in Iraq, and they have been responsible for the vast majority of bombings and shootings aimed at undermining the new government.

The Bush administration initially attempted to deal with the guerrillas through search-and-destroy tactics, which were ineffective and fed the war by alienating the civilian population. After January 2007, it attempted a combination of troop escalation ("the surge") and new counterinsurgency strategies (taking, clearing, and holding Baghdad neighborhoods so as to exclude the guerrillas, as well as simply paying tribal and neighborhood groups to turn on the radical guerrillas). These tactics reduced daily death tolls in the capital but allowed the continued Shiite ethnic cleansing of Sunnis. That ethnic cleansing in itself greatly reduced the monthly civilian death tolls, since after a while there were few Sunnis in formerly mixed neighborhoods for the Shiite militias to target. It is often forgotten that the rationale for the surge was to provide a breathing space in which the federal government could make tough compromises without extensive ethnosectarian violence in the capital. Few political initiatives for ethnic or sectarian reconciliation have been taken, however, and the political success of the 2007–2008 American troop escalation is questionable.

One of Iraq's biggest problems—the Kurdish question—so signally lacks a significant religious or Islamic dimension that it has been impossible to portray in the terms of Islam Anxiety, and so U.S. politicians and the press have paid less attention to it. That Iraqis might have mainly secular, subnationalist conflicts with one another in which religion is largely irrelevant defies the conceptual framework erected by the Bush administration. But downplaying these ethnic problems is dangerous, because they may constitute the biggest powder keg of all.

The Kurds have the Peshmerga paramilitary, said to be tens of thousands of fighters strong, which is designated in the new Iraqi constitution as the National Guard for Kurdistan. Although Islam and sectarianism are constantly invoked by commentators on the problems in Iraq, political Islam has been weak in the Kurdish regions. Jalal Talabani of the Patriotic Union of Kurdistan, who became the president of Iraq in 2005, is a socialist and a regular attendee at Socialist International conferences. His sometime rival and current partner, Massoud Barzani of the Kurdistan Democratic Party, is a relatively secular nationalist. The Kurdistan Islamic Union is the next biggest party, but it holds only 5 of 58 Kurdish seats in the Iraqi Parliament.

Iraq as it now stands is an "asymmetrical federal" state.[62] That is, special autonomy is granted to the three provinces of Irbil, Dohuk, and Sulaimaniya, which have joined together in a single superprovince, the Kurdistan Regional Government (KRG). The special prerogatives of Iraqi Kurdistan are greater than in most such federal systems, such as Canada's (in which Quebec has special status). The Kurds want to extend their Kurdistan to at least parts of three more northern provinces and have in fact stationed their Peshmerga troops well beyond their borders in Iraq proper. They want the oil province of Kirkuk to be in this Kurdistan and to annex parts of Diyala and Ninevah provinces (or perhaps the entirety of these provinces) on the grounds that these three have substantial Kurdish populations. The other major ethnic groups in Iraq oppose this Kurdish expansionism.

Interethnic violence, among Kurds, Arabs, and Turkmen, is already occurring in Kirkuk and Mosul, but it is not massive. A greatly heightened interethnic conflict provoked by the expansion of Kurdistan poses the threat not only of domestic instability in the north but also of outside intervention. Turkey views the Turkmen as brethren and would intervene to save them from a massacre if there were extensive violence with the Kurds. Al-Maliki's new assertiveness, which led him to send Iraqi troops into the northern areas of contested Diyala Province, provoked a crisis in late summer 2008. In largely Kurdish cities such as Khanaqin, the Peshmerga were already supplying security, and their presence signaled the interest of the Kurdistan Regional Government in ultimately annexing those cities. Al-Maliki, by sending in government troops, was implicitly reclaiming them for the central government. The confrontation led KRG president Barzani to complain bitterly about al-Maliki's aggressiveness and failure to honor earlier commitments to Kurdistan's prerogatives (such as a referendum over the disputed province of Kirkuk) and to wonder aloud whether the Shiite-Kurdish political alliance was still intact. A Peshmerga commander warned that open fighting could break out between the army and the Kurdish militia.[63]

As long as no determination is finally made about Kirkuk, the looming conflict can be put off. The 2005 constitution (article 140) specified that Kirkuk (Ta'mim) Province should have a referendum by late 2007 over whether its population wishes to accede to the Kurdistan Regional Government. The federal government in Baghdad has dragged its feet on making arrangements for the referendum. Whenever it is held, violence could break out, with the Peshmerga seeking to attain by force what they cannot get by legislation.

The expansion of the KRG is a regional issue because it is opposed by Turkey. Ankara accuses the Kurds of harboring some 5,000 Turkish-Kurdish guerrillas of the Kurdish Workers Party (PKK). The PKK is implicated in continued bombings and killings in Turkey's eastern Anatolia region, part of Turkish Kurds' decades-long struggle for more autonomy from Istanbul. Turkey has bombed northern Iraq several times and even launched limited ground incursions, and has threatened a full invasion if Kurdistan declares independence. Ankara clearly dislikes the prospect of the annexation of Kirkuk. Washington has attempted to cool rising tensions between Ankara and Irbil, but with few U.S. troops in northern Iraq and virtually none in the KRG, it has a limited ability to force agreement. America, insofar as it desperately needs its Kurdish allies in Iraq and is deeply tied to Turkey through NATO, finds its hands tied in this conflict.

Washington opposes any secession of Kurdistan from Iraq, an aspiration of the vast majority of Kurds. It has supported the current asymmetrical relationship of Kurdistan to Baghdad, however, and appears to have no objection to the likely annexation of Kirkuk and possibly other territory by the KRG. Washington seems strangely oblivious to the severe Iraqi and geopolitical tensions and even violence that could ensue from Kurdish expansionism. U.S. military authorities appear to have made no provision for what will happen when they withdraw from Kirkuk. (In all likelihood, the Peshmerga will take it by force.)

Another side effect of the asymmetrical model is that it can be contagious. Seeing that one group has special perquisites can cause other ethnic groups with contiguous territory to seek similar asymmetries. And, in fact, this development has occurred: the Islamic Supreme Council of Iraq is campaigning to create a regional confederacy out of eight provinces in Iraq's largely Shiite south.

Although it has been argued that unbalanced federalism does not necessarily produce violence or secession, many of the typical examples given, such as Canada, are large states with otherwise centralized rule. In those cases, the unequal provincial rights may not be problematic precisely because they are a concession by a powerful, stable central state. In contrast, countries with only a few ethnically based provinces or regions, such as Yugoslavia, Nigeria, Afghanistan, and Lebanon, tend to be unstable. Reducing Iraq's eighteen provinces to only four, with Kurdistan as one of them, is probably undesirable.

Any balance sheet drawn up for the American misadventure in Iraq will inescapably show a lot of red ink. Ironically, after the invasion of Iraq, the United States was forced into continuing to pursue the policy of dual containment that neoconservatives had intended the invasion to obviate. Although the Baath regime in Iraq was deposed, the Sunni Arab population that formed its backbone went into insurgency against the U.S. occupation, and many turned to an alliance with Muslim radical opponents of the United States. And the Baath's fall allowed Iran to exercise influence there and in other Arab Shiite communities. In many ways, then, the task of containment has remained central and become more difficult and complicated. It requires a much greater commitment of resources than before 2003.

The overthrow of the Baath government did not lead, as the Bush administration had hoped, to the emergence of a stable, democratic, pro-American Iraq that could prove a launching pad for the projection of American influence and the penetration of American capital in the Middle East. Rather, a weak state emerged, beset by a range of ethno-sectarian militias. Washington allied with the Shiite fundamentalist parties and the Kurds against the Sunni Arabs, even though Iraq's Sunnis were generally more secular-minded than America's Shiite allies—Bin Laden's al-Qaeda is Sunni, and the U.S. government was selling the war as a fight against "al-Qaeda in Iraq." Some American politicians even went so far as to suggest that it might be possible for radical Sunni fundamentalists to take over a largely Shiite and Kurdish country, even without access to the tanks, helicopter gunships, and chemical weapons that Saddam had deployed to establish his minority-dominated state. The role of bogeymen such as Abu Musab al-Zarqawi was vastly exaggerated, as demonstrated when his death in May 2006 had virtually no effect on the course of the Sunni Arab guerrilla movement in Iraq.

The invasion kicked off a vast new refugee crisis unparalleled in the Middle East since the Israeli ethnic cleansing of the Palestinians in 1948. The U.S. public, deprived by its government and much of the mass media of an accurate view of the situation on the ground with regard to civilian deaths and suffering, remained largely unaware of the magnitude of the catastrophe provoked in our name. The rest of the world wore no similar blinkers, and American prestige sank.

One danger for the future is that sectarian violence could draw in Iraq's neighbors, in a repeat of the 1980–1988 Iran-Iraq War, this time as a guerrilla war. Guerrillas have already shown a willingness to engage in pipeline sabotage as a tool of war, and if this tactic should spread to Iraq's neighbors, it could have a devastating effect on the world economy. There is also some danger that frustrated U.S. and Israeli hawks might launch a preemptive strike on Iran's nuclear research facilities and that an Iranian response could plunge the entire region into war. This eventuality, as well, could substantially roil energy markets at a time when supply is tight and new demand from China and India is growing rapidly.

In short, the military option pursued by the Bush-Cheney administration in Iraq as a means to achieving the country's goals in the Persian Gulf has been a huge disappointment. The security of energy exports from the region clearly has been endangered. U.S. firms are still unable to operate in Iraq, because of insecurity, or in Iran, because of the continued U.S. boycott. China, Russia, India, and European corporations are still in a good position to win Iraqi contracts (especially since the Iraqi government has a public mandate and wishes to avoid being trapped in a subservient relationship to Washington). Iraq's ability to play regional dominant power has been destroyed for the foreseeable future. Iran's ability to play that role has, however, been greatly enhanced. Both Israel and Saudi Arabia have demonstrably been weakened by the insecurity in Iraq and by the rise of Iranian influence in the Middle East. The Bush-Cheney game of dual containment was doomed from the start and was far more perilous than the Clinton-Gore round. The new president now has an opportunity to abandon "containment" as a goal and turn instead to engagement.

Clearly, the diplomatic and economic fortunes of the United States in the Muslim world and possibly elsewhere depend on achieving an orderly withdrawal of its military from Iraq. The prerequisites for this withdrawal include regional diplomacy. Iraq's neighbors, among them Saudi Arabia, Iran, Turkey, Jordan, Syria, and Kuwait, need to continue their regular meetings with Iraq, and the United States and the European Union need to join them. The Bush administration's skittishness about face-to-face meetings with Syria and Iran needs to be abandoned. Iran and Saudi Arabia are in a powerful position to convince their Shiite and Sunni clients in Iraq, respectively, to move more quickly and firmly toward political cooperation, as a means of strengthening the elected government. The Gulf Cooperation Council (GCC), which groups the small oil monarchies, including the United Arab Emirates, Qatar, Bahrain, Saudi Arabia, Kuwait, and Oman, also needs to play a positive role. Flush with an enormous windfall from the run-up in petroleum and gas prices, the GCC has a strong interest in stability in Iraq. The way these dwarf stars of Middle East politics can play the role of honest broker in the furtherance of regional peace was demonstrated in 2008, when Qatar achieved some progress in mediating the conflict in Lebanon.

The Iraqi government needs to be reformed, with an upper house of parliament added that would overrepresent Sunni Arabs, Kurds, and other minorities and would require a strong consensus to pass legislation. This step or something like it is necessary to overcome the permanent tyranny of the majority of Shiites in the current parliament, which has caused a great deal of trouble and is likely to cause more. The existing government in Baghdad needs to reach out and become more representative.

A more positive regional atmosphere and a more representative government would lend the Iraqi executive the legitimacy it needs to establish a monopoly on the use of force. The United States and NATO need to continue to work to strengthen the Iraqi military, not only with ongoing training, but also with better equipment, including more armor and air power. Iraq will not have social peace until the militias are disarmed. This step is also necessary if Iraqis are to return from exile in Syria and Jordan without further violence, since the masses of refugees were largely ethnically cleansed by militias that then grabbed their homes.

Proactive attention should be given to the resolution of the conflicts between Iraqi's Kurds and their neighbors, whether Iraqi Arabs or regional states such as Turkey, Iran, and Syria. Holding a referendum in Kirkuk Province about whether it should accede to Kurdistan is unwise, and the constitutional deadline for it has passed, rendering that article of the constitution null and void. The best resolution for Iraq would be to limit the Kurdistan Regional Government to its current three provinces. That policy would enhance both Iraq's stability and the security situation with regard to Turkey and Iran. At the most, Kirkuk Province could be partitioned along ethnic lines, with part going to the KRG and the rest forming a joint

Arab and Turkmen province. Kirkuk city itself might have to be partitioned in that case. The alternative, of allowing large numbers of Arabs and Turkmen to be dragooned into a Kurdish ministate, is simply asking for trouble.

Likewise, the United States and the European Union should broker a formal treaty between Turkey and Iraq governing relations between the two countries, which must be binding on the Kurdistan authorities. Obviously, if the United States has used Iraqi Kurdish guerrillas against Iran, as some critics have charged, that has to stop. Encouraging Kurdish nationalism could tear apart not only Iran but also Iraq, Syria, and Turkey, in a conflagration from which the eastern Mediterranean (and oil prices) might not soon recover. Why the Bush administration let this situation drift rather than making policy on it is a mystery, but that relative inaction must end.

With agreements hammered out in the arena of both regional diplomacy and domestic ethnic politics, the United States will be in a position to withdraw its troops beginning in 2009. The administration should resist the temptation to keep military bases inside Iraq. They will never be acceptable to the Shiite clerical leaders, such as Grand Ayatollah Ali Sistani and Sayyid Muqtada al-Sadr, nor to most of the Sunni Arabs, who are nationalists. The Kurds may offer a base, but the offer should be rejected. Such a base would be largely inaccessible in landlocked Kurdistan except by air from Turkey, and if conflict broke out between Turkey and the Iraqi Kurds, the U.S. troops would simply get caught in the middle.

The U.S. withdrawal from Iraq could be attended, or followed, by a renewal of guerrilla activity. That danger is one that the Iraqi government and military will have to deal with. The danger will be much less if Iraq's neighbors are cooperating on security matters and making sure fundamentalist vigilantes do not cross their borders.

A U.S. withdrawal may well force various Iraqi factions to make needed compromises with one another and so contribute to growing security. Militant Shiite politicians have often proved unwilling to compromise with Sunni Arabs because they knew that if a fight broke out, the U.S. military would support the Shiites (seeing them as the legitimate, elected government of the country). If the Shiites realized that American troops and planes would not be at their beck and call, they might go out of their way to avoid picking such fights.

Another danger often voiced is that Iraq will become an Iranian sphere of influence. In fact, Iran is likely to be less concerned about threats to its security emanating from Iraq once U.S. troops are gone and so will feel less urgency in developing Iraqi assets beyond the considerable ones it already has high in the Iraqi government. While friendly relations between the Shiite-majority government in Iraq and the ayatollahs in Iran are likely, and even desirable, the prospect of Arab Iraq allowing itself to be subordinated to Persian Iran is far-fetched. For most of its modern history, Iraq has had conflicts with Iran, over border issues, the Kurds, and Iranian meddling in Shiite politics. Those conflicts have not disappeared with the advent of the post-Baath order and are likely to reemerge in ways that complicate Iran's regional ambitions. The United States is, moreover, likely to remain a Gulf power for the foreseeable future, and its military withdrawal from Iraq will actually give it greater clout and options, since it will no longer be bogged down. U.S. policies in the Gulf will continue to offer a counter to Iran in the region. Iraq's politics and security are likely to be fragile for some time to come, but the time when the U.S. military could hope to do anything effective about that has passed.

Some American and European observers have expressed the fear that ethnic conflict on a vast scale might break out in the wake of a U.S. withdrawal or that such a withdrawal will allow al-Qaeda to establish bases in central Iraq or even to take over the country. It is not widely recognized that hundreds of thousands of Sunnis were ethnically cleansed from Baghdad and environs under the noses of U.S. troops in 2006–2007, including during the surge, or troop escalation. It seems clear that the American troops simply cannot affect such big social processes, and so the argument that they should stay in order to do so is flawed on the evidence of what has already happened. As for an al-Qaeda base or takeover, such a development is virtually impossible, since the Shiite-dominated government and its military will not countenance it, nor will the Kurds. With Baghdad's oil profits, moreover, it ought to be able to bribe Sunni Arab elites to suppress the vigilantes themselves. A withdrawal of U.S. troops from Iraq would reduce America Anxiety in the Muslim world and would eliminate a prime cause of Islam Anxiety for the American public, perhaps making possible movement toward real understanding.

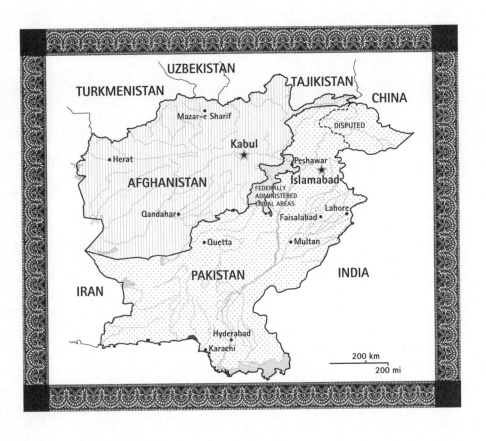

CHAPTER V

PAKISTAN AND AFGHANISTAN

BEYOND THE TALIBAN

The horrific bombing of the Islamabad Marriott in September 2008, continued attacks on United States and NATO military garrisons in Afghanistan, and assassination attempts on Afghan president Hamid Karzai all point to a Taliban resurgence in Pakistan and Afghanistan. Political instability in both countries continues to cause concern about security threats to NATO societies. The Taliban create Islam Anxiety in the West not only because they hosted al-Qaeda but also because they dislike foreigners, oppress women, and practice extreme puritanism. Westerners confuse the social conflict between urban and rural society in these two countries with mere terrorism and tend to assume that the deployment of military might by a praetorian state against rural and tribal peoples is synonymous with a war on terror. In fact, good policymaking would recognize the legitimate social and economic discontents of the rural population and seek to redress them with well considered aid programs instead of with bombs. When Westerners insist on seeing Pakistan and Afghanistan solely through the lens of terrorism, however, they deeply distort the two complex societies, since most people in both countries are not rigid

Muslim fundamentalists. Seeing them as Taliban also creates a carica-ture that gets in the way of practical understanding.

Pakistani Taliban have become active in the relatively small Feder-ally Administered Tribal Areas (FATA) of Pakistan. Though the poli-tics of the FATA tribes is consequential, the fear, often expressed by U.S. pundits, that the Taliban from this region might take over the government in Islamabad, or that Pakistani opinion is shifting in their favor, is wholly unrealistic. The Afghan Taliban are active throughout a much larger expanse of their county than their Pakistani counter-parts, but are very active in only a few southern provinces.

Frustrated that these two South Asian states seem unable to con-trol their militants, the Bush administration pressed both Afghanistan and Pakistan to use their armies to subdue the tribes. It is a fool's er-rand. These rugged regions along the Afghan border are thinly popu-lated by Pushtun tribesmen who are interested in reducing their isola-tion from the outside world only if they can see a benefit. (The tribal areas on the Pakistan side are 10,507 square miles, or a little bigger than Vermont, while Pakistan is 340,403 square miles, a little bigger than California, Oregon, and Washington state combined.) Histori-cally, central governments, whether the old British Empire or the bu-reaucrats in Islamabad, reached out to the Pushtuns primarily to de-mand taxes or offer bayonets and cannonades or economic and social programs framed for very different societies far away. The tribes' seg-mentary politics, whereby they pursue internal feuds with one another, can quickly be put aside to unite against a grasping or belligerent out-sider. This makes the tribes a formidable obstacle to heavy-handed forms of governance imposed from the outside. Even the British Em-pire at the height of its power never subdued them.

Any region where al-Qaeda operatives find refuge is a potential se-curity threat, but making sure that the operatives lack access to airports and monitoring their communications would be more effective than provoking a feud with their tribal hosts. September 11 was launched not from Khost in Afghanistan but from Hamburg in Germany, not by tribal persons or seminarians but by engineers trained in the West. Even in their heyday in the 1990s, the Taliban were seldom directly involved in committing international terrorism. The conflation of Pushtuns, and their love of relative autonomy, with Talibanism frequently obscures the local politics that drive militancy.

Finally, concentrating solely on tribal areas while ignoring developments in the far more populous and central cities and towns of Afghanistan and Pakistan creates bad policy; doing so caused the Bush administration to pamper the military dictatorship of General Pervez Musharraf while signally declining to sympathize with popular demands for the rule of law and democracy. Popular discontent cut the legs from under Washington's pro-military policy when Musharraf was forced to resign in August 2008. He was succeeded as president by a civilian politician he had kept in prison for several years.

During his run for the presidency, Barack Obama continually charged that the Bush administration's obsession with Iraq and expenditures of blood and treasure there had caused the United States to take its eye off the real struggle against al-Qaeda in Pakistan and Afghanistan. He stirred controversy by vowing to strike at the top al-Qaeda leadership in Pakistan if their whereabouts became known to U.S. intelligence, even if no permission was forthcoming from the government of Pakistan. He and his then rival, Hillary Clinton, even sparred over whether they might use tactical nuclear weapons in such a strike, with Obama deciding against it. That U.S. politicians were blithely discussing nuking a U.S. ally seemed not to puzzle or disturb the American public. The Pakistani government for its part called Obama's remark "irresponsible," and the governor of Baluchistan warned that giving Pakistani troops the idea that their sacrifices in fighting militants were not appreciated in Washington might sap their will to carry on the struggle.[1] A thousand tribesmen in the town of Miranshah in FATA demonstrated against Obama, saying they would defend themselves if attacked.

While Obama's comment was probably only a realistic acknowledgment of how the United States would act under such circumstances, it was impolitic for him to say it. Clinton's remarks about deploying nuclear weapons were, in contrast, over the top. The security threat they pointed to, however, is taken seriously by both U.S. and

Pakistani officials (though Pakistanis tend to see the United States as exaggerating the severity of the threat).

Born in the massive violence that attended the partition of British India into Hindu-majority and Muslim-majority states in 1947, Pakistan struggled for decades to overcome a colonial legacy of low literacy and lack of industry.[2] Some of the country is lush, its vegetation fed by monsoon rains and the famed "five rivers" *(panjab)* that descend from Himalayan headwaters to form the geographical framework of Pakistan's biggest province. Other parts, such as the arid, mountainous province of Baluchistan, are more like the Middle East. The parts of Pakistan most resembling India, such as the Punjab, have the water to support large numbers of people.

Pakistan, with a population, as I write, of about 170 million, is the world's sixth most populous country, just after Brazil. Because of its still rapidly growing population, Pakistan is expected to level off at midcentury with some 300 million residents, about the same as the United States in the early twenty-first century. Lush, river- and monsoon-fed Punjab has 55 percent of Pakistan's citizens. To the south of the Punjab, the province of Sindh, benefiting from the Indus River and rainfall agriculture, also has a big peasant population in the hinterlands of the huge port of Karachi; it accounts for about a fourth of the country's population. Baluchistan in the southwest, with its barren wastelands and brooding hills, has less than 5 percent of the population even though it looks huge on a map. Neither as lush as the Punjab nor generally as arid as Baluchistan, the North-West Frontier Province (NWFP) is largely Pushtun in ethnicity, and its proximity to Afghanistan has in recent decades embroiled it in geopolitical conflict; it accounts for about 12 percent of the Pakistani population. Large urban centers such as Karachi and Lahore increase in population every year, and urbanites now make up over a third of the country. Some 97 percent of Pakistanis are Muslim, with small but significant Christian and Hindu minorities. Shiites are variously estimated at between 13 and 20 percent of the population, but Sunnis predominate.

The founders and leaders of Pakistan have had conflicting visions of its purpose and destiny.[3] Founder Muhammad Ali Jinnah, leader of the Muslim League, was a secular lawyer educated at Lincoln's Inn in London, who enjoyed a good stiff drink, fulminated against theocracy, and thought of the new country as a refuge for South Asians with a Muslim cultural heritage. Jinnah, typical of the British-educated elite that led South Asia to independence in the first half of the twentieth century, had long been active and prominent in India's Congress Party. However, he worried that its leaders insufficiently appreciated the danger of a tyranny by the Hindu majority. About a fourth of British India was Muslim, and Jinnah championed their rights. Jinnah played the role of James Madison, insisting on specified rights for the minority while Congress leaders such as Jawaharlal Nehru and Mohandas K. Gandhi played the role of Federalists. They rejected Jinnah's requests, seeing them as a form of special pleading, or a demand for affirmative action for Muslims. Jinnah was also alarmed that Gandhi had begun appealing to explicitly Hindu religious themes and had begun speaking of a Ramraj, or rule of the god Rama—a Hindu theocracy.[4]

In the 1920s, when Jinnah was a leader in the Muslim League, which championed Muslims as an ethnic group, a journalist named Abu'l-Ala' Maududi began promoting Muslim fundamentalism, founding the Jama'at-i Islami (South Asia's analogy to Egypt's Muslim Brotherhood). The Jama'at actively opposed Muslim separatism and the creation of a Muslim-majority state, since its leaders did not believe Indian Muslims were ready to establish a truly Islamic state that would live up to the religion's ideals. After Pakistan was established, however, Maududi did go to live there, and over time his organization reconciled to participating in the nitty-gritty of Pakistani political life.[5]

In contrast to Jinnah's vision of a secular state with a large Hindu population but protecting Muslim culture, Pakistani fundamentalists have pushed for an Islamic state with sharia displacing the tradition of Anglo-Muhammadan law cobbled together from British common law principles and Muslim custom and jurisprudence during the British colonial period. The country has alternated between periods of civilian parliamentary rule and military dictatorship. The military, despite its power and interventions, has never been able to destroy or displace the political parties, including in recent decades the Muslim League and the Pakistan People's Party (PPP), which have the support of long-standing institutions and devoted local activists. The officer corps has diverse views. Fundamentalist officers dominated in the 1980s, but the government of General Pervez Musharraf, established in a 1999 coup, leaned more to the secular side with regard to domestic policy.

Some of the Pakistani military's support for political Islam has been instrumental rather than religious. Western pundits and policy makers too often see Muslim politics as wrought up with militancy, failing to recognize that Muslim elites sometimes use fundamentalism cynically, invoking Islam in their geopolitical struggles with India, for example, whether devout or not. Pakistan's Islam policy derives in part from the quest of the elites in Islamabad to incorporate the Muslim-majority province of Kashmir, which was brought into India by its Hindu ruler in 1947. The Kashmir valley is productive farmland, the area is picturesque and has great tourist potential, and its Himalayan districts have strategic value because they abut China and form the headwaters of the Indus Valley rivers, but the struggle over this area is largely a product of irrational territorial and ethnic nationalism. Pakistan felt cheated of a contiguous Muslim province when India grabbed it, and multicultural India fears that any territorial concessions to ethnic nationalism would break it up. Although the United Nations Security Council in 1948 mandated a referendum in Kashmir on its fate, one has never been held. Pakistan's conflict with India over Kashmir has caused three major wars between the two countries and brought the two to the brink of a nuclear exchange in the summer of 2002. It was also implicated in the November 2008 terrorist attack on the Indian city of Mumbai.

Pakistani leaders see militant fundamentalism as a means of mobilizing both Pakistanis and Kashmiris against Hindu India. Even the Pakistani military's policy of encouraging the Taliban in Afghanistan and winking at al-Qaeda's presence in the mid- to late 1990s was in part aimed at creating strategic allies for Pakistan in its struggle against India. Elements in the Pakistani military began secretly deploying Muslim terrorist groups in Kashmir against Indian troops there in the 1990s, and were happy enough for them to get training in the al-Qaeda camps of Afghanistan late in that decade and at the beginning of this century.

Today's Pakistan is an enigma to many in the West. Its government maintains that it is an ally in what the Bush administration called "the war on terror," and it is true that Pakistani forces have helped capture some seven hundred Arab al-Qaeda operatives who fled south from Afghanistan in 2001–2002. Some of those taken, including Khalid Shaikh Muhammad and Ramzi Bin al-Shibh, were top operatives in the organization. Pakistani troops have also repeatedly fought remnants of the Taliban and their Pakistani tribal allies in the northwest of the country. At the same time, one cannot help noticing anti-American demonstrations in the country's streets and the persistent reports that the Pakistani military is backing some Taliban forces in southern Afghanistan.

The Pakistani public has severe problems with U.S. foreign policy.[6] About half of all Pakistanis blame the United States for most of the violence in their country, while 14 percent think India is stirring things up. A State Department diplomat who attended Friendship Day, hosted by the Pakistani American Congress in Washington, D.C., in June 2008, was probably surprised when one attendee asked sharply, "How long will [the United States] keep fighting, until you destroy everything so there is nothing left?"[7] Only one in six Pakistanis told pollsters in 2008 that al-Qaeda and the Pakistani and Afghan Taliban formed the greatest threat to their country. Given that Pakistan has fought three major wars with India and many Pakistanis obsess about the threat their large Hindu-majority neighbor poses to the survival of their country, the Pakistanis' view that the United States is three times more threatening than India is an eye-popping result. Still, if it is remembered that the United States has invaded and occupied two Muslim countries in the vicinity of Pakistan in the past decade, and for many years propped up an unpopular dictatorship in Pakistan itself, the America Anxiety of Pakistanis might be easier to understand.

Incidents like the June 2008 air strikes launched by U.S. forces in Afghanistan that killed eleven Pakistani troops who had fired on American forces in support of the Taliban, or strikes by U.S. forces at targets inside Pakistan that have sometimes also killed Pakistani villagers, have soured the Pakistani public on the U.S. war effort. As the United States became more aggressive about cross-border raids and strikes in fall 2008, in the run-up to the American presidential elections, the public outcry against Washington's belligerence grew louder. A spokesman for Prime Minister Yousuf Raza Gilani told the press bluntly in September 2008, "The Pakistani people and government will not endure foreign attacks on Pakistani provinces."[8]

Another irritant in relations between Pakistanis and the United States was the Bush administration's determination to put virtually all its eggs in the basket of General Musharraf, whom three-quarters of the Pakistani public viewed unfavorably by the time he was forced to resign in late summer 2008.[9] Indeed, the three-decade-long U.S. project of building up the Pakistani military, training its officers, and equipping it with high-tech weaponry has helped unbalance the Pakistani state, creating a vast military-industrial complex that makes repeated claims on the prerogative of rule, rather as if it were a political party in its own right. Governments in Pakistan have long declined even to reveal the exact size and details of their military budgets.[10]

The Pakistani public and the Bush administration also differed greatly in their views of Pakistan's neighbors. Washington considers the government of Afghan president Hamid Karzai as a positive actor in the region and depicts Iran as a menace. Yet 69 percent of Pakistanis view Iran favorably and only 42 percent see Afghanistan in that same positive light. Among the few pieces of good news for Washington in this poll is that al-Qaeda and Bin Laden have suffered a steep decline in popularity, with only 7 percent of Pakistanis saying they would vote for al-Qaeda, though a third said they had a favorable view of the organization, which they saw primarily as having the goal of standing up to the United States. Since many Pakistanis do not believe that al-Qaeda was behind the September 11 attacks, this attitude does not indicate support for terrorism. That so few said they would actually vote for al-Qaeda suggests that even the minority that sees it as an anti-imperialist organization would not want to live under its harsh puritanism themselves.[11]

Asaf Ali Zardari, the president of Pakistan, ascended to power despite a checkered career marked by accusations of corruption and two murder charges. The awkward trailing spouse of the charismatic Benazir Bhutto, he seemed doomed to live in her shadow. The son of a minor Sindhi clan chieftain, Zardari in his youth loved the nightlife scene in the metropolis of Karachi and became a notorious playboy. He even put a disco in his own mansion. (I was in Pakistan in the early 1980s and remember that among the more popular songs on the charts then was Nazia Hasan's "Disco Divani" [1982] or "crazy about disco.") That he was modern, secular, and tribal all at once may have suggested him to the Bhutto family as a suitable match for Oxford- and Harvard-educated Benazir, though many pundits complained that her family made her marry down for the purpose of a Sindhi tribal and landlord alliance.

Zardari, who spent nine years of his life in prison and says he was tortured, has never been accused of cowardice. Once he was out riding in the countryside with a party that included the daughter of a German diplomat. Her horse lost its footing, and steed and rider both went into a swamp. Out of a party of forty persons, Zardari was alone in throwing himself into the muck and rescuing the German and her horse, risking drowning himself.[12]

In 1988, a year after Zardari wed Bhutto, she became prime minister. While she was in power, he was alleged to have demanded a percentage of government contracts with foreign firms, and even to have engaged in mafia-like activities. One (uncorroborated) accuser said he strapped a bomb onto the leg of a businessman and thus forced him to withdraw money from his bank for a payoff. When the president of Pakistan dismissed Benazir Bhutto in 1990, Zardari went to jail. However, his wife came back to power in 1993, released him, and picked him to serve as her minister of the environment (he launched a campaign to have schoolchildren plant trees). When she was again dismissed in 1996, Zardari went to prison again, charged with a cloud of crimes, including demanding kickbacks from a French arms manufacturer and a Dubai gold merchant, not to mention plotting the murder of his leftist, radical brother-in-law, Murtaza Bhutto, with whom he had a feud. Bhutto supporters proclaimed his innocence, however, and alleged that Zardari was held in prison by General Musharraf as a means of controlling Benazir, whom he kept in exile, threatening her with imprisonment if she returned. Zardari was finally released on bail in 2004, after which he relocated to London and Dubai (he had sumptuous mansions in both cities). Gradually the cases against him have been dropped for lack of evidence or, some allege, because of his renewed political power.

Because of his besmirched reputation, Zardari was seen as a liability by Pakistan People's Party (PPP) leaders in the last year of Musharraf's reign. Although he benefited from a wave of sympathy after the December 27 assassination of his wife, Benazir, he largely kept out of sight before the February 2008 parliamentary elections. Yet on September 6, 2008, both houses of the Pakistani legislature and members of all four provincial assemblies assembled in Islamabad to elect Zardari president to succeed General Musharraf, who had been forced to step down to avoid impeachment.

Zardari faces grave challenges. Pakistan is not an oil state and must import much of its energy. Its farmers and factory workers have been badly hurt by the rise in energy prices during the past decade. Food prices have also skyrocketed. The radical Tehrik-i Taliban, based in the tribal areas, regularly attacks government troops and checkpoints and has attempted to encroach on Peshawar, the capital of the North-West Frontier Province. Out-of-control cells within the Pakistani military are still supporting covert jihadi groups as a means of extending Pakistani influence into Afghanistan and Kashmir. The arbitrary and dictatorial actions of General Musharraf left a legacy of uncertainty and instability in the country's legal institutions, which must be repaired. Martial law decrees also gave the presidency far too much power, and most Pakistani politicians and voters want to see those prerogatives reduced in favor of the prime minister.

Furthermore, the country is divided politically. Some tribes in Baluchistan have separatist tendencies—Sindhis, whom Zardari represents, feel deeply discriminated against on ethnic and economic grounds. They went on an antigovernment rampage in late December 2007 in the wake of the assassination of Benazir Bhutto, who was one of their own. Much of the populous, wealthy, and powerful Punjab province supports the Muslim League rather than the PPP, and the province's chief minister, Shahbaz Sharif, is the brother of Zardari's most important political rival, former prime minister Nawaz Sharif. The latter announced in September 2008 that his party will sit in the opposition in parliament. Zardari gave assurances that he would not attempt to impose PPP governance on Punjabi provincial politics, but rivalry between the two major parties there could produce political gridlock. Given Zardari's frivolous, avaricious, and possibly violent past, many in the public and the press ask whether he is up to the task of successfully tackling all these pressing issues.

Pakistanis had been hoping for a breath of fresh air as they worked for the end of military dictatorship and a government policy less subservient to the United States. Instead, the wind that swept over them from the professional politicians in Islamabad was stale indeed. Despite Zardari's overwhelming popularity among Pakistan's legislators, an opinion poll carried out in early September 2008 by the ARY satellite television channel showed that he trailed his two opponents in the contest for president among the public at large.[13]

It is striking that the major discontents of the vast majority of Pakistani public, in the Punjab, Sindh, Baluchistan, and even much of the North-West Frontier Province, have little to do with Islam. It is also noteworthy that a majority sees the demand by a small minority for a Talibanization of their country as a threat to their way of life. The image often met with in the American press, of Pakistan as a nation of religious fanatics, makes no sense at all in the light of the political developments since 2007. Whatever else Zardari may be, the democratically elected current victor in the political struggle in that country is the farthest thing from a fundamentalist one could imagine. The remarkable story of how Pakistan moved toward parliamentary rule and away from military dictatorship in recent years tells us a great deal about why Pakistanis view the West as they do and what would be necessary to improve relations.

Islam Anxiety about Pakistan derives from Westerners' looking at the country solely in a cultural and religious context and not understanding the social and economic dynamics that drive its tensions with the West. Pakistan faces two big political challenges, one urban and the other rural. The urban crisis springs from the rapid growth of a literate, well-informed, and densely connected middle class. Ironically, the military dictatorship of Musharraf helped greatly expand this class, fostering an average growth rate of 7 percent a year from 1999 to 2007. In that period, the gross domestic product doubled. In the opening years of the twenty-first century, 5 percent of the population—some 8 million persons—moved from the poor and working class to the lower middle class. Urban Pakistanis adopted globalization with alacrity. Literacy has risen to 54 percent overall. In the past decade, the number of cell phones in the country went from 600,000 to 50 million. Families bought televisions and motor scooters in the millions. Cable television channels proliferated, and some families gained access to satellite channels. Instead of depending solely on the government PTV (Pakistan Television) and its state-produced news, Pakistanis could view a wide range of television news programs, including CNN, India's ZeeTV, and private Pakistani channels such as Geo (the production studios of which are in Dubai in the Gulf).[14] Despite these advances, the widening middle classes labored under the authoritarian government of Musharraf, who was backed to the hilt by the United States. Aspirations for more say in how they are governed appear to have driven their discontent, inasmuch as they give their newly elected leaders much higher marks than they used to give Musharraf, who came to power in a coup.

The newly wealthy owners of textile workshops in Karachi and the expanding urban middle classes as well as the landlords in the countryside depended on Pakistan's shaky rule of law for the security of their business and professional dealings. Despite the nation's ethnic and regional diversity and its great extremes of wealth and poverty, the institutions and networks that tie together the wealthiest 5 percent of the population constitute a relatively cohesive national elite. Generals, landlords, businessmen, judges, and politicians tend to be produced by the same extended clans, many of them springing from the long-standing rural gentry. Political leadership tends to rotate among representatives of these big clans and the generals in the military.

Pakistan has an extensive legal infrastructure that employs tens of thousands. There are commercial courts, drug courts, and labor courts, among others. Nothing could have been more contradictory to this legal edifice and the rule of law than a military dictatorship. Over the years, Musharraf came into increasing conflict with Chief Justice Iftikhar Mohammad Chaudhry of the Supreme Court. The feisty justice had ruled against the government's attempt to privatize the state-owned Pakistan Steel Mills, on the grounds that it was carried out with undue haste. He blocked a plan by the fundamentalist religious parties to institute an Islamic public morals court in the North-West Frontier Province on the grounds that it was unconstitutional. Perhaps most important, Chaudhry forced the government to produce hundreds of supposedly missing persons who were apparently actually in the custody of the domestic intelligence forces or possibly the American FBI or CIA, accused of involvement in Muslim radical groups.

It was likely the missing persons issue that finally provoked Musharraf to suspend the chief justice on March 9, 2007. The suspension was widely viewed as unconstitutional among Pakistani jurists and the middle classes. Musharraf had struck at the judicial foundations that sustained the professions and businesses of the new middle classes he had helped to create. Attorneys and white-collar professionals mobilized to protest the action despite Musharraf's ban on rallies. In early June, 7,000 demonstrators came out to greet Chaudhry at a public appearance, as attorneys and others staged a sit-in in the eastern city of Lahore. In response, Musharraf moved to curb Pakistani press freedom, cutting the transmissions of private channels such as Geo to prevent honest coverage of the demonstrations. This move further endangered the personal freedoms and access to information of the expanded middle class, heightening their anger and the crisis rather than tamping it down.

As the urban crisis over the rule of law progressed, a second crisis unfolded in the northwest. Pakistan has one of the more unequal distributions of land in South Asia, with 5 percent of the population controlling 66 percent of the land.[15] And while the urban service sector has been economically dynamic, agriculture has been stagnant. Incomes are crushingly low in the countryside. A third of Pakistanis make less than a dollar a day. Inflation, which has been running at 10 percent, hits rural folk especially hard. Rural poverty is worst in the northern Punjab, the North-West Frontier Province, and Baluchistan, as well as in the FATA areas, all of them near Afghanistan, which is the terrain of the neo-Taliban.

The northwest is dominated by Pushtuns, the ethnic group from whom the Taliban have largely emerged. They speak an eastern Iranian language and organize themselves loosely by clan. Their ethos is unusually egalitarian, however, in part as a result of their emphasis on small farm ownership. They avoid the inequality of tribal hierarchy because their tribal councils are open to membership by any propertied male. Also, their small clans have a tradition of engaging in feuds that prevent the emergence of large dominant political blocs among the tribes. (One American ethnographer compared them to Americans in that they all think they are as good as everybody else and his uncle, even though they obviously do live in a society with social hierarchies.[16]) Their ethnic group straddles the Hindu Kush mountain range, with big populations in both Pakistan (28 million, where they are called Pathans) and Afghanistan (12 million). Pushtunwali, their traditional code of tribal law, does not always accord with the Qur'an, though most Pushtuns would never acknowledge that.

The mountain Pushtun populations of FATA labor under the rule of the federal government, having key local development decisions taken out of their hands by Islamabad bureaucrats. The origins of this direct rule over FATA lay in British colonial policy, which had signally failed to subdue the northern Pushtuns, despite building a string of forts. The tribes of the area revolted in 1897–1898, attacking government facilities, and the British had to commit 60,000 troops to putting them down. The Mahsud tribe staged an uprising in 1919–1920, which forced the British to send in 80,000 troops and spend several times what it had cost them to prosecute the Third Anglo-Afghan War in neighboring Afghanistan. Nor was this a story of steady imperial progress. The 1940s saw more challenges to British rule and less British control in the region than earlier in the Raj.[17] The inability of the British Government of India to subdue these regions prevented them from devolving the administration on local politicians. They were finally given individual adult franchise in 1997 with respect to the federal parliament, though political parties are forbidden to operate in these regions. FATA is directly ruled by the federal government through appointed officials, and the local population is still governed by a colonial-era legal code and is not affected by Supreme Court decisions. Living in an arid region, they face challenges in water management. Their agricultural goods and lumber are expensive to transport in and out, and in order to escape poverty, they will need better roads and transportation infrastructure—a need that, to say the least, the central government has not met.

This combination of governmental intrusion and neglect in the region has sometimes provoked lawlessness. The British-drawn Durand Line (1893) arbitrarily cut the Pushtuns off from their hinterland and markets in southern Afghanistan, but they have never recognized it in practice. They conduct a vast peddling and smuggling trade across those borders. Yet, while they seek regional autonomy, some of their demands are for better integration into Pakistan and the global economy. Their remoteness, their special geographical and ecological challenges, their unequal status in the Pakistani system, and curbs on their ability to make their own development decisions have each played a greater role in provoking their occasional militancy than the forms of Islam that they have followed.[18]

The Muslim seminaries in this region tended to adopt the reformist Deobandi school of Islam, which concentrates on the sayings and doings of the Prophet Muhammad as their main source of law and practice, in part as a reaction against the syncretic cultural atmosphere of nineteenth-century British India.[19] The Deobandi school had been fairly quietist for much of the twentieth century but became radicalized in this area by the Soviet invasion of Afghanistan in 1978. The arrival of 3 million Pushtun refugees from the Afghanistan wars during the 1980s and 1990s put severe strains on regional resources, despite the desire of Pakistani Pushtuns to be hospitable to their Afghan cousins. The ongoing neglect by the central government in Pakistan was another grievance. The Taliban, or "seminary students," initially arose among those refugees, whose sons or orphans were taken in by Deobandi seminaries (some of them funded in part by the Saudis), at a time when the rudimentary Pakistani civil educational system simply would have been overwhelmed by so many new students.

The U.S. invasion of Afghanistan in 2001, and its consequent heavy military presence just across the border, angered Pushtuns on nationalist grounds. After 2001, Washington's push to ensure heavier Pakistani central government intervention in the region against the remnants of al-Qaeda and the Taliban further enraged even tribesmen previously unconnected to either. That is, American policies that thwarted tribal aspirations for more input with the Pakistani state about how they were to be ruled have themselves pushed some in this population toward greater radicalism.

Although Pushtuns have a reputation for religiosity, until recently their voting patterns in Pakistan had not favored political Islam. Indeed, one major anticolonial party attracting Pushtun followers in the 1930s and 1940s, the Red Shirts, was inspired by the nonviolent philosophy of Mahatma Gandhi. In the period after Pakistan's founding in 1947, Red Shirt adherents formed the core of the later Awami National Party, a secular-leaning vehicle for Pushtun nationalism. Otherwise, in recent decades, the inhabitants of the North-West Frontier Province tended to vote like other Pakistanis, mainly for the Muslim League, a conservative party representing big landlords and rising industrialists, or for the Pakistan People's Party, which had a left-of-center, relatively secular platform.

Pakistan's major fundamentalist party, the Jama'at-i Islami, did not make substantial inroads into the Pushtun areas until after the U.S. invasion of Afghanistan. In 2002, the residents of the North-West Frontier Province voted heavily for the United Action Council (Urdu initials: MMA), a coalition of religious parties, the most important of which was the Jama'at-i Islami. This turn to the fundamentalist parties, which promptly attempted to implement sharia as much as they could, appears in the main to have been a protest vote against Washington's Afghanistan War and Musharraf's complaisance toward it. Pushtuns were not primarily radicalized by the neo-Deobandi seminaries or madrasahs coming under Wahhabi influence, as is often charged by pundits and politicians in the West. They voted in large numbers for parties promoting political Islam only when they saw their compatriots on the Afghan side of the border conquered by the United States.

From 2004 until early 2008, the Pakistani province that was most crucial to the fight against the remnants of al-Qaeda and Taliban was governed by parties that had difficulty believing those two movements were as evil as Washington alleged. From the point of view of the American war on terror, this political development was a first-class disaster. Qazi Husein Ahmad, the leader of the biggest religious party, the Jama'at-e Islami, routinely denied that al-Qaeda actually existed or that there were any such operatives in the northwest. One leader of the MMA had long run a seminary that produced many Taliban. Even though the religious parties of the MMA themselves were not violent and rather had entered into the mainstream Pakistani political process, the MMA government clearly could not be depended on to help against the remnants of al-Qaeda and the Taliban.

Although the elected MMA government was an impediment to fighting the Taliban, it should not be assumed that North-West Frontier Province Pushtuns concurred with MMA policies. Many Pakistani Pushtuns in the NWFP were dismayed to find that the MMA fundamentalists did not stand strongly for Pushtun subnationalism, rather putting their efforts into imposing puritanism. They banned secular music concerts, chased great Pushtun crooners out of the province, and forbade the public advertising of Bollywood films (made in Bombay, India), which they considered too racy and too focused on romance and sex, and thus made themselves unpopular over time.

Federal troops loyal to General Musharraf arrested radicals in the area and put pressure on tribes in the rugged regions to the west that were hosting radical escapees (often, apparently, more because the escapees were willing to pay exorbitant sums for renting rooms or because they had intermarried with local tribes than because of ideological affinity). The military attempted to curb what became known as the Pakistani Taliban, but the fighting in that area involved hard slogging. FATA's population is 3.5 million, or about 2 percent of Pakistan's population. It is only 3 percent urban, and 30 percent of the territory is so rugged that it is beyond the reach of the government. Although the militants among the tribes were capable of causing trouble and attacking police checkpoints, they and their power base were far too small to actively menace the Pakistani government. At the same time that the military was fighting the neo-Taliban in Pakistan, it appears to have deployed Pushtun Muslim activists across the border into Afghanistan as a means of retaining influence in that country.[20] It may be that some of that money and materiel found its way back to the growing Pakistani Taliban movement. That is, the Pakistani military's schizophrenic policies of fighting their own Taliban at home while encouraging them and like-minded groups to attack inside Afghanistan produced what the CIA calls "blowback"— when a covert operation boomerangs to harm its own backers. The FATA tribes began inflicting significant casualties on Pakistani troops who were attempting to bring them under control of the central government. The apparent hopelessness of the task of militarily subduing the fractious tribes in their immense and craggy homeland led Musharraf to make a controversial truce with the chieftains in September 2006, which lasted for about a year.

In fall of 2006, the rural crisis made itself felt in the capital. Militants of the neo-Deobandi school of radical theology came from rural areas and established themselves in the Red Mosque and seminary of the capital, Islamabad, seeking to impose themselves as a sort of local Taliban-style morals police. They eventually turned violent, capturing police on May 19, 2007, and then taking Chinese acupuncture workers captive on June 23. They accused the acupuncturists of prostitution. The capture of Chinese nationals caused an international incident. Pakistan is closely allied with China, and, given its tensions with India, Iran, and Afghanistan, Islamabad could ill afford a souring of relations with Beijing. Musharraf responded by ordering an invasion of the mosque and seminary on July 10. Over a hundred people died in the ensuing skirmish, which outraged other Deobandis in the Pushtun areas of the north and brought out thousands of protesters in towns of the NWFP.

After the government captured the mosque, suicide bombers targeted Pakistani security forces in the north in a campaign that ultimately killed hundreds of people. Angered by the massacre at the mosque and the military crackdown in the north, Waziristan tribal leaders cancelled their truce with Islamabad on July 15. Clashes between Pakistani troops and militants near the Afghanistan border became common again. At the same time, the Afghan guerrillas dubbed Taliban by the United States were resurgent on the Afghan side of the Hindu Kush, repeatedly attacking NATO troops and kidnapping foreigners.

Faced with accusations that Pakistan had not done enough to track down al-Qaeda figures in the northwest, and responding to hints that the United States might intervene itself, Foreign Minister Khurshid Mehmood Kasuri heatedly pointed out in summer 2007 that Pakistan had sacrificed seven hundred troops to the fight against extremists in the tribal areas. He warned that any U.S. incursion would infuriate the Pakistani public and remove any hope that Washington could win local hearts and minds.

Most Pakistanis appear to have had no sympathy for the hard-line ideology of the Red Mosque vigilantes, and few joined demonstrations on their behalf in provinces such as Sindh and Punjab. In a summer 2008 poll, some 60 percent of Pakistanis said they would oppose further Talibanization of their society, and only 15 percent wanted a substantial increase in such puritanism. The Pakistani public is worried about the influence of the rigid and authoritarian seminaries, or madrasahs, and 64 percent favor requiring them to register with the government and modernize their curriculum so as to include contemporary sciences.[21] Still, the mosque invasion and continued unrest and militarization did not sit well with people. Musharraf was further weakened on July 20, 2007, when the Supreme Court reinstated Chief Justice Chaudhry, only four months after Musharraf suspended him. This bold move, in defiance of a military dictator, underlined the commitment of the justices to hew to principle whatever the cost.

The twin urban and rural crises profoundly weakened the Musharraf regime, raising questions about its ability to survive. The mobilized, highly interconnected middle class was vehemently opposed to the military's interference with the rule of law, striking and holding rallies despite martial law. The neo-Taliban of the northwest deeply sympathized with the Red Mosque puritan vigilantes and turned to active rebellion against the regime, deploying suicide bombers against military checkpoints with unprecedented frequency. Both urban and rural dissidents profoundly resented American backing for Musharraf, seeing the Bush administration as an impediment to political change. America was coded as standing for arbitrary decree as opposed to rule of law and for brutal repression as opposed to political compromise.

Washington began asking if Musharraf was another Mohammad Reza Pahlevi, who tried to hold on to dictatorial power too long and found himself overthrown by a popular revolution. Then Secretary of State Condoleezza Rice was reported to have come up with the idea of convincing Musharraf to allow exiled former prime minister Benazir Bhutto to return to the country and run in the approaching parliamentary elections.[22] Rice appears to have unrealistically hoped for cooperation between Musharraf as president and Bhutto as prime minister.

In the 2003 elections, Musharraf's goons had actively interfered with the PPP and Muslim League campaigns, and the restrictions his military dictatorship had clamped on the bigger and more popular parties helped the Muslim League (Qa'id-i A'zam), a branch of the original Muslim League that supported Musharraf, dominate parliament. Qa'id-i A'zam, or "great leader," is the affectionate epithet by which Muhammad Ali Jinnah, the country's founder, is known, so Musharraf and his supporters wrapped themselves in the flag and thereafter referred to their party as Muslim League (Q).

Ironically, Musharraf's interference in the election also unexpectedly resulted in a protest vote in the North-West Frontier Province in favor of the fundamentalist United Action Council, which, as we've seen, went on to oppose Musharraf. Bhutto's Pakistan People's Party, however, still had a formidable political organization, with cadres, grassroots supporters, and backbenchers who could swing into action if given the opportunity. That the haughty and flamboyant Benazir could have played junior partner in Musharraf's presidency for life was rather unlikely. On Benazir's return in mid-October 2007, her convoy was targeted by a bombing, probably by al-Qaeda or the Pakistani Taliban, but she escaped harm.

In the meantime, Saudi Arabia appears to have had concerns that Benazir's installation as prime minister with, potentially, a PPP-dominated parliament might lead to an Americanization and liberalization of Pakistani society. There are a million Pakistani guest workers in Saudi Arabia, and the royal family sees the country as an important regional ally. Riyadh's candidate for prime minister was Nawaz Sharif, a Punjabi steel magnate who had alternated in power with Benazir in the 1990s. He had shown increasingly dictatorial leanings in the late 1990s, assaulting press freedom and bullying political opponents. His Muslim League, despite the name, was not a fundamentalist party but, as noted, represented the interests of the landed and industrial elite. Sharif's alternative to the Jama'at-i Islami was the Prophet's Order (Nizam-i Mustafvi) Movement led by Tahir al-Qadri, a religious thinker and law school professor who loudly denounced al-Qaeda and Bin Laden. Sharif was overthrown by Musharraf in 1999, in part because he was not seen by the military as sufficiently hawkish against India, and went into exile in Saudi Arabia.

George W. Bush opposed Sharif's return, incorrectly intimating that he was implicated in religious extremism and lacked both an understanding of the requirements of today's world and a strong commitment to fighting the war on terror.[23] Washington had for years solidly backed Musharraf but excoriated Sharif, erasing Islam Anxiety from the general and inscribing it on the civilian prime minister deposed by Musharraf's coup. Musharraf in any case allowed Sharif to return from exile. On his arrival in November 2007, Sharif explored the possibility of an alliance with Bhutto.

Information reached Musharraf that the Supreme Court was planning to declare his October 2007 election as president null and void because he ran while still a general. Musharraf's refusal to resign from the military and rule as a civilian president had long been an embarrassment to Washington, which had, as noted, strongly supported him despite its rhetoric about democratizing the Muslim world. His subsequent dismissal of the existing Supreme Court on November 3, 2007, and appointment of a more compliant one, produced a new crisis, since civilian politicians felt uncomfortable participating in parliamentary elections under a corrupt judiciary. The Jama'at-i Islami's leader, Qazi Husein Ahmad, announced that his party would boycott the elections unless the original justices were restored to office. It is remarkable that Pakistan's major fundamentalist religious party risked self-destructing as a parliamentary force on behalf of a secular rule of law. Ahmad was defending the very justices who had struck down his plan for implementing sharia in the North-West Frontier Province. The attorneys and their supporters attempted to demonstrate against Musharraf but were suppressed by the army. Musharraf tightened press and television censorship. Nawaz Sharif began suggesting that his Muslim League (N) might boycott the elections as well.

Then disaster struck. On December 27, 2007, Benazir Bhutto was assassinated while campaigning. Sindh Province (her political base) erupted in protests and attacks on government offices, railroads, and banks. Her assassination was blamed by the Musharraf government on Baitullah Mahsud, a guerrilla leader of the Pakistani branch of the Taliban, the Tehrik-i Taliban. In the aftermath of this dramatic assassination and the violence that ensued, 72 percent of Americans told a Gallup poll that they had a negative view of Pakistan.[24]

After the assassination, Musharraf intimated that parliamentary elections might have to be postponed for a year. Washington, alarmed at the way the security situation was spiraling out of control, appears to have convinced him behind the scenes that the elections needed to be held. A poll of Pakistanis in January 2008 found that 88 percent thought it was important or very important to live in a democracy with elected representatives in parliament, so delaying the elections for so long would probably have risked substantial social turmoil.[25] The government reluctantly scheduled elections for February. Benazir's young son Bilawal, studying at Oxford, was anointed leader of the PPP, but it was Zardari who served as his regent and the actual leader of the party. He was widely viewed as corrupt, but the public appears to have given Benazir's party a sympathy vote nevertheless.

The Pakistani public dealt a stinging rebuke to Musharraf's party, the Muslim League (Q), in the February 2008 elections. The party that received the most votes, and the only one that was well represented in more than one province, was the PPP. Sharif's Muslim League (N), the branch loyal to Nawaz, came in a strong second.[26] The two parties put together a ruling coalition with some small or regional parties, attaining not just the majority needed to elect a prime minister but the supermajority that would allow them to overturn Musharraf's veto and even amend the constitution. Baluchistan was the only province where the Muslim League (Q) did well (and even they later went into coalition with the PPP). The North-West Frontier Province, which had been ruled for over five years by the fundamentalist United Action Council, gave about a sixth of its votes to the secular, left-of-center PPP and a third to the secular Pushtun nationalist party, the Awami National Party. The fundamentalist party got only about 10 percent of the seats in the provincial assembly and only four of thirty seats allotted the NWFP in the federal parliament. This volatility with regard to political Islam suggests that the heavy fundamentalist vote among Pushtuns in 2002 had been a mere protest against the U.S. invasion of Afghanistan; or possibly that the people of the NWFP did not think that the Jama'at-i Islami and its rivals had done a very good job of governing.

That the electorate would give secular parties a majority in the National Assembly in 2008 demonstrates that political Islam is not nearly as strong in Pakistan as most Western observers assume. Most urban, middle-class Pakistanis are either religious liberals or not interested in mixing religion into politics. The outcome in the villages of the Punjab and Sindh underlines the difference between fundamentalism, or political Islam, on one hand, and Muslim traditionalism, on the other. For example, the more traditional, rural Pakistanis most often value visiting the tombs of saints to ask for blessings, a practice that the Jama'at-i Islami and the neo-Deobandis denounce. In Sindh and some parts of the Punjab, they voted heavily for the PPP.

Many Punjabis and Sindhis follow a form of Shiite Islam tinged with Sufi mysticism. Most Pakistanis love religious music (qawwali) and poetry readings, which the Salafi-minded denounce. They also swoon over Bollywood movies (in the old days when Pakistan had an economic boycott on India, these were pirated on VHS, but they are now freely available). These films are the opposite of puritanism in every way, and to the extent that the MMA attempted to ban them in Peshawar, it likely sealed its political doom.[27]

The Pakistani government elected in February 2008 initially consisted of a coalition between the PPP and the Muslim League (N), who, however, engaged in lively disputes over when and whether to reinstate the justices Musharraf had dismissed from the Supreme Court. PPP leader Zardari feared the destabilizing consequences of this move. His coalition partner, Nawaz Sharif, however, demanded immediate action, hoping that the court would declare Musharraf's earlier election to the presidency null and void.

Because of the commanding position attained by the PPP in the February elections and the other allies it attracted among smaller parties, Zardari was able to avoid reinstating the Supreme Court, which he may have feared would revive corruption charges against him. Zardari and Sharif did agree on ousting Musharraf, forcing him to resign, after which Zardari became president in September 2008.

Washington was well known to have supported Musharraf almost to the last, and its backing for the military and officer coups raises America Anxiety among a Pakistani public weary of arbitrary rule. Most of the $11 billion in foreign aid that the American government gave to the Musharraf regime benefited the military without helping ordinary Pakistanis. The pressure the United States has put on the military to attack other Pakistanis in the northwest inspires nationalist objections, even from middle-class people that have no sympathy for the Pakistani Taliban. Worse, in the summer of 2008, the U.S. military began launching air strikes at Taliban and al-Qaeda targets inside the Pakistani border. These actions were called "terrorism" even by otherwise friendly Pakistani politicians.

At a time when Washington was claiming to back democratization in the Muslim world, it was clear to a Pakistani public actively working toward free and fair parliamentary elections that the United States was an impediment, not an aid, to popular sovereignty. Bush depicted mere conservatives such as Nawaz Sharif as allied to al-Qaeda and deployed Islam Anxiety as a reason to keep the military in power. Yet when the Pakistani public went to the polls, they turned the country over to the secular, reformist Pakistan People's Party, and almost no one voted for the fundamentalist parties. They want U.S. aid and investment and more travel between Pakistan and America—but they want those programs to be structured so as to help ordinary people rather than corrupt generals living the high life in Karachi mansions.

The political crisis in Pakistan is deeply intertwined with that of its neighbor to the northwest, Afghanistan. In both countries, rural tribal groups resist the penetration of the countryside by the bureaucratic state just as they stand up to foreign influence. The presidents of both countries have in recent years suffered from being seen by many in their publics as puppets of the American superpower. The political and security challenges in the two differ enormously, however.

Pakistan has the advantage of a cohesive national elite, a large, disciplined army, a long if troubled tradition of party politics, and a significant, cosmopolitan urban population. For Pakistan, the FATA Taliban are a small provincial revolt and are rather unlikely to take over the government in Islamabad. In Afghanistan, in contrast, the Taliban ruled the country in the late 1990s, and their potential political base is much larger. However despised they are now, they have shown an ability to take, hold, and rule large swaths of territory. The Taliban remnants benefit from substantial resentment in the Pushtun countryside roused by efforts to eradicate the lucrative poppy crop and by the actions of U.S. and NATO troops in their regions. The foe they face in the form of the Afghan government is weak, and its newly built army is largely ineffective.

Everyone remembers that al-Qaeda hit the United States after training at camps in Afghanistan, and the substantial U.S. military presence in that country is not nearly as controversial in the United

States and Europe as are the troops in Iraq. Despite the installation of the friendly Karzai government after the fall of the Taliban, Americans gave Afghanistan high unfavorability ratings, as though it were still an enemy country.[28]

In 2008, the situation there took a turn for the worse, with a growing Pushtun guerrilla movement in the south that opposed Karzai's government. The U.S. troop presence grew to over 30,000, with a similar number of NATO soldiers on the ground, but they continued to face increasing violence. Although the foreign troops were ostensibly committed to fight the resurgent Taliban and Pushtun guerrillas, their search-and-destroy missions and air strikes, which often killed innocent villagers, may have instead strengthened the antigovernment movement.

In April 2008, Karzai himself was the target of an assassination attempt. Emblematic of the growing instability in the country was a spectacular jailbreak staged in Qandahar in June 2008. Taliban set off bombs at the main prison there, killing 15 guards. The attack allowed 1,100 inmates to escape, including about 400 captured insurgents. Observers suggested that the operation must have been an inside job, casting doubts on the loyalty of at least some prison officials or guards. The operation also cast into doubt the commitment and effectiveness of NATO troops in the region, since the escapees fled with virtual impunity. Soon thereafter, another large truck bomb killed over 50 people and wounded over 100 at the Indian embassy in Kabul. (The Taliban denied responsibility.) In May and June 2008, more U.S. and allied troops were killed by guerrillas in Afghanistan than in Iraq. The Karzai government was accused of being riddled with corruption and near collapse.

Seasoned observers had for some time warned of catastrophe in Afghanistan, blaming the ever-increasing alienation of the southern Pushtun population on U.S. and NATO search-and-destroy tactics, which made it impossible for the West to win hearts and minds. They worried that Kabul could lose control of the south, leaving security tasks almost entirely to the International Security Assistance Force (ISAF) troops from NATO.[29] It is indeed unclear what the U.S. military hopes to gain from these continued missions in the south, for it is unlikely that a foreign military force could repress rebellious Pushtun tribes by main force. Afghanistan is a big, rugged country, and much of the population is organized by clan and tribe. It has never had a strong centralized government, and the last regime that even attempted such a thing was probably the communists of the 1980s, who were overthrown by angry mujahideen and executed.

Afghanistan expert Barnett Rubin argues that some of the fighting in the south has little to do with NATO or with ideology. He points to subtribes of the Alizai in Helmand who are feuding with one another despite all being Pushtun and even though they have no ideological differences. He quotes a fruit trader in Qandahar who said in 2007, "Those Afghans who are fighting, it is all because of unemployment," adding, "A drought in some parts of the country has also led to displacement and a decline in agricultural employment."[30] In addition to drought and unemployment, the fighting is impelled by the lack of an economic infrastructure, which allows overgrazing, and by forced migration and drug trafficking. Local economies in the south offer few sources of income besides the money proffered by various outside actors for militia activity, producing what Rubin calls a "jihad economy." He points out that the devastated economy of Afghanistan, which lies behind much of the continued instability there, could have been addressed by big international aid and investment programs after the defeat of the Taliban in 2001, but Washington chose instead to put the big money into the Iraq War.

The NATO project to set up a stable government in Afghanistan faces numerous obstacles. Among them is the competition for influence in the region between NATO and rivals such as Iran and Pakistan. In the fall of 2001, the United States installed in Kabul what was called the Northern Alliance. This coalition grouped Tajik, Hazara, and Uzbek guerrilla groups, drawn from ethnic groups that predominate in the center and north of the country. Tajiks, who speak a form of Persian and are largely Sunnis, account for about 30 percent of Afghans. Hazaras also speak Persian, but have the East Asian features that suggest their origin in the Mongol invasions of the medieval period. They are Shiites, and constitute perhaps 20 percent of the population. Uzbeks, who speak a Turkic language, are more secular-minded and more industrialized than other Afghans. They constitute about 10 percent of the population. The Tajiks were organized in part by the Jami'at-i Islami, the Afghan offshoot of the Egyptian Muslim Brotherhood, and were led before September 2001 by Ahmad Shah Masoud. That revered leader, who had fought against the Soviets and then the Taliban, was assassinated by al-Qaeda on September 9, 2001. The Hazaras were organized by the Hizb-i Vahdat, which was formed under Iranian guidance in 1988 as an umbrella group for Shiite activism in Afghanistan.

The Bonn conference of late 2001, convoked by Afghanistan's neighbors along with the United States and the United Kingdom to establish a provisional government after the fall of the Taliban, installed in power Pushtun leader Hamid Karzai. Karzai had been a key adviser to the Union Oil Company of California (Unocal—now part of Chevron) in the late 1990s when it was exploring the possibility of the Turkmenistan gas pipeline through Afghanistan. In 2002, a congress of Afghan tribal elders and leaders, called a Loya Jirga, made Karzai interim president of Afghanistan. Another Loya Jirga convened in 2003 to hammer out a constitution, which recognized Afghanistan as an Islamic Republic and forbade the Afghan parliament from passing any legislation contrary to "the laws of Islam." In 2004, Karzai was elected president, and in 2005, Afghans voted for a federal parliament. No political parties were recognized by the government, however, and all the candidates had to run as independents. The ethnic groups that made up the old Northern Alliance are numerous in both the government bureaucracy and the parliament, though their initial overwhelming dominance has lessened as Karzai has made a place for more Pushtuns.

The Northern Alliance guerrillas had depended for military aid in fighting the Taliban in the 1990s on India, Iran, and Russia, and had especially strong connections to New Delhi.[31] The Hazaras, and the Tajiks of the west, have continued in recent years to have especially strong relations with Iran. From the point of view of the Pakistani military, the fall of Kabul to the Northern Alliance in 2001 was a catastrophe that delivered what should have been a Pakistani sphere of influence to India and, to a lesser degree, to Iran. The Taliban had in the 1990s been in large part the project of a Pakistani military intelligence organization, the Inter-Services Intelligence, or ISI. Although some of the officers who promoted the orphaned Afghan seminary graduates as a military force were themselves fundamentalists, others went along for geopolitical reasons. Many Taliban had lost their families to Soviet bombardment, and the seminaries supported by Islamic charities (including, famously, Saudi ones) were the only family the students knew. As Pushtuns, they had the linguistic tools and the religious charisma to establish legitimate governance in the warlord-ridden southern provinces of Afghanistan near the Pakistani border.

As noted earlier, the Pakistani military plays the double game of fighting Pakistani Taliban and al-Qaeda on Pakistani soil, while at the same time giving aid to Afghan Pushtuns fighting an insurgency against the United States, NATO, and Karzai. They see the Taliban as an avenue for the possible reestablishment of Pakistani hegemony over its northern neighbor and thus a means of pushing Indian influence out of Afghanistan. After September 11, 2001, the United States may have hoped that steady diplomatic pressure and the grant of billions in military and civilian aid would be a sufficient enticement for the Pakistani military gradually to give up its promotion of Talibanism in southern Afghanistan. At the moment, however, it appears that cells within the ISI disregarded both the pressure and the enticements.

Although Pakistani geopolitics are an important context for the resurgence of the Taliban, the insurgency in southern Afghanistan also grows out of local Afghan grievances. There is some question in my mind as to whether it is even legitimate to refer to all the some 4,000 Pushtun guerrillas now active in southern Afghanistan as Taliban. Many do not appear to have been displaced to Pakistan during the 1980s, or to have attended Deobandi seminaries there. Many just seem to be disgruntled villagers from Helmand and other provinces who have been inconvenienced by the U.S. and NATO troop presence or who resent the ways that the Karzai government is newly dominating their local politics.

The insurgent attacks have been most frequent precisely in those provinces most affected by the Afghan government's forcible poppy eradication campaigns. Afghanistan's poppies are its most lucrative crop, and account for perhaps half of its cash economy. They supply 85 percent of the opium demand in Europe. International pressure and Kabul's fears of a rise of narcoterrorism impelled forcible eradication measures in which government troops burned fields. That campaign seems to have been a significant contributor to the insurgency. So in addition to facing neo-Taliban, the United States and NATO are also confronted by Afghan and Pushtun resentments over the devastated economy and reduced local autonomy, combined with the economic grievances of poppy farmers who have lost their crops and thus their livelihoods.[32]

One of the goals of the U.S. presence in Afghanistan is to put pressure on Iran, which Washington has been attempting to isolate economically and diplomatically since the 1979 Khomeinist revolution. A large U.S. troop presence just to Iran's east functions as a form of pressure on Tehran, giving teeth to U.S. threats of exercising a military option if Iran does not cease its uranium enrichment research program. The downside of the American use of Afghanistan for this purpose is that it motivates Iran to cultivate clients in its eastern neighbor so as to create a security buffer that might protect it from Washington's designs. Iran has invested substantially in developing Herat Province and is accused by the United States of training and arming insurgents. On the face of it, however, the idea of Tehran actively helping the Taliban does not strike me as plausible, given the history of hostility between Shiite Iran and the neo-Deobandi Sunni radicals. That Iran is backing tribes in western Afghanistan that have a poor relationship with NATO would not be surprising. Iranians are also concerned about the large numbers of Afghan refugees who remain in their country, as well as the spread of drugs and drug trafficking into Iran.[33]

The Pentagon has sought to use its position in Afghanistan to forge new military relationships in Central Asia, which would give it the ability to intervene in security affairs. One subsidiary advantage of this American forward policy is that it might reassure the American private sector that it is safe to invest billions in gas pipelines in Central Asia. Washington sought bases in Afghanistan's northern neighbors and now has a base in Kyrgyzstan. Base rights granted to the United States by Uzbekistan after September 11 were withdrawn by the government of Islam Karimov when Washington criticized his May 2005 brutal crackdown on protesters at Andijan that left five hundred dead.[34] Karimov had become suspicious that Washington was behind the pro-democracy demonstrations.

Although competition for political influence in Afghanistan sets its neighbors and the great powers against one another, one key energy project brings some of these actors together. India and Pakistan are hoping that a stable government in Kabul might give them access to Central Asia's natural gas. In late April 2008, Turkmenistan, Afghanistan, Pakistan, and India signed off on a deal that would involve spending an estimated $8 billion to build the aforementioned TAPI pipeline, with construction slated to begin in 2010. The United States strongly backs the project, which would likely make the rival Iranian pipeline plan a dead letter and would reduce Russia's leverage on the natural gas market. Canadian energy economist John Foster rang the alarm soon after the deal was initialed, warning that the Canadian NATO contingent in the Qandahar region would likely be drawn into defending the pipeline from "massive" terrorist attacks. He said Canadians were being drawn into a "geopolitical game in Central Asia" and were "babes in the wood."[35] Because of continued instability in southern Afghanistan, the prospects for the TAPI pipeline are deeply uncertain, and it seems increasingly likely that Turkmenistan will pipe its gas north to Moscow for sale to Western Europe.

The Pakistani public has already told pollsters what the United States needs to do to have better relations with their country.[36] The negative views that have built up among Pakistanis toward the United States during the past eight years can be reversed. As cited earlier, if the United States provided more educational, medical, and disaster aid, increased its business investment, lowered tariffs on Pakistani goods, and gave Pakistanis visas to visit America more easily, two-thirds of Pakistanis said they would form a more favorable view of the United

States. This result held true even for those Pakistanis who said that they had a positive view of al-Qaeda! It is remarkable that whereas many Muslim countries are suspicious of American corporations, a supermajority of Pakistanis actively crave their investments. Note that although the United States has given the country billions in military aid since September 11, that sort of help is not what the public is asking for.[37]

The United States needs to support civilian politics, not a return to military rule. It needs to focus its foreign aid on medical, educational, and relief projects that benefit ordinary people, not on supplying fancy weapons and perquisites to the officer corps. The United States will get more support from the Pakistani public for its struggle against al-Qaeda remnants in the tribal agencies if it works through the Pakistani government and military rather than launching unilateral air strikes that infringe on the country's sovereignty. That is, the belligerent rhetoric of Clinton and Obama during the presidential primaries needs to be put away. Given the return of an elected parliament at the mercy of the popular vote, public support for American policies in Pakistan is crucial. In addition, holding the Pakistani military to higher standards of accountability and curbing the fundamentalist and pro-jihadi cells within it will be key to resolving the political crises in South Asia.

In return for U.S. educational aid, the Pakistani government should be induced to build more state schools so that villagers do not have to send their children to fundamentalist seminaries. As noted, most Pakistanis favor requiring seminaries to register with the government and to broaden their curriculum to include modern subjects, in hopes of making them more cosmopolitan and less likely to turn out fanatics.

The parties victorious in the 2008 elections all favor negotiating with the Pakistani Taliban and the FATA tribesmen who often support them. If those negotiations can lead to better relations between Islamabad and these regions, and if they can lead the tribal chieftains to cooperate in rooting out al-Qaeda remnants among them, then they should be given a chance. It is highly unlikely that Pakistani military attacks can subdue this region any time soon, and the very attempt may further radicalize the population.

If the primary concern of the United States with these regions is rounding up the remnants of al-Qaeda, then it would be more cost effective to implement better security at Karachi and other airports, which are, after all, the ports from which any al-Qaeda operative would embark for Europe or the United States. Highway checkpoints and aerial surveillance on the border between FATA and the North-West Frontier Province would be more effective than trying to take and hold the territory itself, which is likely impossible. If the goal is to prevent the FATA tribesmen from making trouble in Afghanistan because of the pipeline, then some carrots of development aid are probably as important as military action.

The struggles in Afghanistan appear to be much more about geopolitics than about culture or religion. Virtually all the people in this region are Muslims, after all. The Karzai government is deeply influenced by the Jami'at-i Islami, or Afghan Muslim Brotherhood, and many of its judicial and other practices have been fundamentalist in character. It has overseen blasphemy prosecutions and has heavily censored television programming. The constitution forbids parliament to enact civil legislation that contradicts "the beliefs and laws of Islam." The implication, which Westerners have mostly missed, is that sharia is unchallengeable. Although the Afghan constitution also in principle recognizes the Universal Declaration of Human Rights, in practice (as with the blasphemy or censorship cases), sharia has so far tended to trump the latter. While the Taliban are entirely unconcerned with international human rights thinking, the ideological struggle between them and the Karzai government is over the interpretation and the limits of Muslim fundamentalism rather than over whether Muslim fundamentalism should be the center for law and domestic policy.

The conflict also has a strong, if not determinative, ethnic coloration, with some Pushtun tribesmen resentful of what they see as the Tajik-dominated government in Kabul even though Afghan bureaucrats representing that government in the southern provinces are themselves Pushtun. The ethnic lines are not drawn in an absolute way, since Karzai and many of his officials are Pushtun and they have many Pushtun tribal supporters. In some ways, the fighting in the south is a

Pushtun civil war between pro- and anti-Karzai tribes. Still, ethnicity is one element in the struggle—there are no Hazara Shiite Taliban, and the spread of neo-Taliban violence to northern provinces such as Kunduz, where German troops have come under repeated attack, has tended to occur through Pushtun clan networks.[38] The conflict also has an imperial context, with proud Pushtun villagers rejecting U.S. and NATO domination and their often-murderous search-and-destroy tactics, and an economic dimension, with U.S. opposition to poppy growing conflicting with farmers' hopes for prosperity.

Although forcible poppy eradication may on the surface appear to be a reasonable response to the threat of narcoterrorism, it is in fact counterproductive.[39] It raises the price of poppies and so does nothing to impede the drug economy. The farmers involved in it are mostly engaged in subsistence agriculture and are otherwise dirt-poor. If their poppy crops are put under flame-throwers, they are cast into profound debt. One in seven Pushtun farmers in Helmand who saw their poppy crops eradicated reported that they had had to sell one of their children as a result (likely it was a girl child who was trafficked).[40] Some 38 percent said that they had become more sympathetic to the Taliban after the crops were forcibly destroyed. Instead, Afghan expert Rubin argues, the Kabul government and its international backers need to go into the provinces they control, fire corrupt government officials, and work to provide farmers with alternative crops and livelihoods, as well as work to get assent from local populations that the poppy-growing and drug trafficking must stop. Of course, the Afghan government does not control some areas of the country. There it will have to establish itself and its authority while giving local populations incentives to give it their loyalty and to accept from it the kind of aid and investment that might wean farmers off poppies. Better global cooperation in stopping the poppy flow is also important, as is international investment in the Afghan economy and the marketing of other Afghan agricultural products. All together, the only solution for Afghanistan is a significant international aid program combined with intensive strengthening of good governance.

Until the United States and NATO give up their counterproductive search-and-destroy tactics, and until they instead invest heavily in reconstruction, they will make no progress in winning Pushtun hearts and minds. There is even an increasing danger that the massive number of foreign troops in the country will make it a magnet for radical vigilantes; already, foreign volunteers are being found among the neo-Taliban, from places such as Chechnya and the Arab world. That is, the immensity of the U.S. and NATO footprint in this fiercely proud tribal Muslim region may actually be creating the threat it ostensibly seeks to avoid: the reconstitution of al-Qaeda and the revival of the 1980s discourse on holy war that proved so deadly to the Soviet Union.

CHAPTER VI

FROM TEHRAN
TO BEIRUT

THE IRANIAN CHALLENGE

President Mahmoud Ahmadinejad, a Holocaust denier who believes the coming of the Shiite messiah is imminent, has been the face of Iran since his election in 2005. Ahmadinejad's Iran is among the biggest generators of Islam Anxiety in the Western world. The theocratic regime of Supreme Jurisprudent Ali Khamenei stands accused of obsessive anti-Americanism, of pursuing nuclear weapons, of cultivating guerrilla cells in Iraq that have deployed sophisticated roadside bombs to kill U.S. soldiers, of funding Hizbullah and Hamas terrorism against Israel. It is charged with being an implacable and even "eternal" foe of the United States, of wanting to "wipe Israel off the face of the map," and of being a nation full of anti-Semites. Some pundits have even spoken of Iran as the antagonist in a new cold war with the United States. Washington is trying to strangle the Shiite regime with a wide-ranging economic boycott. Some have suggested darkly that the United States or Israel, so provoked by all Iran's misdeeds, will soon have no choice but to strike at it militarily.

President Ahmadinejad is accused of holding beliefs about the end of the world that make him dangerously irrational. Tehran is depicted as a military colossus astride the Gulf that menaces U.S. allies such as Saudi Arabia, Bahrain, and Kuwait, and which could, if it so chose, close the Straits of Hormuz to the supertankers that carry Gulf petroleum to the United States and its allies. It has been seen by local rulers such as King Abdullah II of Jordan as promoting a "Shiite Crescent" in the Middle East, utilizing its branch of Islam as a form of soft power to mobilize Arab Shiites against Sunni-ruled regimes. Domestically, the regime is portrayed as a puritanical dictatorship and among the world's worst abusers of human rights, its population in the grip of an unrelenting religious fanaticism.

The problems between the United States and Iran are rooted partially in the 1979 overthrow of Mohammad Reza Pahlevi Shah and the implementation of the theocratic Khomeinist ideology. Khomeinism consisted of several themes, including anti-American populism, insistence on national autonomy against globalization, rule of the nativist Shiite clergy, and state socialism, with much of the economy nationalized. A form of sharia, or Islamic canon law, was implemented as national law, with extensive restrictions on individual behavior and draconian punishments for infractions against them. Such a nativist posture, aimed at putting restrictions on foreign investment and halting the subordination of Iran's political elite to the global dominant power, helps ensure enmity with the United States.[1]

Ironically, Washington's own policies in recent years have profoundly benefited Iran and allowed it to emerge as a regional player on a scale unprecedented since the 1970s. Iran has been much strengthened by the destruction of the Taliban and the Iraqi Baath governments, Tehran's primary regional enemies. The American invasion of Iraq tore down the wall of containment built by the Sunni Arabs during the Iran-Iraq War of 1980 to 1988 and allowed extensive Iranian influence to be exercised inside Iraq (among the Kurds as well as among the Shiites). The Shiite government in Baghdad is a natural ally of Tehran; regional U.S. partners such as Saudi Arabia and Jordan feel betrayed because they have lost an ally and seen their Iranian rival gain one. Iran is now strong not only in Iraq, but also has clients in the Hizbullah party militia of south Lebanon and the Shiite communities of the Gulf. The Bush administration therefore has made the containment of Iran much more difficult and increased the likelihood of hostilities between the United States and Iran.

In addition to its anti-Americanism, critiques of consumerism, and restrictions on U.S. investments, the Islamic Republic of Iran also is pursuing a nuclear energy research program aimed at achieving the ability to enrich uranium. Iran's leadership believes that the only way for the country to maintain its independence in the long term is to have an independent nuclear enrichment capability and a network of nuclear energy plants. Iran is pursuing nuclear enrichment for fuel purposes through the use of centrifuges. There is no evidence that it has a nuclear weapons program, though it is not being entirely transparent to UN inspectors and in the past it has sometimes neglected to report experiments that are required to be made public by the Nuclear Non-Proliferation Treaty (NPT).

Despite the lack of good evidence for an Iranian nuclear weapons program, both Washington and its regional allies, Israel and Saudi Arabia, are consumed with anxiety about this possibility. Nuclear weapons would enhance Iran's growing role as a regional dominant power, undermining and displacing the current regional leading military power, Israel, as well as the dominant global power in this region, the United States.

Iran's alleged support for Shiite fundamentalist parties in Iraq adds to the tension. Although the U.S. Department of Defense accuses Iran of training rogue militia elements and of supplying them with deadly explosively formed projectiles (an especially effective type of roadside bomb), the evidence it has offered for this activity so far is not conclusive. Nor is it logical that Iran would be attempting to undermine the Shiite-dominated government in Baghdad, which is composed of two parties that are very close to the ayatollahs in Tehran. Nevertheless, the accusation that Iran is more or less deliberately killing U.S. and British troops by giving arms and training to anti-American Shiite militias has gained some political purchase in the United States.

In the winter of 2007, the Bush administration announced that American troops in Iraq were henceforth authorized to "kill or capture" any Iranian intelligence agents they discovered. The announcement came on the heels of Bush's pledge in the 2007 State of the Union address to shift another aircraft carrier to the Persian Gulf, a move that clearly targeted Iran. A prominent Iranian parliamentarian responded to Bush's threat by saying "Such an order is a clear terrorist act and against all internationally acknowledged norms."[2] This and other belligerent steps have set the stage for growing conflict with Iran, which could turn violent even with a new administration in Washington.

Islam Anxiety surrounding Iran has been woven into U.S. law, institutions, and public nightmares. In the fall of 2007, the U.S. Senate passed by a margin of seventy-seven votes the Kyl-Lieberman resolution calling on the president to declare the Iranian national guard, the Revolutionary Guards Corps (IRGC), a terrorist organization. Since the technical definition of terrorism is violence targeting civilians for political purposes carried out by nonstate actors, the resolution seemed nonsensical. Bush nevertheless gladly followed through, designating the Revolutionary Guards as terrorists.

The IRGC has given training to Hizbullah's paramilitary in Lebanon, a thorn in the side of Israel and the United States, and U.S. commanders maintain that it has trained Shiite militiamen in Iraq, though they are vague as to how many or to what effect. Ironically, the Badr Corps paramilitary of the Islamic Supreme Council of Iraq, a key U.S. ally and a pillar of the elected Iraqi government, formed part of the IRGC while its members were in exile in Iran during the Saddam period and until they returned to Iraq in 2003. The United States almost never criticizes the Badr Corps, since it has been helpful in Iraq, even though its training and ideology would be difficult to distinguish in any other way from those of its Iranian counterpart.

The constant drumbeat of negative and menacing stories about Iran on American television and the dramatic flourishes of political rhetoric have gradually instilled a sense of alarm in the public. By summer 2006, nearly half of Americans said they would approve of going to war to stop Iran from getting a bomb if that development seemed imminent. By October 2007, 77 percent of Americans insisted that Iran was attempting to acquire nuclear weapons.[3] Put the two polls together, and they seemed to equal war.

While the regime in Tehran is indeed authoritarian and implements hidebound laws in harsh ways, most of the other charges against Iran are either completely untrue or need to be qualified so extensively that they may as well be. Nor should the vitality of Iranian civil society be underestimated, despite the political setbacks visited on the reform movement in recent years. For example, an assertive and impressive movement for greater women's rights has achieved increases in women's university education, their election to municipal office, and their participation in the economy.[4] What is most mystifying about the rap sheet against Iran produced by Western power elites is why the charges are repeated with such alacrity and lack of elementary reflection or fact-checking by the American and European media. Islam Anxiety appears to operate so powerfully in this instance as to make the most implausible accusations, wholly unsupported by genuine evidence, seem plausible, even inevitable.

In 2008, only one-fifth of Iranians said that they had an unfavorable view of the American people, but three-quarters expressed negative sentiments toward the Bush administration. (Note that about three-quarters of Americans also slammed the former administration in its last year.) Iranians overwhelmingly believed that Washington wanted to dominate their petroleum and gas resources and that it was intent on dividing, weakening, and humiliating Islam. The Iranians are, however, hopeful that the situation can be improved. In 2008, some 65 percent thought it was possible to find common ground, and only 12 percent thought that conflict was inevitable, showing an increased optimism over 2006. Solid majorities wanted more cultural exchange, favored direct negotiations between the United States and

Iran on matters of mutual concern, and thought more Americans and Iranians should visit each other's country as tourists.[5]

Iran is hardly a military giant of the sort with which the United States could be plausibly locked in a cold war. Iran's annual military budget, at a little over $6 billion per year, is in the same range as that of Norway and Sweden, and less than that of Greece or Singapore. Defense expenditures are smaller per capita than any other country in the Gulf except for the United Arab Emirates. That statistic does not offer much support to the idea of Iran as a military threat to other Middle Eastern countries. U.S. military expenditures total about $1 trillion annually, nearly two hundred times those of Iran.

Although its detractors in the West constantly hint that Iran has unconventional weapons capabilities, the evidence is thin to nonexistent. The UN Organisation for the Prohibition of Chemical Weapons (OPCW) certified in 2000 that Iran was in compliance with the chemical weapons ban. Although Iran admitted to having produced some chemicals for weapons in the late 1980s and early 1990s as a reaction to Iraq's deployment of these weapons in the Iran-Iraq War, it maintains that it dismantled the production facilities, and most of these claims have been explicitly investigated and confirmed by the OPCW. Iran is a signatory to the Convention on Biological Weapons and denies having such weapons. In recent years, U.S. intelligence estimates have not accused Iran of producing or stockpiling chemical weapons, though they raised concerns about dual-use factories that could ramp up their production if the regime so decided.[6]

Since U.S. intelligence on Iran is highly politicized and many Iranian expatriate groups wishing to overthrow the regime provide wild allegations to U.S. officials, it would be unwise to accept charges in this regard without very firm proof, especially in view of the weapons of mass destruction (WMD) scams pulled on the CIA by Iraqi expatriates and American neoconservatives. There is no proof that Iran has ever transferred unconventional weapons to groups designated as terrorists by the United States, and there is every reason to believe that it would not do so even if it had them.[7] Indeed, belligerency has not been typical of Iranian statecraft traditions, in part because it is a large country with many deserts and mountains and poor transportation networks, making its population hard enough to rule, let alone mobilize for foreign wars. Iran has not launched an aggressive war of conquest against a neighbor for at least 150 years, and some say not since 1785, when tribal warlord Karim Khan Zand briefly took Basra from the Ottoman Empire.

When the United States under the Bush administration repeatedly told its Arab allies that Iran was menacing them, regional governments for the most part declined to take the bait. During Iranian cleric Akbar Hashemi Rafsanjani's visit to Riyadh in June 2008, King Abdullah explicitly rejected the American charges against Iran. He said that Saudi Arabia and Iran could work together to thwart Muslim extremism and offered to expand bilateral relations on a range of fronts. Since both Shiite Iran and pro-Western Saudi Arabia are menaced by al-Qaeda and similar fundamentalist vigilante groups, the quest for coordination in fighting the challenge is not surprising. The Arab public is also clearly not afraid of Iran, for the most part. A 2008 poll of six Arab countries found that a plurality did not believe Iran was seeking nuclear weapons, and 67 percent said that international pressure on Iran should cease. Some 44 percent maintained that even if Iran acquired a nuclear weapon, it would be positive for the Middle East (only 19 percent thought it would be negative).[8]

In 1997, Iran's youth, women, and social liberals elected reformist president Mohammad Khatami, who worked for greater personal liberties for Iranians, many of whom resented the regime's puritanism. Although Khatami's movement, the Second of Khordad (named after the date of the electoral victory), went on to have great success in parliamentary and municipal elections, it could never overcome the determined opposition of the clerics who controlled the judiciary and had the power to close reformist newspapers. After a while, the hard-liners simply began forbidding liberals to run for office, vetting candidates ever more closely for ideological purity. Predictably, this technique produced a swing to the right in subsequent elections, and Khatami's movement, effectively stymied, gradually lost its popularity.

Khatami had repeatedly reached out to the United States, suggesting vigorous people-to-people exchanges to begin with, but Washington showed little interest in a rapprochement and gave the reformers no diplomatic breakthroughs on which they could campaign at home. The most extensive proposal for a new relationship was conveyed to the United States through the Swiss embassy early in 2003 in the buildup to the Iraq War. Iran proposed to the United States an alliance against Saddam and a move toward normalizing relations. Tehran even intimated that it might recognize Israel as part of the deal.[9] The Bush administration rejected the overture out of hand, apparently because it still hoped to overthrow the Iranian government after taking Baghdad. Hawks quipped in the spring of 2003 that "everyone wants to go to Baghdad. Real men want to go to Tehran."[10]

Khatami, a relatively liberal theologian, had served many years as a chaplain for Iranian students in Germany and studied the work of sociologist Jürgen Habermas. He urged a more open society in Iran and a dialogue of civilizations. In the summer of 2005, Khatami had to step down after two terms, and the presidential elections produced a successor who was in many ways his polar opposite: Mahmoud Ahmadinejad, with a Ph.D. in traffic engineering and top grades at the Iran University of Science and Technology in Tehran, knew little of the outside world and favored religious literalism over Frankfurt School philosophizing.

Ahmadinejad, largely self-taught when it comes to subjects such as world history, immediately gained notoriety for his ignorant and often bigoted pronouncements. He charged that the human toll of the Holocaust had been exaggerated and that in any case the logical response to this tragedy would have been to give the surviving Jews some German territory on which to erect their state. He could not see why the Palestinians should have been expelled from their homes and punished for Europe's sins. It is, of course, outrageous that Ahmadinejad should have questioned whether the Nazis really killed as many as six million Jews, and his ideas on the subject are hardly universal in Iran.

Former president Khatami found it difficult to believe that Ahmadinejad intended to reject the reality of the genocide against the Jews, telling *Time* magazine, "I personally believe that he really didn't deny the existence of Holocaust. I believe the Holocaust is the crime of Nazism."[11] Iranian television subsequently ran a widely watched serial on the Holocaust, *Zero Degree Turn*, which told the story of a love affair between Habib Parsa (from a mixed Iranian and Palestinian family) and Sarah Stuck, a French Jew, who met as students at a university in Paris before the war. Habib pursued Sarah, quoting mystical Persian poetry to her. After the Nazis took France, Sarah had to go underground. Habib, who had a position in the Iranian embassy in Paris, managed to get them counterfeit Iranian passports, and they escaped to Iran. The enormously popular serial was based on true accounts of the role Iranian diplomats in Europe played in rescuing thousands of Jews in World War II.[12]

Ahmadinejad attended a conference on the end of Zionism in the fall of 2005, in which he gave a speech counseling Palestinian activists not to lose hope. He pointed to the fall of the shah in Iran and the collapse of the Soviet Union as examples of how powerful regimes that appear unassailable are often in fact houses of cards. He affirmed that what he called the Zionist regime in Israel was similarly fragile. He clearly felt that just as Iranians had wished away the shah, and the Russians had wished away the Soviet politburo, so Palestinians could wish away the Israeli regime. Then he quoted Ruhollah Khomeini's saying, "This Occupation regime over Jerusalem must vanish from the page of time."[13] Earlier wire service translators had rendered Khomeini's saying into English as "Israel must be wiped off the face of the map." The same phrase was used in Western reporting and even in English-language Iranian articles about Ahmadinejad's speech, triggering a global outrage. The translation is obviously extremely inexact and misleading. Khomeini had spoken about the "Occupation regime," not about "Israel." Moreover, the verb he used, "must vanish" *(bayad . . . mahv shavad)*, is intransitive. That is, Khomeini was expressing a wish for the regime to go away, but was not making a threat to actively wipe it out. A regime can vanish without anyone much coming to harm, as happened in Pahlevi Iran and the Soviet Union; wiping a country off the map sounds rather more ominous.

The wire service mistranslation was then picked up and used by a wide range of American and European press. Indeed, it became a tagline at the end of virtually all articles about Iran. It is hard to know whether the American politicians who kept repeating it realized that they were engaging in propaganda or whether they really believed that Iran's president hoped to annihilate ordinary Israelis. Ironically, at the time Khomeini originally made the statement in the 1980s, there was no international outcry and Israel was tacitly allied with Iran.

Ahmadinejad repeatedly attempted to make clear that he did not want to kill any Israelis or Jews, much less wipe them off the map. In an interview with French radio, the Iranian president was pressed on his vision of the future for Israel. He replied with a call for the stateless Palestinians to be added to the Israeli electorate and for the Palestinians of various religions living between the Jordan River and the Mediterranean to participate in a referendum on the future of Israel/Palestine: "I think the people of Palestine also have the right to determine their own fate. Let them choose for themselves, the Christians, the Jews and the Muslims. That is, all the Palestinians who belong to that land can participate in the referendum."[14]

Whereas in the West the word Palestinian refers only to Christian and Muslim inhabitants of geographical Palestine, Ahmadinejad uses the word to refer to longstanding Jewish residents of that territory as well. Thus Jewish families who had lived in Jerusalem for five generations would be considered Palestinian Jews by Ahmadinejad, but he excludes European Jewish immigrants from this status. He is not clear, and he has said various things about, what date would be the cut-off between these so-called Palestinian Jews and those he views purely as European outsiders. He wishes the "Palestinian Jews" to retain the franchise in the single state of Palestine but wishes to see those he codes as "European Jews" repatriated to Europe. I regret having to spill ink on explaining this crackpot plan, which will vanish from the pages of time as soon as Ahmadinejad leaves office, but here too, it is important to understand exactly what he is saying rather than to engage in hyperbole and polemics. Calling for some variant of a one-state solution via elections is not the same as military aggression, however offensive the call may be. Referendums similar to the one he proposes for Israel and Palestine have been suggested for Kashmir, which is claimed by both India and Pakistan, and for the Kirkuk province of Iraq, claimed by the Kurdistan Regional Authority as well as by Arab and Turkmen residents.

Ahmadinejad's views on these matters are out of the mainstream in Iran. Khatami argued that "the peaceful solution to the problem of Palestine is to recognize Palestinian rights." When asked, "And a Palestinian state to exist alongside Israel?" he replied, "Yes."[15] That is, Khatami accepted a two-state solution. Even Ahmadinejad appears at times to say he would as well, if that was what the Palestinian people wanted.

Ahmadinejad explicitly denies being a bigot: "No. I am not anti-Semitic. Like all other human beings, Jews are respected."[16] He points out that Jews and Christians are represented in the Iranian parliament: "You know that according to the Law in Iran, every 150,000 people have one representative in the Majles [parliament]. But the number of the Jews is not even 20,000 people and they have a representative. We say that the life and belongings of all people should be respected. We condemn all crimes."[17] Given that Iran has nearly 20,000 Jews, one has to wonder why—if Ahmadinejad were genocidal in the way he is often depicted—he would not start at home. Iranian Jews are free and unthreatened enough that community leaders have dared write Ahmadinejad letters of protest concerning his allegation that the number of Jewish deaths in the Nazi genocide has been exaggerated.

One reason that Ahmadinejad's ideas are so unrealistic is that he does not understand Israeli society. Of 7.2 million Israelis today, about 75 percent, or 5.5 million, are counted in the census as Jews. Some 20 percent, or 1.46 million, are Arabs, with three-quarters of them being Muslim. While Arab Israelis face discrimination, they are full citizens and have 12 members in the current Knesset, or parliament, which has 120 seats. About 39 percent of the Jewish population, or 2.1 million, are Eastern Jews originally from Iberia or the Middle East.[18] Another million Israelis are Russians and Ukrainians who have largely come since the collapse of the Soviet Union in 1991; about half are widely thought not to have significant ties to a Jewish heritage or be Jewish at all (some 300,000 such non-Jewish "others" are listed in the 2008 census). From 2001 to 2003, some 50,000 of these mainly economic immigrants reemigrated.[19]

About 1.5 million Israelis are central and western European Jews of the sort who formed the core of the original Zionist movement in the first half of the twentieth century. Many of their families originally came to British Mandate of Palestine with the help of British policy;

Ahmadinejad appears to be thinking mainly of them when he speaks of Israelis. In recent years, thousands of refugees and guest workers have also come to Israel, but they do not have citizenship and are not counted in the 7.2 million.

Moreover, Israel's demography is changing rapidly. Jewish out-migration is significant, and there are between 400,000 and 900,000 Israelis outside the country, depending on whether the second generation is entered into the equation.[20] It is not clear whether these emigrants are still counted as being in Israel by the census bureau. Rates of conversion to Judaism of the secular or Christian economic immigrants from the former Soviet Union are low, and some proportion of the Russians may stay nonreligious or turn to the Eastern Orthodox Christianity of their ancestors.[21] (A Christian Arab originally from Jaffa told me in Tel Aviv in June 2008 that he had seen Russian congregants at his own church in Tel Aviv.) Because Arabs have higher population growth rates than Jews, they may well constitute a third of the population by 2030, making Israel even more multicultural than it is now.

The idea that Iran's cocky, diminutive president is about to change into khakis and lead a military attack on Israel is bizarre. Part of the reason Ahmadinejad's views on Arab-Israeli issues are mistakenly perceived as genocidal is due to the failure of corporate news in the United States. The American press almost never allows figures such as Ahmadinejad to speak on the air and in their own words, and the pundits who dissect statements such as his are more interested in scoring political points with domestic audiences than in explaining what the foreign leader actually meant by his words. CBS's *60 Minutes* cut from its interview with Ahmadinejad his extended explanations of his stance on Israel and Palestine, making him look more extreme than he is. Ironically, *Larry King Live,* an ostensibly entertainment-oriented interview program on CNN, has probably done the best job in presenting Ahmadinejad frankly and honestly on U.S. television, in September 2008.[22]

It is often said that Ahmadinejad is more dangerous because he is a millenarian; that is, he believes in the near advent of the messianic

Twelfth Imam, the promised one of the Shiites. But in fact, most millenarians are fatalists and are willing to wait passively for God's will to intervene in history. So, Ahmadinejad's belief in the near advent of the last days may actually make him less dangerous than a practical, hard-nosed secularist might be.

In an article for the *Wall Street Journal* in 2006, British Orientalist Bernard Lewis, an emeritus professor at Princeton, put forward the argument that Ahmadinejad's millenarian beliefs make mutual assured destruction inapplicable as a security doctrine, saying that for someone to be deterred by the threat of retaliation requires that he be a rational actor. Someone who believes that the world is about to end may not care so much about the possibility of a reprisal. Lewis asserted, without any evidence, that Iran had been working assiduously on a nuclear weapon for fifteen years, and he suggested that Ahmadinejad might deploy this weapon against Israel on August 22, 2006. That was the anniversary, in Muslim belief, of the Prophet Muhammad's miraculous night journey to visit heaven by way of Jerusalem. Lewis suggested that it would make a fitting date for Iran's nuking of Israel.[23] Lewis's beliefs about Iran are even more bizarre than Ahmadinejad's about Israel, but unfortunately he had the ear of the Bush administration. Of course, nothing came of his ridiculous prophecy, which said more about the irrational anxieties of Western ultra-Zionists than about Iranian political reality. In fact, a fifth of U.S. Christians expect to see the end of days during their lifetimes, and some prominent American politicians have held such beliefs. Thus, even if Lewis's argument has any validity, we should be more worried about Christian millenarian officeholders in the most powerful nation on earth than about a weak, relatively small Iran.

The clerical establishment in Iran deeply dislikes Ahmadinejad's belief that the hidden Twelfth Imam, the Messiah of the Shiites, will appear shortly. Some ayatollahs have mobilized to campaign against his election to a second term, on the grounds that he is a heretic.[24] The Speaker of the House in Iran, Ali Larijani, is reportedly furious at Ahmadinejad for his confrontational approach on the nuclear energy research program, and he resigned as chief negotiator with the Europeans in late 2007 for that reason.[25] That a parliament led by Larijani would allow Ahmadinejad to go to war for his strange theology is not plausible. Also a nonstarter is the idea that the Supreme Leader, Ali Khamenei, would make a military decision on the basis of the quirky little president's exotic ideas about the end of time.

Not only has Ahmadinejad not suggested annihilating civilian populations, he lacks the authority to do so. In the Iranian system, he is not the commander in chief of the armed forces. Supreme Jurisprudent Khamenei is the one who would decide on troop deployments and missile strikes, and he has pledged a policy of no first strike. And although Ahmadinejad is more popular than his predecessor, Khatami, with the aforementioned Iranian Revolutionary Guards Corps (IRGC), the country's national guard, which has a structure and history distinct from the regular army, he could not independently order the IRGC into action abroad. Khamenei would simply dismiss him if he overstepped his bounds. Ayatollah Khamenei appoints over five hundred key officials in the judiciary, the expediency council, and the military and security forces. He can dismiss the prime minister and the parliament at will. Ahmadinejad has direct influence only over the shape of his own cabinet and their ministries.

Khamenei's patience with Ahmadinejad's more weird and provocative statements and actions is said to have been stretched thin. It may be that he chose not to move against the president because Ahmadinejad's removal would weaken the hard-liners, and damage Khamenei's own prestige, given the hard-liners' earlier support for him. For American and European pundits to speak about Ahmadinejad as though he were in a position to launch a war or even independently set major policy is profoundly misleading.

But let us just imagine for a second that the image of the Islamic Republic as a praetorian regime with aggressive ambitions were true. It is not, but let us do a thought experiment. If Iran wanted to attack Israel, how could that even be accomplished? Iran does not have much of a tank corps, and it is separated from Israel by rugged territory in several countries, including some combination of Turkey, Iraq, Syria, or Jordan. Those countries would not allow an Iranian army through. Turkey is an ally of Israel. Jordan has a peace treaty with it. Iraq is now an American sphere of influence. Obviously, a conventional attack by the Iranian Army and IRGC is out of the question. Even if it were not,

Israeli fighter jets and missiles would reduce the Iranian armor to burned-out hulks in a matter of hours.

Iranian jets do not have the range to reach Israel, and Iran's fleet of fighters is small and old, with many planes dating from the days of the shah. Despite persistent rumors that it will purchase state-of-the-art fighters from Russia, there is no good evidence that it has done so. Iran does appear to have some missiles that might be able to reach Israel, though their range and accuracy are in question. The Iranian regime knows that it cannot attack Israel with missiles without killing Palestinian Arabs. Since Israel, according to former president Jimmy Carter, has 150 nuclear bombs, it would in any case be suicide for Iran to attack Israel militarily; Israel has the capability of incinerating Tehran, with 12 million residents in its metropolitan area, in retaliation. The scenario has no plausibility whatsoever if one does not accept the Islamophobic premise that Iranians by virtue of being Muslims are insane and undeterrable by mutually assured destruction.

The key judgments from the U.S. National Intelligence Estimate (NIE) on Iran, declassified in late 2007 stated, "We continue to assess with moderate-to-high confidence that Iran does not currently have a nuclear weapon." The estimate was that Iran had done some work toward a weapon before 2003 but had ceased early in that year. It added, "We assess with moderate confidence Tehran had not restarted its nuclear weapons program as of mid-2007."[26] It concluded that Iran backed off its exploratory program under international pressure and was therefore more susceptible to such pressure than had earlier been thought. The sense of international crisis over this issue is difficult to understand, since any serious breakthroughs seem likely to be distant. A previous U.S. NIE, issued in 2005, concluded that even if the regime had been trying to develop nuclear weapons, and if the international environment had been conducive to that quest (that is, Tehran could freely import the needed materiel), it would still take Iran at least ten years to get there.[27]

Some Republican politicians, visibly disappointed at losing a bogeyman with which to scare the American people, declared, undeterred, that the NIE changed nothing. They appear determined to go on marking Iran as a source of anxiety and danger for the U.S. public, in the face of all evidence to the contrary, and to plan for a war on that country that would be truly catastrophic for American interests. Washington politicians continue to accuse the regime of attempting to acquire the bomb, and both major candidates in the 2008 presidential campaign pledged to prevent Tehran from going nuclear.

In June 2008, Barack Obama told the annual convention of the American Israel Public Affairs Committee, "The danger from Iran is grave, it is real, and my goal will be to eliminate this threat. I will do everything in my power to prevent Iran from obtaining a nuclear weapon—everything."[28] At the same conference, John McCain said, "Tehran's continued pursuit of nuclear weapons poses an unacceptable risk, a danger we cannot allow." He explained his reasoning: "Emboldened by nuclear weapons, Iran would feel free to sponsor terrorist attacks against any perceived enemy."[29] These American leaders were committing themselves to deploy enormous resources to combat a threat that the NIE had already determined, in the fall of 2007, did not exist.

So what are the Iranians doing that causes so much anxiety? They are seeking to enrich uranium 235 to low levels for the purpose of creating fuel for civilian nuclear reactors. Article IV, paragraph one, of the Non-Proliferation Treaty, first signed in 1968, specifies that "Nothing in this Treaty shall be interpreted as affecting the inalienable right of all the Parties to the Treaty to develop research, production and use of nuclear energy for peaceful purposes without discrimination." The Iranians maintain that they are in complete conformity with the treaty and that the United States, in demanding that they stop their attempt to enrich uranium to fuel peaceful nuclear reactors, is attempting to abrogate Article IV retroactively and unilaterally.

In a major policy speech in June 2006, Supreme Jurisprudent Ali Khamenei called the American assertion that Iran seeks a nuclear bomb "a sheer lie." He affirmed, "We consider using nuclear weapons against Islamic rules. We have announced this openly." Khamenei was instancing the chivalric law of Islamic warfare, wherein jurists had forbidden the killing of innocent noncombatants such as women, children, and unarmed men. Since a nuclear bomb dropped on a contemporary city would inevitably annihilate hundreds of thousands or millions of innocents, he was saying, it cannot be used by an Islamic state that has any regard for Islamic law. Further, he said, a nuclear weapons program is extremely expensive, and he could not justify imposing that expense on the Iranian people, since there were no policy purposes for which Iran would find such a weapon useful. He concluded, "We do not need those weapons."[30] Khamenei pledged no first strike with conventional weapons against Iran's enemies, saying "We will never start a war. We have no intention of going to war with any government." At the very end of his speech, he did say that if it were wantonly attacked, Iran would strike back and "the energy flow through this region will be seriously in danger." Typical American reporting on the address ignored the pledge of no first strike and headlined Khamenei's threat of reprisals, making it look as though he gave a belligerent speech.

Khamenei's conviction that nuclear weapons are contrary to Islamic principle is shared by three-fifths of Iranians. In a spring 2008 opinion poll, less than one-quarter of Iranians felt that the two could be reconciled. Only 10 percent of Iranians said that the country should withdraw from the Nuclear Non-Proliferation Treaty (NPT), which forbids development of nuclear warheads. Another three-fifths of Iranians favored making a deal with the UN Security Council about the nuclear program, whereby the International Atomic Energy Agency would have full access to all the Iranian facilities.[31]

President Ahmadinejad has not challenged Khamenei's pledge of no first strike. Again, the president in Iran is relatively powerless, does not control policy on security and energy issues, and serves at the pleasure of the Supreme Jurisprudent. Still, since the Western press has focused on the president, it is important to note that he speaks just as Khamenei does on the issues of war and peace. He said in a 2006 speech, "Iran is not a threat to any country, and is not in any way a people of intimidation and aggression." He insisted, "Weapons research is in no way part of Iran's program."[32]

In September 2007, when he addressed the UN General Assembly, Ahmadinejad again asserted that Iran's nuclear research program is "completely peaceful and transparent."[33] Far from threatening to develop nukes and then use them against Israel, the strategy of which he stands accused by his critics, Ahmadinejad explicitly said, "Even with regard to the Zionist regime, our path to a solution is elections."

Of course, the Iranian leaders may be lying when they condemn the atom bomb as satanic and insist they want nothing to do with it. But to make honest policy, American and European politicians must at least acknowledge the disavowals of Tehran on this matter. In March 2008, George W. Bush asserted of Iran's leaders that they have "declared they want a nuclear weapon to destroy people."[34] It is embarrassing that the press had to correct the former leader of the Free World on his facts even as they reported his false allegation.

In his 2006 speech, Khamenei was reaffirming the ruling of his predecessor, Imam Ruhollah Khomeini, who had shut down Iran's nuclear research program in the 1980s, calling it the work of the devil. In the 1960s and 1970s, Washington had actively urged Mohammad Reza Shah, Iran's monarch, to develop nuclear technology. The Ford administration produced a memo saying that the shah's regime, a key cold war ally, must "prepare against the time—about 15 years in the future—when Iranian oil production is expected to decline sharply."[35] Iran's petroleum reserves are extensive, so that fear was misplaced. But Iran already uses domestically 2 million of the 4 million barrels a day it produces, and it could well cease being an exporter and even become a net importer in the relatively near future. Ford authorized a plutonium reprocessing plant for Iran, which could have allowed it to close the fuel cycle, a step toward producing a bomb.

In the 1970s, General Electric and Westinghouse won contracts to build eight nuclear reactors in Iran. The shah intimated that Iran would seek nuclear weapons, without facing any adverse consequences beyond some reprimands from the United States or Western Europe.[36] In contrast, Khomeini was horrified by the idea of using weapons of mass destruction, and he declined to deploy chemical weapons at the front in the Iran-Iraq War of the 1980s, even though Saddam had no such compunctions and extensively used mustard gas and sarin on Iranian troops. While it is easy to dismiss the ethical concerns of ayatollahs as irrelevant to policy making and to see them as a dishonest cover for nefarious designs, when discussing a theocracy there is at least some reason to take such religious motivations for policy seriously.

The Ford administration memo from the 1970s on Iran's need for nuclear energy as a backup for its petroleum reserves explains why Iran is pursuing a civilian nuclear research program that alarms the rest of the world. Ayatollah Khamenei explained in his 2006 address, "To say that no country has the right to have access to nuclear technology means that in twenty years' time, all of the countries of the world will have to beg certain Western or European countries to meet their energy demands." That is, Khamenei views the sophisticated nuclear power plant infrastructure in France, Russia, and the United States as the future of energy, and fears that if his country does not develop its own plants and close the fuel cycle so as to be able to produce its own fuel, Iran will be drawn into dependence on Western technology for its future energy needs. In an ironic turn of phrase with which people in the Americas and Europe surely can empathize, he complained that once Iran's oil is gone, it and countries in a similar position "will have to beg for energy in order to run their lives. Which country, nation, or honest official is ready to take that?" I argued earlier in this book that nuclear energy cannot in fact resolve the global energy crisis, but since Iran has its own uranium supplies, it would not be irrational for it to build some nuclear power plants to enable it to extend the life of its lucrative petroleum exports.

Iran's thirst for independence, political and technological, goes far beyond that of the other Gulf oil states. This impulse can be explained by its modern history of being dominated by Britain, Russia, and the United States.[37] In the nineteenth century, Britain established hegemony over southern Iran, reaching up from its Indian empire and from the Gulf, where it had naval supremacy. At the same time, Russia, moving into the Caucasus and later into Central Asia, exercised profound influence in Iran's north. The British and Russian empires were engaged in a hard-fought struggle for supremacy in Asia, known as the Great Game. Their colonial administrators feared what might happen if the two empires came to share a common border. In order to avoid a potentially debilitating conventional war, the minions of St. Petersburg and London sought buffer zones. Iran and Afghanistan were therefore kept neutral, or at least the interiors of the countries were.

For the same reason, Russian and British diplomats forbade Iran to build a railroad in the nineteenth century, since each empire feared that Iranian trains could be commandeered by the other for troop transport. That is, a railroad network would in essence destroy the value of Iran as a buffer state between the colonial possessions of London and St. Petersburg. Iran desperately needed a railroad, however, since, as noted, it is a large (four times the size of France) country of desert, steppe, and mountain ranges and lacks much in the way of rivers for transport. In other countries, such as Egypt and India, nineteenth-century railroads served as economic "multipliers," accelerating the circulation of goods, people, and money that added to prosperity. Iran was denied that benefit by Anglo-Russian imperial rivalry. Educated Iranians still chafe at the idea that imperial powers want to go on denying them key technology and its economic benefits.

In 1907, Russia and Britain formally partitioned Iran into zones of influence, leaving the shah with complete sovereignty only over a strip of the interior. From 1905 to1911, Iranians staged a Constitutional Revolution against their absolute monarch, Muzaffar al-Din Shah of the Qajar dynasty, and against his son, Muhammad Ali Shah. Despite the support given the shah by his British and Russian patrons, the Iranian people won a constitution and the right to elect a parliament in 1906. In 1908, Muhammad Ali Shah, regretting his father's surrender of royal prerogatives, prorogued parliament and suspended the constitution. A citizens' militia rose up, especially in the cosmopolitan northern entrepôt city of Tabriz, marched on the capital, and deposed him. Iran remained a constitutional monarchy until 1925.

In the wake of the revolution, Iranians were dismayed to discover that parliamentarians could be bribed and pressured by the Russians and British just as easily as the shah had been when he was absolute monarch. The Iranian quest for independence was repeatedly foiled by imperial interventions. In 1910, the British Royal Navy adopted petroleum as the chief means to power its ships, replacing coal. Thus the British government became extremely interested in Iranian petroleum, which had been discovered by a British concern in 1908. London and St. Petersburg were still competing for influence in Iran, however. In the late teens, the newly established Soviet Union inspired peasant guerrilla revolts in the north of Iran. A soviet was even declared at Rasht. Alarmed, and with one eye on the precious oil fields of Abadan, the British armed and funded a strongman, Colonel Reza Khan, who defeated the pro-Soviet Iranian leftists. In 1925, he deposed the last Qajar dynast and declared himself Reza Shah Pahlevi, "the Great." Reza Shah banned labor unions and disallowed socialist and communist parties. He usurped large amounts of land and built up the army as a power base. He reduced the parliament to a debating society that never dared defy him. In 1934, he signed a deal with the Anglo-Persian Oil Company that paid Iran a small stipend for its oil rather than a share of profits.

In 1941, Britain deposed Reza Shah, suspecting him of Axis sympathies. The United Kingdom joined with the United States and the Soviet Union in placing his shy young son, Mohammad Reza Pahlevi, then eighteen, on the Peacock Throne. They jointly occupied Iran, using it to provision the Soviet Union from the south. The Americans reformed the Iranian finance ministry, and Norman Schwarzkopf of the New Jersey police helped train a modern police force. The weak young shah, his country militarily occupied, was in no position to stop the reemergence of a lively parliamentary and intellectual life.

In the late 1940s, a strong nationalist trend emerged in the Iranian parliament as a reaction against foreign dominance. Iranians complained that the Anglo-Iranian Oil Company (AIOC) was not sharing profits on Iranian petroleum with Iran equitably. Parliament pressed for a revision of the 1934 agreement. The AIOC absolutely refused to entertain this demand. In 1951, exasperated, the MPs simply nationalized Iranian oil. They then elected Mohammad Mosaddegh, a patrician from an old aristocratic family, prime minister. Britain and the United States organized a global boycott of Iran in response. Mosaddegh looked around for domestic political allies and found that, in addition to the secular nationalists, he could get support from Shiite fundamentalists led by Ayatollah Kashani and from the Tudeh Party (the

Iranian Communist Party, but the Pahlevis forbade it to call itself that). His willingness to accept support from the Tudeh, however, caused the Eisenhower administration to view him as a "pinko," that is, as leaning toward the Soviet Union. Mosaddegh was in fact just a liberal nationalist and was acting as the prime minister of a democratically elected parliament. He came into increasing conflict with the shah, who fled into exile in Italy.

The boycott of Iranian petroleum orchestrated by the British and U.S. governments and the oil majors sent the Iranian economy into a tailspin. By 1953, it was relatively easy for the CIA to buy some crowds, network with some generals, and stage a coup against Mosaddegh, who was overthrown and placed under house arrest. Over five decades later, in 2006, the Bush administration asked Congress to appropriate $75 million for democracy-promotion programs in Iran. Congress responded by funding them at a slightly lesser level of $66.1 million.[38] That is, the U.S. government opined that its dearest wish for Iran was the establishment of a parliamentary democracy, just like the one the Eisenhower administration had overthrown.

The United States put the shah back on the throne in 1953, helped train his secret police, and enabled one of the more repressive capitalist dictatorships in modern history. The shah became more and more megalomaniacal, favoring gaudy costumes that would have put a Las Vegas lounge lizard to shame. He built up a coterie of billionaire cronies, while millions of villagers, unable to get government loans for their small farms, were forced to migrate as day laborers to squalid urban slums. A massive apparatus of domestic spying and surveillance filled the shah's jails with prisoners of conscience. The shah began assaulting, in the name of secular nationalism and the monarchy, key symbols of Islam, including the calendar.

By the mid-1950s, Britain and the United States had put the Pahlevis on the throne three times and had summarily deposed a shah once. As late as 1966, when Mohammad Reza Shah started complaining that Iran was not receiving a fair shake in the petroleum sector, American ambassador Armin H. Meyer immediately reminded him of what happened to Mosaddegh: "I said, that Consortium treating Iran very well. Saying it not necessary to make speeches re what happened in 1951, I noted Iran would probably be even better off today had it not on that occasion fomented confrontation with oil companies."[39]

The shah recognized Meyer's implicit threat and backed off, pledging that there would be no similar "impasse" this time. In reaction to Meyer's report, British and American diplomats met in 1966 about whether they might wish to replace the shah if he got too big for his britches. In the end, at that meeting in Washington, D.C., U.K. diplomat "Mr. [Willie] Morris, in considering US and UK strategic interests in Iran, saw no persuasive alternative to the present regime."[40] Morris and the others could not have come to this conclusion unless they had already considered and rejected the possibility of another CIA coup.

Iranians had long grown tired of having their government and economic policies dictated to them by foreigners, for the benefit of foreigners. They had rebelled in 1905 and again in 1951, only to have their hope for autonomy and freedom crushed. In the 1970s, a new nativist rebellion was taking root. Ali Khamenei became a revolutionary as a young man and helped Ruhollah Khomeini overthrow the shah in 1979. His generation of Iranians saw Mohammad Reza Shah as a mere American puppet who squandered Iran's oil wealth on American weapons and contractors. Khamenei's generation of Iranians remembers very well what it is like to be subordinated firmly to the great Western powers and their corporations, and they see the attempt to deny Iran its right to develop peaceful nuclear energy as a means of returning them to the status of virtual slaves.

International suspicions of Iran's nuclear intentions, however, are also understandable. Despite being a signatory to the NPT, Iran in the past was not always forthcoming in fulfilling its obligations under the treaty. In late 2002, the world was surprised to discover that Iran was far more advanced in its nuclear research than anyone had known. Either the Israelis or the dissident Mojahedin-e Khalq organization (to which Saddam had given a base in Iraq) had gained effective intelligence on the Iranian facilities and experiments at Natanz near Isfahan and blown the whistle. Iran had been obliged to inform the International

Atomic Energy Agency (IAEA) of its "intention" to enrich uranium, but had not done so. President Khatami confirmed the findings of the spy reports in February 2003.

With the revelations of its program ricocheting through European capitals, the Iranian leadership moved aggressively to shut down those experiments, apparently fearful that the Europeans would otherwise join the United States in imposing severe sanctions.[41] The Iranians also likely had been interested in a nuclear weapon in part to counter Saddam's alleged program, but it was clear by the spring of 2003 that his government was living on borrowed time and that the unconventional weapons threat to Iran was over. It is not sure that the illicit weapons-related experiments had been cleared with Khamenei, which could help explain the alacrity with which they were discontinued when they became public, given the Supreme Leader's stated opposition to such armaments as un-Islamic.

Of course, two other possibilities present themselves. One is that Khamenei came by his conviction that nuclear weapons are impermissible only after 2002. Another is that he is lying when he says he is opposed to the atom bomb as un-Islamic. The latter possibility, while it cannot be discounted altogether, is unlikely—if such hypocrisy became known and acknowledged among Iranian Shiites, it would entirely destroy his authority as a theocratic leader.

Four years after the initial revelations about Iran's nuclear program, British intelligence intercepted the telephone call of an Iranian hard-liner talking to another official, who complained bitterly that for some years no experiments with weapons implications had been performed.[42] The CIA also ran a program for defectors from Iran who had been involved in the nuclear program, some of whom brought out documents in 2007 showing that the nuclear research effort was being conducted solely as a civilian energy program.[43] Still, the use of centrifuges for enrichment raises suspicion. That technique is not the best one for creating fuel (though it can serve that purpose), but was used successfully by Pakistan at its Kahuta plant to create a bomb. Centrifuges are also open-ended as a technique for enrichment, since the uranium can be fed back through them and whirled around with hexafluoride gas until it is highly enriched enough to be fissionable.

That mere possibility is hardly a cause for panic, however. As long as there are no secret facilities, and as long as the existing facilities continue to allow inspections by the IAEA, any highly enriched uranium could be detected. So far Iran has allowed such regular inspections. The IAEA cannot find any evidence of Iranian noncompliance with NPT protocols during the past five years but remains frustrated that Iranian authorities have not been completely forthcoming in a way that would allay all doubts about their intentions. This frustration is often misinterpreted by American hawks as positive evidence of Iranian noncompliance with the inspection regime.

Better access to the some 2,500 Iranian scientists involved in the project, and especially to the engineers doing centrifuge design and construction, would help establish more trust. In and of themselves, the sorts of research facilities maintained by the Iranians are common in industrialized countries, and the nuclear labs of the Netherlands also use centrifuges that in theory could be used for proliferation. Were Iran to withdraw from the NPT and cancel inspections, it might precipitate hostilities. The issue is trust and transparency rather than purely one of technology, so that is where the solutions lie.

An important contributor to anxiety around Iran's civilian nuclear research program and to Islam Anxiety in general is the harsh discourse about Israel in the speeches of Ahmadinejad and many other Iranian leaders. The Khomeinist revolutionary tradition has a hostile rhetoric about Israel that is not, however, always matched by policy. Ruhollah Khomeini, having helped overthrow the shah in 1979 and come to power as theocrat in chief, put forward some basic ideological principles to guide Iran. The first was rule by high clerics in accordance with medieval canons of Islamic law. Government was to be run for the benefit of the people, including the barefoot, and so had a strongly populist cast, with state ownership of banks and large industries. This populism and nativism went hand in hand with anti-imperialism, a distrust of the great Western powers, and a discomfort with direct foreign investment in the Iranian economy.

Khomeini distrusted the state of Israel, the preconditions for which had been created in Palestine by the British Empire and the establishment of which had ethnically cleansed hundreds of thousands of Palestinians. Israel had been a firm ally of the United States and of the shah.

In one of his speeches in the 1980s, as noted, Khomeini expressed the sentiment that "this Occupation regime over Jerusalem must vanish from the arena of time."[44] Khomeini and other pious Shiite activists had been able more or less to wish away the shah's repressive regime. The remarkable revolution of 1979 involved many techniques of popular opposition, but none was more impressive than the revolutionaries' ability to put a million protesters in the streets of Tehran, paralyzing the capital and presenting an impossible challenge to the shah's military.[45] Even the hard-line generals could not take a million people out and have them shot, and their own soldiers increasingly became unwilling to fire on unarmed protesters. Unable to keep order, and clearly unpopular, the shah ultimately went into exile. Khomeini was urging a similar model of resistance upon the Palestinians, encouraging them to wish away the Israeli regime.

For reasons that are understandable, given the Nazi destruction of the vast majority of European Jews, Israelis and Western Zionists often view sentiments such as those expressed by Khomeini as a dire existential threat, especially since the phrase was mistranslated as "Israel must be wiped off the face of the map."

Yet Iran under Khomeini not only did not attack Israel, it made an alliance with the Zionist state. In the early 1980s, Khomeini supplied Israel with petroleum in return for American spare parts for the American-supplied Iranian arsenal.[46] Iran and Israel had a tacit alliance against the Saddam regime during the first phase of the Iran-Iraq War of 1980 to 1988.

Israeli and Iranian go-betweens tempted Ronald Reagan into the Iran-Contra scandal, whereby the American president stole war materiel such as TOW antitank weapons from Pentagon storehouses and sold them to Khomeini's Iran (designated by the United States as a terrorist state that should be boycotted). In return, Iran used its good offices to persuade Shiite radicals in Lebanon to release U.S.

hostages. Reagan used the Iranian black money, deposited in secret bank accounts, to support right-wing guerrillas trying to overthrow the government of Nicaragua in defiance of the Boland Amendment, through which Congress had forbidden U.S. government funding for that purpose.

For all Khomeini's rhetoric against Israel and the United States, his government behaved in a pragmatic way, doing a lot of business with both. He never acted on his wish for the Israeli regime to collapse, and, indeed, he helped prop it up. Iran has become less ideological since the 1980s; the idea that it is more rigid and less willing to compromise now than then is an unlikely one.

Iranian support for Hizbullah and Hamas is certainly a fact and a legitimate concern for the North Atlantic states and their allies. In Europe, the Middle East, and much of the rest of the world, that support is deemed less important, and less illegitimate, however, than it may seem in Washington and New York.

Hizbullah in southern Lebanon is a political party that contests elections against rivals, and over time it has won substantial popularity among Shiites. It has Maronite Catholic political allies; sits in parliament, currently holding 14 out of 128 seats; and its Shiite ally, the Amal Party, has another 14 seats. The Lebanese population is on the order of 4 million, and something like 1.8 million of them are Shiites. Most Shiites support Hizbullah. Many Shiites of a secular bent vote Hizbullah even though they do not share its fundamentalist precepts, because it represents their material and political interests ably. The party formed part of national unity governments in 2005 and 2008, with cabinet ministries under its control. In the underdeveloped south of Lebanon, it runs many clinics and offers community services. To see the party as merely a terrorist organization is to ignore its major role in Lebanese national politics. In fact, the European Union has declined to designate it as a terrorist organization.[47]

The fears about terrorism derive from Hizbullah's maintenance of a small paramilitary of about five thousand fighters. The government in Beirut did not demand that Hezbollah disarm at the time of the 1989 Ta'if Accords that ended the civil war, implicitly accepting the paramilitary's deployment of roadside bombs and other guerrilla techniques to end the illegal Israeli occupation of south Lebanon, which lasted from 1982 to 2000.

The Israelis invaded Lebanon in 1978 and again in 1982, then stayed, as part of their struggle against the Palestine Liberation Organization and other Palestinian refugee groups mounting guerrilla attacks on Israel from Lebanese territory. Israeli leaders' decision to continue the occupation in the 1990s raised fears in Lebanon that Israel sought a permanent annexation of Lebanese territory. Before the Israeli invasion and occupation, many Lebanese Shiites had been relatively pro-Israeli, and the community had not been very politically mobilized. Lebanese Shiites in conflict with Palestinians even garlanded Israeli tank turrets at the beginning of the 1982 invasion. But the long Israeli occupation of south Lebanon squandered that goodwill and created a clever and dogged enemy.

In 1983, radical Shiites of Husayn al-Musawi's Islamic Amal splinter group bombed the U.S. embassy in Beirut, killing 63 persons. Later that year, they used a truck bomb to kill 241 marines who had come as a peacekeeping force to Beirut in the wake of the Israeli invasion. In 1984, Islamic Amal was absorbed by the newly established Hizbullah organization, which had earlier been more of a clique, formed under the influence of Iran and of the radical Shiite Da'wa (Islamic Mission) Party of Iraq. In 1985, Imad Mughniyah, who was alleged to have been a senior intelligence officer in Hizbullah, was among the hijackers of TWA Flight 847. (The plane was made to shuttle between airports in Beirut and Algiers, and a passenger on board, a U.S. navy diver, was killed.) Long involved in pro-Palestinian activism, Mughniyah had been further radicalized by a bombing earlier that year. That attack, allegedly backed by the CIA, was aimed at killing Ayatollah Muhammad Husayn Fadlallah (tagged as Hizbullah's spiritual guide, a charge he denied), but missed its target and killed 80 others, including friends of Mughniyah, who was Fadlallah's bodyguard. Mughniyah was later accused of being involved in the horrific bombing of a synagogue in Buenos Aires in 1992.

It is unarguable that Hizbullah had a terrorist phase in the 1980s through the early 1990s, but since then it has evolved into a Lebanon-centered parliamentary and militia force. It maintains that its guards-men are still needed to confront continued Israeli territorial aggression at the border with Lebanon and to recover from Israel the occupied Shebaa Farms. That territory, conquered by Israel in 1967, had largely been owned by Lebanese farmers and had been disputed between Syria and Lebanon. Syria, however, relinquished its claim in favor of Lebanon in May 2008.[48] Beirut demands its return under the UN Charter, which forbids member states from acquiring the territory of their neighbors through military force. This provision was intended to forestall any repeat of the abuses that occurred in the 1930s and 1940s in Europe and Asia.

In August 2008, the Lebanese government formalized its relationship to Hizbullah's paramilitary, recognizing its contributions to fighting continued Israeli occupation of Lebanese territory and affirming "the right of Lebanon, its people, its army and its resistance to liberate its land in the Shebaa Farms, Kfarshuba Hill and Ghajar." The phrase "its resistance" refers to Hizbullah. In return, the cabinet manifesto underlined that "the unity and the authority of the state would be the guiding principle of all government decisions and actions"—that is, that Hizbullah would not unilaterally drag the country into any wars.[49]

In March 2002, the U.S. State Department listed Hizbullah as a terrorist organization. But since about 1998, the party has done little or nothing that would qualify as international terrorism. In 1992, it came under new leadership, that of Hasan Nasrallah. The violence it deployed against Israeli occupation forces is not considered terrorism in international law, but rather a form of national liberation struggle. Hizbullah has attacked Israeli troops in the disputed Shebaa Farms territory, but said it did so as an agent of the Lebanese people, who have no peace treaty with Israel and who have continued territorial disputes with it. Hizbullah has fired mortars into the Shebaa Farms, killing some civilian Israeli colonists there—which is a war crime if the civilians are specifically targeted. Hizbullah's spokesmen maintain that they are aiming at military facilities and personnel. Since the party is now a formal agent of the Lebanese state, it does not conform, with regard to its border conflict with Israel, to the technical definition of a terrorist organization.

Iran provisions Hizbullah with katyusha and other small rockets—which were used against Israel in self-defense when Israel launched a war against Lebanon in the summer of 2006—but insofar as the Hizbullah guardsmen are an arm of the Lebanese state, Iran's provision of arms and training to them is not obviously illegal. Israel launched the war in reprisal against the killing of Israeli troops by Hizbullah, but critics considered this Israeli response, which involved bombing Beirut, Jounieh, Tripoli, and other cities much to the north, where Hizbullah was not in control, to be vastly disproportionate to the provocation. Hizbullah maintains that the troops were in the Shebaa Farms and therefore illegally on Lebanese territory. Its small rockets, Iranian supplied or not, can be used effectively only for harassment or as a defensive weapon, deterring Israeli bombing campaigns. Were Hizbullah suddenly to launch a barrage of rockets aggressively, it would meet with a crushing Israeli military response. Hizbullah is unlikely to risk it.

Despite the conviction in Washington, D.C., that Lebanon is becoming an Iranian outpost, the reality is more complex. The Levantine country is a playground for oil-rich governments and investors. Smaller than Connecticut, and with a population of only about 4 million, it is uneasily wedged between Israel and Syria. Its employed workers are mainly in the financial services and tourism sectors (three-fourths of the labor force), while nearly a fifth work in industry and only 5 percent still farm. A fifth of Lebanon's population is unemployed, and over a fourth lives below the poverty line. Its major city, Beirut, consists of boxy white towers crowding the edge of the indigo Mediterranean and extending up rolling hills. In times of political calm, Beirut hosts summer music festivals for European youth and pilgrims from nearby puritanical societies seeking the profane shrines of nightclubs and casinos. Smart hotels and fashionable shopping districts lace through a city reeling from the negative effects of wars and bombings.

Lebanon's sectarian and ethnic divides, between Christian and Muslim, Sunni and Shiite, Armenian and Palestinian, do not produce polarization so much as kaleidoscopic alliances and feuds that shift with head-spinning alacrity; they often pit members of the same group against one another. A little less than a century ago, Lebanon was a majority Christian society carved out of Syria by French colonial masters. Today its population is probably only 30 percent Christian. Among the Muslim majority, the fastest-growing group is the Shiites, who are also the poorest community. Good statistics on Lebanon's population are not easy to come by, but my own estimate is that Lebanon is now 45 percent Shiite and that in twenty years it will likely be a majority Shiite society.

Despite their political support for Hizbullah, Lebanese Shiites should not be assumed to share its puritanical attitudes. Many Shiite young women are every bit as chic and oriented toward Paris fashion as their Maronite Catholic peers, and cosmopolitan Shiite families often have outposts in Brazil or West Africa. One of the more scandalous video music stars in Beirut, known for her baby face and steamy dance moves, is Haifa Wahbi, whose father is a Shiite. In December 2007, I flew to Lebanon to give a talk at the American University of Beirut. On my trip I had a conversation with a Shiite graduate student from the village of Qana in the south, who was studying comparative literature at Lebanese American University and enjoying Arundhati Roy's *God of Small Things*—an Indian novel about a star-crossed romance that transgresses caste taboos.

In 2006, the Pew Charitable Trust's Global Values Project released the results of a poll showing that nearly half of Lebanese Muslims are secular in outlook. It concluded, "Although Lebanese Muslims consider Islam an important part of their lives, they place less emphasis on their faith than do Muslims elsewhere."[50] Only 54 percent of Lebanese Muslims said that "religion is very important." In societies such as Pakistan and Morocco, over 90 percent of respondents assent to this sentiment. Likewise, less than a third of Lebanese Muslims say they think of themselves first as Muslims and only secondarily as Lebanese. An equal number openly assert that being Lebanese is more important to them than their religious identity. Fully 86 percent of Lebanese Muslims have a favorable view of Christians (which is natural since they have far more Christian neighbors and friends than Muslims in most other countries in the region).

Nevertheless, the U.S. mass media cannot mention the word "Hizbullah" without showing stock footage of its small paramilitary marching in ski masks. Former president George W. Bush denounced the movement as a form of "Islamic fascism." But it is obvious, as noted earlier, that large numbers of Lebanese Shiites who vote for Hizbullah are not very religious and that they back the party for secular reasons. Likewise, they may take money from Iran, but they are mostly uninterested in Khomeinist puritanism, at least for now.

During my 2007 trip, I spoke on a Tuesday afternoon at the university, and Wednesday was a Muslim holy day, so I had it free. My host, the geographer Patrick McGreevy, and his wife, Betsy, kindly took me on a whirlwind afternoon tour of Shiite areas south of the capital. McGreevy, who sports a shock of gray hair, a salt-and-pepper mustache, and a chic black wardrobe, heads the university's innovative Center for American Studies and Research, endowed by Saudi billionaire al-Walid bin Talal to promote knowledge of the United States in the Arab world. McGreevy and his wife had bravely stayed in Beirut during the 2006 war to show their devotion to their new home, unlike most foreign residents of the capital and unlike a lot of middle-class Beirutis, who headed for Syria.

On July 23, 2006, McGreevy circulated to friends a poignant meditation on how the war affected the Shiite slums and rural south far more deeply than it did swanky Ras Beirut, referring to that part of the capital as the uppermost, least uncomfortable ring of hell. He described how some 50,000 refugees had streamed into the port of Sidon. The far south, from which many of the refugees came, was the lowest rung of hell, an inferno of exploding munitions and villagers set on the road by horror. At the end of that war, in its last three days, the Israelis dropped a million cluster bombs on south Lebanon, an act that had no legitimate military purpose but rather was designed to discourage Shiite villagers from returning to their homes. The ploy failed, but the cluster bombs did kill civilians, including children. It was a war crime, since the bombs were clearly intended to harm civilians.

A year and a half later, as we headed through Beirut on our one-hour journey to Tyre, we could see to the west, along the seashore, massive piles of rubble that bulldozers had cleared from the slums of south Beirut (the Dahiya quarter). Those residential neighborhoods had been so heavily bombed by the Israelis during the summer war that the damage was visible even from outer space. Entire city blocks began to look vacant in satellite photographs. The Hizbullah offices were the primary Israeli targets here, but these administrative centers were located in the midst of crowded civilian tenements.

The intensive Israeli bombing campaign inflicted $3.6 billion in infrastructural damage and killed as many as 1,100 persons, most of them civilians. Hundreds of thousands of Shiites huddled in schools and other public buildings, having fled their homes in the south. A cruel joke circulated in Beirut during the war that asked which was the best-educated sect in Lebanon. The answer? The Shiites, because they live in schools 24/7.

Hizbullah's impressive emergency fund, to which Iran is said to have contributed, allowed it to give out food and other aid to Shiites displaced by the war. Afterward, some of the rebuilding of south Beirut was carried out by Hizbullah's Holy War for Reconstruction, which receives funding from Iran as well as from Qatar and the United Arab Emirates. One engineer working with the organization, Yasser al-Hajj, boasted to an American reporter, "We are going to rebuild Dahiya before you [Americans] rebuild New Orleans from Katrina."[51] On the road through the southern suburbs, I saw wooden posts placed in highway islands that bore images of the Iranian flag.

A pan-Arab London daily alleged recently that Iran gives Hizbullah $400 million a year and that, in the eighteen months ending in December 2007, Tehran had transferred $1.5 billion extra to the Shiite party to help with war and reconstruction costs.[52] The first estimate is at the higher range of what U.S. diplomatic sources have asserted to the press, suggesting that Iran has been sending $20 million to $40 million a month to Hizbullah. Others say that these estimates are too high, though no one denies that Iranian money comes into Lebanon. Some of the donations pay for the katyusha rockets that Hizbullah uses to deter another Israeli attack. But much of the funding is used to provide hospital care and other services.

Iran has to compete with many other forces in Lebanon, however, and its role is sometimes exaggerated. A Lebanese scholar who worked on reconstruction told me that, in south Beirut, "the initial rubble removal was funded by different agencies," including, she said, the United Nations Development Programme and the Lebanese Ministry of Public Works. She also noted that "the Iranian government pledged some money for the rehabilitation of gardens (which they have done, so you see the flag plastered across these areas with notes of thanks)."

She explained that Lebanese Shiites were given compensation funds by the government, which many invested in the Hizbullah real estate cooperative "in return for which they will get housing in the complex once it is built." Since the Lebanese government received grants to replace housing from many donors, including Sunni oil monarchies such as Saudi Arabia, Qatar, and Kuwait, as well as from Europe and Japan, persuading Shiite families to donate their compensation to a Hizbullah cooperative is a clever way for the organization to take credit for the philanthropy of others. Another aid worker observed to me that, despite their designation as nongovernmental organizations, the "Iranian NGOs in southern Beirut are connected to Iranian government." He cautioned, "What sucks about the Iranian funds that go to Hezzies [Hizbullah] is that they mainly help Hezzie supporters."

If Tyre is Hizbullah territory, the nearby port of Sidon is largely Sunni, dominated by the Muslim Brotherhood, probably with Saudi encouragement and funding. Saudi Arabia typically supports the Sunni prime minister of Lebanon, and during the 2006 Israel-Lebanon War, King Abdullah deposited $1 billion in Beirut's central bank as a way of shoring up the Lebanese pound. In 2007, the kingdom pledged another $1 billion in reconstruction aid.

Although Tyre had been repeatedly bombed by the Israelis during the war, only a year and a half later there was no obvious sign of the damage. Among the reasons for the rapidity of the reconstruction was the influx of foreign aid, including that from Iran. David Harbin, an aid worker helping with the clearing of Israeli cluster bombs in the south, observed of the Iranians, "I know that they've been rebuilding some rural roads in south Lebanon." These projects included widening two-lane roads to four lanes. A colleague of his was more emphatic: "Man . . . Iran is all over the south! They fund Hizbullah pretty heavily." He added, "The mayor of Khiam," a village in the south, "is the director of the Khomeini Institute, which also funds pretty cool programs such as schools and orphanages."

Khiam village is only about three miles from the Israeli border. Heavily Shiite, it was part of the territory Israel occupied in south Lebanon between 1982 and 2000. It was the site of a fierce battle between Israeli troops and Hizbullah's paramilitary in July 2006. Khiam maintains a Web site where it posts village news and events, including wedding pictures. It also proudly announces foreign aid from Saudi Arabia, Qatar, Kuwait, and Iran for the postwar reconstruction of the south, of the city of Baalbek in the Biqa' Valley, and of Dahiya in Beirut. It reprinted a late 2007 article from a major Beirut newspaper, which reported that the Iranian Committee to Reconstruct Lebanon has funded over 1,500 projects that are under way or completed, including repair of 22 main roads and 666 rural ones, 20 main bridges, 164 schools, 69 "mosques and churches," and 67 municipal buildings.[53]

Early in 2007, the English-language *Daily Star* reported that the Iranian Committee to Reconstruct Lebanon had pledged to rebuild eight bridges destroyed by Israeli bombers. Abbas Harb, director of the Nabatieh office of the organization, explained, "Our work started soon after the end of the war on August 14, 2006. It included roads and bridges ravaged by Israel in Nabatieh, Tyre, and Bint Jbeil."[54] Lebanese Shiites evince gratitude for Iran's help, which also extended to the provision of medicine, food, generators, and water tanks. Iran's petroleum revenues in 2007 rose to over $50 billion, and since the petroleum industry is in government hands, this massive infusion of cash gave the ruling ayatollahs plenty of money to devote to public diplomacy.

Interestingly, although Tyre is, politically speaking, Hizbullah territory, bars were open for the United Nations troops and unveiled young women could be seen in the streets. Shiite activism in Lebanon does not typically take the form of imposing puritanism. The carrot of oil money and the attractions of soft power in the form of Muslim authenticity and care for the downtrodden were obviously more important than the tools of coercion often deployed by other movements of political Islam.

Oil money is only one source of Tehran's influence in the Shiite south of Lebanon. Religious authority is another. The Iranian leader, Ali Khamenei, enjoys the sort of standing among members of Hizbullah that is accorded the pope by pious Catholics. Most adherents of the Shiite branch of Islam hold that the laity, persons without higher seminary degrees, must follow the rulings of a trained religious jurisprudent on the practice of religious law. Laypersons would not try to treat themselves for a serious medical condition, they argue, and it is equally foolhardy for them to risk their souls attempting to treat their spiritual problems on their own. Ideally, according to the principles of jurisprudence, each believer would find the most upright and most learned clergyman and follow his rulings on Islamic law without question. Such a figure enjoys the rank of grand ayatollah, and is called an "exemplar" *(marja')* to be imitated *(taqlid)* and obeyed in matters of religious law. Most Shiites follow Grand Ayatollah Ali Sistani of Najaf in Iraq, though he is less popular in Iran itself, which boasts several top clergymen.

Khamenei was not widely accepted among Shiites as a clerical exemplar when he became the supreme leader, and, indeed, the constitution had to be amended to allow him to serve despite his lack of erudition. Because he is outranked by so many ayatollahs in Iran with regard to learning, he does not seek lay followers for his informal rulings on law and practice in Iran, only abroad.[55] Those Shiites who follow Khamenei do so for mainly political reasons. (Even beginning in the 1980s, some Shiites in Pakistan began saying that they were splitting their allegiances, following Khomeini as their political exemplar and the grand ayatollah in Najaf as their religious exemplar.) Khamenei's claims to being an exemplar form a sort of soft power for Iran among Shiites in places like Lebanon, Bahrain, Iraq, and Pakistan.

The leadership of Hizbullah accepted Khamenei as its spiritual guide and directs party members to obey his strictures. That loyalty to Khamenei can be seen in daily life. After Khamenei prohibited the controversial practice of cutting the forehead during mourning rites for the martyred descendants of the Prophet, or imams, Hizbullah members gave up the practice. Other Lebanese Shiites, such as members of the rival Amal Party, went on doing it, ignoring Khamenei, because they rejected his authority.[56] The power of this bond to Khamenei was evident after Nasrallah's attack on a handful of Israeli troops in July 2006 provided the Israeli government of Prime Minister Ehud Olmert with a justification for its war on Lebanon. Khamenei was reported to have lost confidence in Nasrallah's military judgment as a result and removed him from control of the paramilitary.[57] Hizbullah vigorously denied the report but did not deny that Khameini had the authority to make such a decision if he so chose.

Some form of Palestinian resistance to Israel has been a powerful feature of regional politics since the late 1960s, when the second generation of those ethnically cleansed in 1948 came to consciousness in their refugee camps and began to be influenced by revolutionary movements such as the ones in Algeria and Latin America. The Palestinian resistance was active when Iran was pro-American and pro-Israel under the shah. It has so much support from the Arab middle classes and the wealthy that it would never lack the resources to mount a challenge to Israeli policies, even if Iran did not exist. Iranian leaders have expressed support for Hamas and are said to have funneled millions of dollars to it. But Iran did not create Hamas, and it is not clear what proportion of Hamas's resources come from Tehran; Iran is certainly not the only sponsor of the organization. Moreover, Israel itself gave financial and other support to Hamas in the 1980s in hopes of using it as a foil against the secular Palestine Liberation Organization.[58]

The Gaza Strip has become the primary political base for Hamas. Israel occupied Gaza in 1967 and, over time, put several thousand Israeli colonists into this poverty-stricken area. Its military occupation of the

Palestinians in Gaza was brutal, and Israeli policies interfered with the economic and social development of Gazans. In 2005, the Israeli military unilaterally withdrew from the strip and forced several thousand colonists to relocate (many went to the Palestinian West Bank). Since the Israeli government had made no deals with the Gaza politicians, a political vacuum ensued.

Thereafter, Islamic Jihad and other militant groups bombarded nearby Israeli towns such as Sederot with small homemade rockets, occasionally causing property damage or killing civilians. Ultimately, Israel imposed a siege on the territory that sometimes interfered with basic services such as electricity, bringing the 1.5 million inhabitants repeatedly to the brink of a public health crisis. Unemployment in Gaza is rife, and Israel blocks the building of needed infrastructure such as an airport or port facilities. Apparently, until they agree to accept Israeli hegemony, the Gazans are to be half-starved into submission. While Israeli brutality toward the Palestinian civilian population does not excuse Palestinian violence, decades of Israeli occupation, followed by siege and the impoverishment of the population, has understandably produced a good deal of anger in the region.

Meanwhile, Hamas provided social services and gained a reputation for honest management of funds, winning most Gazans' hearts and minds. Hamas won the elections in the Palestine Authority in January 2006 and is therefore a legitimate political player, even though in the aftermath the United States and Israel have attempted to delegitimize it. The Israeli and therefore American critique of Hamas as refusing to recognize Israel seems hypocritical to most observers in the Middle East, since Israel steadfastly refuses to recognize a Palestinian state. Why, they ask, should Hamas give up one of its few bargaining chips in a contest with a much more powerful opponent right at the outset? Hamas leaders have repeatedly indicated a willingness to conclude a very long-term truce with Israel (Hamas's spiritual leader, the wheelchair-bound Sheikh Ahmed Yassin, spoke of a hundred-year truce before he was wiped out by an Israeli helicopter gunship as he emerged from his mosque with followers, including children, in March 2004).

Hamas's ideology is a repressive religious fundamentalism, and Hamas is sometimes involved in violence against civilians, which is condemnable. But it is highly unlikely that if Iran cut it off, its resistance to Israel's virtual siege of the Gaza Strip would miraculously cease. In June 2008, Hamas accepted an Egypt-brokered truce with Israel in return for a lightening of the Israeli blockade of the Gaza Strip. Many outside observers have condemned the Israeli actions over the years as a form of collective punishment, which is illegal according to the Geneva Convention. Israel's massive bombardment of Gaza in December 2008 and January 2009 raised an international outcry because of the high number of civilian deaths, and seems unlikely to destroy Hamas or cow the Palestinians. Israel's unwillingness to negotiate with elected representatives of the Palestinian people, and its brutality toward civilians, gives Iran an opening to establish influence on the Mediterranean region that could be combated by more realistic and less belligerent Israeli policies.

Although the demonization of Iran and its Levantine clients in the Western media has gone to extremes, genuine policy differences between Iran and the North Atlantic states do exist. The Khomeinist model, of puritanical restrictions on personal liberties, clerical dictatorship, repression of dissent, state dominance of the economy, and knee-jerk dislike of foreigners is pernicious, and its influence in the Middle East should be contained through diplomatic and economic means. Since most Iranians are not hard-liners, and since even the government has sensible people in it, the international community should find ways of reaching out to the more reasonable elements while marginalizing the radicals.

Centrifuge technology might allow the production of a nuclear weapon if the Tehran leadership changed its mind and began actively seeking to build one, so it is desirable that Iran be pressured to give up its program altogether. Hizbullah's refusal to disarm its militia contributes to instability in Lebanese politics that in turn acts as a drag on Lebanon's economic and social development, and the Lebanese military's inability to defend the country as ably as a small paramilitary does detract from the state's legitimacy. Hamas's violence has gained nothing for Gazans politically, and its self-defeating opposition to a two-state solution should not be strengthened by a long-term alliance with Iranian hard-liners.

Nevertheless, according to international law, the conflicts that the United States, NATO, and Israel have with Iran do not rise to the level of a legitimate cause for war. Iran is within its rights to maintain a civilian nuclear research program for peaceful nuclear energy. As long as Iran meets its responsibilities under the Nuclear Non-Proliferation Treaty and continues to allow inspections by the IAEA, it is acting within its rights.

Iran should be convinced that nuclear reactors are the wrong path to energy independence. The country is an area of high seismic activity, and reactors could well be hit by earthquakes. Like all reactors, they could be subject to meltdowns, such as the one at Chernobyl, which exposed large numbers of Ukrainians to deadly radioactivity. Iran will have the same problem safely storing spent nuclear fuel that everyone else does. It faces the same danger that the radioactive waste will seep into groundwater or be stolen by terrorists and deployed in a dirty bomb. Iran may have enough uranium to fuel its reactors for a decade or two, but the uranium will run out, and become expensive. If Iran is seeking reactors to guarantee its independence from the American-dominated global economic system, then it will surely fail.

Iran is much more likely to achieve energy independence in the short to medium term by giving up its nuclear program and developing its natural gas fields. Those fields are estimated to be very large, but the international sanctions that the nuclear program has provoked are interfering with the development of the gas industry. As with the rest of the world, Iran's energy security will best be guaranteed in the medium to long term by the development of inexpensive solar energy and more efficient batteries. Given the solar energy generation potential of Iran's Great Salt Desert (Dasht-i Kavir), it could be an energy giant for centuries if the right breakthroughs were made. Moving quickly in this direction would also allow Iran to avoid the potentially severe disruptions of global climate change from increased atmospheric carbon dioxide, which could interfere with agriculture and threaten the country with food shortages. If the Iranian nuclear program is in the end actually about geopolitical security, it is also wrongheaded. As Saddam discovered, having a reputation for possessing weapons of mass destruction may deter enemy attacks in the short term but expose the regime to even more severe danger in the long run.

Both with regard to human rights and on the nuclear issue, U.S. engagement with Iran will be more productive than military confrontation. Any attempt by the United States to invade or occupy Iran would likely stretch American resources beyond the breaking point. Such a war would also raise the price of petroleum considerably, perhaps tipping the world economy into an even deeper recession.

Already in the opening years of the twenty-first century, the European Union has demonstrated that engaging and negotiating with Iran is a much more effective method of obtaining changes in behavior than saber-rattling.[59] The European Union made it clear to Tehran that trade and cooperation agreements depend on an improved human rights situation in the Islamic Republic. In response, the Iranian judiciary announced a moratorium on stoning as a punishment for adultery, saying that other penalties would be imposed instead. While the moratorium has not always been observed by the courts, the agreement has reduced the use of this punishment. The regime released dissident Ayatollah Hosain-'Ali Montazeri from house arrest at the urging of the Europeans. The European Union has also pressed for an improvement in the treatment of Iranian women. A loosening of U.S. unilateral sanctions on Iran should be tied to specific progress on some of these human rights issues.

Iran's ties to the two activist organizations that are most troublesome to Israel create further tensions between Israel and Tehran. Israel could, however, fairly easily undermine such Iranian initiatives. If it followed through on recently begun negotiations with Syria, making a deal that returned the Golan Heights to Damascus and the Shebaa Farms to Lebanon, it would remove the major remaining pretext for continued Hizbullah militancy.

An Israeli peace treaty with Syria like the one it already has with Egypt and Jordan would be a step toward ending external funding of

Hizbullah and Hamas and might begin the process of weaning Syria away from its Iranian ally. If Israel resolved its disputes with the Palestine Authority and moved quickly to statehood for the Palestinians, with guarantees that Palestinian police would keep order in Gaza and stop rocket attacks by guerrillas on Israel, it would remove a major irritant in its relations with Syria and other Middle Eastern countries.

In short, the Israeli refusal to pursue a comprehensive peace with the Palestinians and local Arab neighbors creates an opening for hardliners in Iran to assert their interests in the Levant, which, while not "evil," are not helpful to the Palestinian-Israeli peace process, since they discourage compromise. Worse, Israeli intransigence is rapidly making a two-state solution implausible, as continued Israeli encroachments on the West Bank leave it increasingly moth-eaten as a potential site of Palestinian nationhood. An end-state of apartheid looms, with millions of poor, stateless Palestinians living among affluent Israelis who control their airspace, water resources, and borders. Such a final outcome for Israeli-Palestinian relations would be unacceptable to the world, might well lead to widespread economic boycotts of the Zionist state, and would begin to lend greater credibility to Ahmadinejad's misrepresentations of Israel. American and Israeli hawks imagine that strikes on Iran, or a war, or forced regime change in Tehran will solve all of Israel's problems. In fact, Iran would become irrelevant if Israel traded land for peace, which is the actual solution to Israel's problems.

Israel's leadership recognizes that the continued colonization of Palestinian territory is not a viable strategy, since it likely will end with Israel being forced to offer the Palestinians Israeli citizenship. (If Palestinians cannot have a state of their own, and since their remaining stateless and without basic rights is increasingly unacceptable to the world, Israel may be forced to absorb them to avoid a ruinous economic and diplomatic isolation of the sort the South African apartheid regime suffered before its collapse.)

That realization impelled then prime minister Ariel Sharon to withdraw colonists from the Gaza Strip in 2005. His successor, Ehud Olmert, was unable to effect a similar decisive policy in the West Bank because of political weakness and dependence on small parties invested in the continued Israeli settlement of Palestinian territory. When Olmert was forced to resign over corruption charges in September 2008, he delivered a poignant farewell interview in which he declared the dream of "Greater Israel" (that is, expansion into the territories occupied in 1967 and perhaps beyond) to be over. He admitted that Israel would have to withdraw to something like its 1949 borders and concede a state to the Palestinians if it is to retain a Jewish majority: "After great internal conflict, I've realized we have to share this land with the people who dwell here—that is if we don't want to be a binational state."[60]

The most effective role a U.S. president can play is to give Israeli governments the cover to do what they need to do. The previous administration refused to play that role, discouraging Israeli negotiation with neighbors such as Syria and helping undermine the Palestine Authority. This administration needs to restart the Israeli-Palestinian peace process immediately and to think boldly about what a final accord would look like in the region. Statehood for the Palestinians, peace with the new Palestinian state, and a peace accord between Israel and Syria would lead to a rapid drop in opportunities for intervention by Iranian hard-liners' in the eastern Mediterranean. An Israeli peace with Damascus and a settlement of territorial issues would likely also lead to a peace treaty with Lebanon, which in turn might lead to a further evolution of Hizbullah toward being a civilian political party rather than a resistance movement. In other words, reducing the influence of Khomeinism must begin at home, in the Levant.

As for Iran itself, there is little alternative to patient diplomacy. The regime is flush with petroleum profits, has $70 billion in currency reserves, and seems unlikely to be overturned by any domestic movement any time soon. UN and European sanctions and incentives, implemented in a targeted and scaled fashion, have more hope of persuading the Iranians to reconsider their nuclear program than does American belligerence, which rather impels the Iranians to make sure they have the means of repelling an aggressive war. It is a mystery why the North Atlantic states, which contained and waited out a powerful, large, and nuclear-armed Soviet Union, find it intolerable to deal with a small, weak Iran in the same way. Iran's political system, moreover, contains more potential for positive evolution than did that of the Soviet Union. Although Iran's electoral system is highly circumscribed and the hard-liners have proved skilled and clever in forestalling a reformist challenge, the overall system is not totalitarian, and the public still delivers some surprises.

The best hope for Iran is a gradual strengthening of its democratic elements and a weakening or moderating of its theocratic ones. A new generation of Iranians less hostile to the West could come to power in a decade or so. Whether outsiders can influence this process is doubtful, but we certainly cannot do so through wars and violent covert operations, and we will not do so if we view Iran only though the lens of Islam Anxiety.

CONCLUSION

As I write, NATO's worsening conflict with neo-Taliban and other Pushtun tribal groups in southern Afghanistan is spilling over into Pakistan. Al-Qaeda leaders such as Ayman al-Zawahiri continue to issue calls for terrorism against Europe and the United States, using young Muslims' disgust—with the Iraq, Afghanistan, and Pakistan conflicts and the civilian casualties they generate—as a recruiting tool. A poll done for the BBC in 23 nations and released in September 2008 found that only 22 percent of those polled believed that al-Qaeda had been weakened since the beginning of the "war on terror" in 2001, whereas 29 percent believed that it had maintained the same strength and 30 percent asserted that it had become stronger.[1] The American invasion of and military presence in Iraq is condemned by most Muslims and most other people in the world.

In a 2007 poll, an average of 79 percent of respondents in Egypt, Morocco, Pakistan, and Indonesia agreed that America seeks to "weaken and divide the Islamic world." The same average percentage in these countries believed that the United States wants "control over the oil resources of the Middle East." An average of 64 percent asserted that Washington wants to spread Christianity among them. Three-fourths of respondents in the four countries supported the goal of getting all American troops and bases out of their region.[2] Obviously, hundreds of millions of Muslims suffer from America Anxiety; they believe that a superpower is seeking to undermine and destroy their religious identity and control their resources.

In order to improve relations, the United States and NATO must repudiate the Bush doctrine of "preventive war," which appears to Muslims as a warrant for aggression. Washington and its allies must recognize that killing civilians creates terrorists. Above all, basic fairness is crucial. The United States must be as willing to condemn Israel for infractions against international law as it is to castigate Palestinians for violence. Western demands for a dismantling of Iran's nuclear program are mere hypocrisy if the West is not working toward reducing, then ending, nuclear weapons everywhere.

Once, I saw an Iraqi tribal leader interviewed on Al-Jazeera. He said, "There is good and bad in America." I was struck by how pragmatic and realistic his response was, and how different it was from so much of the fundamentalist vigilante propaganda about the United States posted on radical Internet bulletin boards. If Washington could reach out to all Muslims and bring them around to this more nuanced—and clear—view, in which America is not simply demonized, it would be a major accomplishment. The point is not that they should see the West through rose-colored glasses, but that they be willing to see good and bad.

We also need a more clear-sighted approach in the West. The bigoted way in which some politicians have dealt with Islam, denigrating Muslims by speaking of "Islamofascism" and attempting to shoehorn the Muslim world into an unlikely role as the new Soviet Union, profoundly betrays modern values such as freedom of religion and neutrality on religious issues. Modern European figures as diverse as Napoleon, Goethe, and Carlyle found things to praise in Islam.

Ben Franklin wrote in his autobiography of how he founded in Philadelphia a nondenominational preaching hall, "the design in building not being to accommodate any particular sect, but the inhabitants in general; so that even if the Mufti of Constantinople were to send a missionary to preach Mohammedanism to us, he would find a pulpit at his service."[3] No doubt a leader of any community organization today who dared follow through on Franklin's suggestion and actually invited the Mufti of Istanbul to preach in public would be pilloried.

Franklin's willingness to hear a Muslim point of view flew in the face of centuries of anxiety in Christian Western Europe about the encroachments of the Muslim Ottoman Empire. His response to the

Islam Anxiety of his own times was a serene open-mindedness. The tradition of tolerance exhibited by some Enlightenment thinkers derived from the premise that freedom of worship and multiplicity of religious traditions forms no threat to the health of society but rather strengthens it. Thomas Jefferson was disgusted at the persecution in Virginia, by the establishment state religion, of Quakers who refused to be baptized.

As early as 1797, the U.S. Senate (in which several Founding Fathers sat) and the Adams administration approved a peace treaty with Tripoli (now Libya) that noted:

> As the Government of the United States of America is not in any sense founded on the Christian religion; as it has in itself no character of enmity against the laws, religion, or tranquility, of Musselmen; and as the said States never have entered into any war or act of hostility against any Mehomitan nation, it is declared by the parties that no pretext arising from religious opinions shall ever produce an interruption of the harmony existing between the two countries.[4]

This treaty pointed out that there was no religious or ideological basis for conflict between the United States and the Muslim world, since the U.S. government is neutral with regard to religion and takes no sides in metaphysical disputes. As an Enlightenment republic, the United States had no reason to want to continue the Christian tradition of the Crusades or of anti-Ottoman warfare on specifically religious grounds.

If the United States and its allies are to thrive in the twenty-first century, they need to reaffirm this tradition of religious neutrality and to cease construing the Muslim world as an object of political rivalry; they need to overcome their Islam Anxiety. The United States and many of the world's industrialized democracies are admired by numerous Muslims for their political institutions and their constitutional ideals, even if Muslims shake their heads at our failure to live up to them consistently. That admiration is a valuable source of soft power that should not be squandered in a bid to gain votes in domestic elections from the least enlightened sectors of the electorate. By abandoning the politics of distrust and fear, the new administration in Washington has the opportunity to repair America's relations with the Muslim world, and should give that task the highest priority.

The pressing problems facing the North Atlantic and Muslim countries can be addressed successfully only by mutual cooperation. Putting aside the more irrational forms of America Anxiety and Islam Anxiety is a prerequisite for such teamwork in tackling the energy crisis, reining in religious fundamentalists, bringing stability to postwar Iraq and Afghanistan, bringing Khomeinist Iran in from the cold, and resolving the six-decades-old Israel-Palestine conflict.

The world is facing twin crises: a growing demand for energy that will outstrip available clean sources and the threat of climate change. They form the greatest challenge humanity has confronted since the last Ice Age, which ended ten thousand years ago. Putting aside the bigotries of Christian and Muslim, Arab and Jew, secular and religious, and choosing positive engagement over polarization and war may be the only way to spare the world the catastrophic consequences of failing to resolve these crises.

The United States could foster an economic and political alliance of energy-consuming states—such as the European Union, Israel, China, Japan, and itself—with hydrocarbon producers to make a swift transition to solar energy. Doing so would position Washington as a new kind of moral leader globally, recalling its key role in fostering economic growth in war-torn Europe with the Marshall Plan after World War II. The creation of the low-carbon city, Masdar, in the United Arab Emirates shows the way in which states now dependent on fossil fuels often have the resources to implement a greener future.

The dilemma of fundamentalist vigilantism and radicalism in the Muslim world can also be addressed only through cooperation between the North Atlantic and Muslim worlds. While religious fundamentalism is a fairly stable feature of modernity, the social problem of violent fundamentalism in the Muslim world is probably a short-term phase—like the era of the Red Brigades and the Baader-Meinhoff left-ist radicals in Europe during the 1970s and 1980s or the heyday of the "Patriot" gun culture in the United States in the 1980s and 1990s.

The struggle against violent radical groups requires not only the cooperation of security agencies in the Muslim world with Western or-ganizations such as Interpol and the FBI but also cultural interchange. Religious and judicial authorities in Egypt and Yemen have had some success in simply arguing young radicals out of their extreme views by appealing to authoritative Islamic texts. Obviously, Muslim norms of disputation are beyond the competence of Westerners, and only coop-eration with knowledgeable Muslim authorities can produce progress in this regard. For Western politicians to denounce "Islamofascists" alienates mainstream thinkers and makes reasoned approaches to quelling radicalism more difficult. Important testimonies such as the pamphlets of former activists of the Gama'ah Islamiyah arguing for peaceful social activism rather than vigilante violence also should be widely translated into European, African, and Asian languages and made inexpensively available to Muslim readers. Arabic speakers, after all, comprise a minority of Muslims.

Institutions such as the National Endowment for the Humanities should create special programs for the academically sound transla-tion of the great works of Islamic civilization and contemporary Middle Eastern religious and political thought. While some funding is available for such purposes and some brave translators have made important contributions in this regard, the enormity of these press-ing needs dwarfs the current resources and efforts dedicated to these tasks. If the range of reliable literature on Islam in the West were widened, students and the public could have access to solid sources of Muslim thought rather than the fevered tracts of crackpots and provocateurs. Since so many of the world's Muslims know only En-glish, it would benefit them to have the thinking of Muslim liberals available, not just the more frequently translated and published polemics of the fundamentalists.

Likewise, the key works of democratic political thinking that are the Western world's precious heritage need to be widely translated and effectively disseminated.[5] It is tragic and bizarre that no translations into Arabic can be found in Cairo and Beirut bookstores of the works and speeches of Thomas Jefferson and Martin Luther King Jr., of German sociologist Jürgen Habermas and British cultural thinker Stuart Hall—all key contributors to global thinking on contemporary democracy.

Educational and training exchange programs for lawyers and judges in North Atlantic and Muslim countries could also be effective. Legal reform can play a key role in increasing conformity to international human rights standards in Africa and Asia and tolerance of Muslim minorities in the West. Insisting on big immediate changes in state policy is unlikely to produce fruitful dialogue, whereas working at the level of the judiciary for an increased rule of law lays an essential foundation for positive change. There is little point in demanding that Saudi Arabia move toward representative government and international human rights standards if the Saudi legal establishment is unfamiliar with what those institutions and practices entail. If we take care of the pennies, the dollars will take care of themselves.

Finding a wise and constructive way to extract U.S. troops from Iraq must be high on the agenda of the new administration. It must involve continued training of Iraqi officials and security forces and support for the building of representative institutions. Clarity of vision and continued engagement with regard to Iraq requires a recognition that the North Atlantic intervention has introduced severe instability and promoted ethnosectarian conflict. A wise policy will promote a grand compromise among the Sunni Arabs, Shiites, Kurds, and Turkmen of the sort achieved in Lebanon in 1989, which ended the civil war there. The Lebanese compromise gave greater representation to the previously underrepresented Muslims. An Iraqi compromise would have to reassure the Sunni Arab minority that it is not doomed to live forever under a tyranny of the Shiite majority.

Some of the unwillingness of the Shiite-dominated government in Iraq to compromise with the Sunnis derives from an overconfidence born of the certainty of U.S. close air support should fighting break out between the two. An American withdrawal may well force the Shiite government into a fruitful compromise with the Sunni

Arabs. If a relatively smooth U.S. withdrawal can be accomplished and if the aftermath does not produce turmoil in the Gulf region, the image of the United States in the Muslim oil states will begin to improve markedly.

The United States and its allies must follow through on their public commitment to democratize the Middle East by supporting the civilian parties and parliamentary government in Pakistan and helping to rebuild Afghanistan. In both instances, a different vision and a new kind of engagement is desperately required. The United States granted $10 billion to the military government of General Pervez Musharraf, which ended in 2008, but it is not clear that Washington and its allies are willing to commit similar resources to support a democratically elected civilian government that is less enthusiastic about deploying military force to subdue the Pushtun tribes of the northwest.

The dangerous policy of encouraging allies like Pakistan to spend billions in high-tech arms purchases from U.S. firms should be ended. Flooding the region with sophisticated weaponry will only provoke arms races among neighbors, and it may well encourage conflicts to break out. Moreover, Pakistan would be better encouraged to put its money into expanding the government school system. That step would raise the country's embarrassingly low literacy rate, create literate workers for the new information economy, and divert students from conservative madrasahs where they are more likely to have their minds closed than opened.

NATO has made major troop commitments to the struggle to support the Karzai government in Afghanistan but has committed relatively few resources to rebuilding the country. The United States may have already invested as much as $1 trillion in the fruitless and unnecessary Iraq War. It has spent, in comparison, a miniscule sum on development aid for Afghanistan. That country could be a key to developing a trans-Asian trucking and rail trade. It would benefit from tolls and money spent in transit but would need security to reassure drivers and investors.

NATO tactics for dealing with rebellious tribes—mainly search-and-destroy missions and aerial bombardment—have been counterproductive. Military attacks alienate village populations and tribes and attract to the region Arab volunteers eager to defend Muslims from what they see as Christian oppression. Western donors need to give the tribes aid in escaping their hardscrabble lives if they are to gain a stake in stability. Failing that, they need to be bribed, cajoled, and played off against one another, not bombarded from the air.

Engagement can also work in Iran. As attractive as a war to change regimes might be to hawks, launching one in Iran would be the riskiest enterprise ever undertaken by the United States and could drastically overstretch our resources, weakening it rather than strengthening it. The Iranian regime has shown itself open to negotiations. Ensuring Iran's energy independence and assuring the government that the United States will not attempt to overthrow it would be steps toward reestablishing at least correct relations between the two countries and reducing the threat of war. Inducing Israel to give up its nuclear arsenal would be crucial to convincing Iran to cease its enrichment program, and would be a necessary step toward making the Middle East a nuclear-free zone.

A careful U.S. withdrawal from Iraq will create new opportunities for better relations with Iran, since that country will feel less surrounded and menaced by a large American troop presence on its doorstep. Better relations between the North Atlantic states and Iran will discredit the paranoid fantasies of the Iranian right wing and will strengthen Iranian moderates.

There is not much time left for the new administration of President Obama to achieve an equitable resolution of the Israeli-Palestinian conflict, which must certainly end the scandal of Palestinian statelessness while safeguarding Israel's security. Demonizing Palestinians and refusing to talk to them will never lead to peace, and keeping Gaza under siege will only turn it into a violent, fourth-world failed state. If the Israelis themselves cannot see the inhumanity and self-destructiveness of creating such a situation right on their border, the international community has an obligation to press wiser alternatives on them. There is not much territory left in the West Bank for a Palestinian polity, and given the rate of Israeli colonization of Palestinian land, in a few years no viable Palestinian state will be possible.

Despite the wholly unrealistic hopes of the Israeli right, the international community (including the European Union and its member states) is not going to put up with Israel keeping the Palestinians stateless for very much longer. If they cannot have a state of their own, then Israel will have to grant them citizenship. Israel has avoided significant economic boycotts over the growing apartheid situation in the Occupied Territories only because the world has accepted the fiction that there is an ongoing peace process. If the current situation in Gaza and the West Bank is, in fact, the endgame, then it is completely unacceptable, and will produce boycotts of and sanctions on Israel.

If figures on the Israeli right such as former cabinet member Avigdor Lieberman follow through on their dream of "transporting"—that is, ethnically cleansing—the Palestinians, there will certainly be a war, and perhaps several.[6] All this turmoil will expose the United States to more threats of terrorism and polarize the world further. A wise American administration would therefore risk everything to lead the two parties kicking and screaming into a peace agreement, for the good of the United States.

In a peculiar atmosphere in which it is controversial even to urge Washington to be more even-handed and act as an honest broker in Middle East disputes, it will take courage and clarity of vision on the part of President Obama to engage the parties vigorously and helpfully. Resolving this conflict in a way acceptable to all the major parties involved should be the highest priority of his administration. This step would resolve 90 percent of America's problems with the Muslim world and would potentially lead to improved relations with states such as Syria and Iran, relations that would stand the United States in good stead in its competition for a favorable position in Muslim energy markets during the next two decades.

Engagement and peacemaking will position the United States to play the role of broker in Africa and Asia in the next generation. In the past decade, the United States has lost the confidence of most Muslims and cannot function as an honest mediator, a failing that has allowed France and even Qatar to step into that role. Rather than facing hostility, losing contracts, and being frozen out as Muslim states turn to Russia, China, and India as better political soul mates, an engaging, peace-seeking United States could reemerge as the indispensable country in the region.

The diverse cultures and polities of the Muslim world and those of the North Atlantic have had conflicts at times and achieved mutually beneficial forms of cooperation at others. There were times and places where social and political interchange among Christians, Jews, and Muslims created impressive advances in science and politics, as in eleventh- and twelfth-century Toledo and Cordoba in Spain. At other times and places, as in the Crusades, there was polarization resulting in Christian-Muslim conflict (though even then there were occasional alliances of Christian and Muslim kingdoms against rivals). Nor is an artificial division between Europe and the Muslim world a useful way to think about history. In the 1500s and 1600s, the Muslim kingdom of Safavid Iran allied with European Christian maritime empires against another Muslim power, the Ottoman Empire. It is now mostly forgotten that British Muslim troops fought in the British army against the fascist army of Italy in World War II and that Senegalese Muslim troops aided the Free French.

The media focus on conflict between the North Atlantic countries and Muslim-majority ones ignores the thick web of cooperation and exchange that increasingly connects them. European economies today would be much less vibrant and would face severe labor shortages without Muslim immigrants. For its part, the Gulf monarchy of Qatar has created an "education city" filled with branch campuses of Western schools, such as Cornell University Medical School and Northwestern University's School of Journalism, training a regional elite of professionals and specialists that will owe its success in part to a grounding in a Western education.

The contemporary world offers unprecedented opportunities for political and cultural teamwork between the North Atlantic countries and the Muslim world, and the pressing problems we face can only be resolved through such collaboration. Doing so will require a setting aside of Islam Anxiety and America Anxiety, a return to wise and persistent diplomacy, and a spirit of compromise on all sides. We can do it, if we engage.

ACKNOWLEDGMENTS

This book was written with the resources, intellectual and technological, made available to me by the University of Michigan. I want to thank my colleagues and students in the History Department as well as at the Center for Middle Eastern and North African Studies and the Center for South Asian Studies for their enrichment of my intellectual life and their friendship. Some of the research for this book (especially on Iraq and Iraqi refugees, carried out in Jordan in summer of 2008) was supported by my collegiate professorship from the School of Literature, Sciences and the Arts (LSA). Likewise, the professorship enabled me to attend some relevant conferences that enhanced my understanding of key issues. The colleagues, departments, centers, and library resources of a university are a crucial matrix for academics, within which our analyses are honed and our horizons widened.

Conferences have been important to this book. I benefited from the conference on Islamophobia and Islamophilia organized by Andrew Shryock and Alexander Knysh in October 2007 at the University of Michigan as part of the Islamic Studies initiative of LSA and a conference with a similar theme hosted by John Esposito at Georgetown University the same month. I presented some of the material in this book first at conferences in Japan, at the Meiji, Kyoto, and Doshisha universities in July 2007, and at the Japanese Institute of Middle East Economies (JIME) in Tokyo, October 30–31, 2007. These were occasions for vigorous and searching questioning, and my Japanese colleagues were most hospitable and gracious. I am especially grateful to

Professors Tomoko Yamagishi, Keiko Sakai, and Kazuhiro Arai for the summer appearances, and to Koichiru Tanaka at JIME. I gave a paper on American foreign policy at the American University in Beirut on December 17, 2007, that prefigured some of the arguments in Chapter Four. I am grateful to Patrick McGreevy for that invitation. I polished my thoughts further on the challenge of the contemporary Middle East for Washington in a keynote address to the British Middle East Studies Association Conference in London, on April 19, 2008, and spoke on Shiite movements in Iraq at a conference on Shiite Islam at the University of Glasgow on April 26. I am grateful to Rob Gleave for his unfailing help with those appearances. The generous invitation of the BBC and the Qatar Foundation to participate in the Doha Debates on April 29, 2008, allowed me to clarify my thinking on Islam and violence in Iraq and to do interviewing with Al-Jazeera editors and staff. My eyes were opened to the full severity of the energy crisis at the "Energy and the Social Sciences Workshop" sponsored by the University of Michigan's Institute for Social Research on May 19, 2008, in Ann Arbor.

Because this book grew out of my research on the contemporary history of the Muslim world conducted in conjunction with my Web log, "Informed Comment," I have acquired innumerable debts to kind readers and interlocutors. Fellow bloggers on Middle East issues—Farideh Farhi, Barnett R. Rubin, Marc Lynch, Helena Cobban, Tom Engelhardt, Andrew Arato, Raed Jarrar, Jenny White, Colin Kahl, Joshua Landis, Abbas Kadhem, Leila Hudson, Michael Schwartz, A. Richard Norton, Jenny White, Charles Smith, As'ad Abu Khalil, Laura Rozen, Josh Marshall, Steve Clemons, Pat Lang, Markos Moulitsas, Dan Drezner, Michael Klare, George Packer, Andrew Sullivan, and Joe Klein—and a cloud of email correspondents, especially Frank Domoney, have through their writings or messages tipped me to issues and informed my analyses. Nikki Keddie made important suggestions for the conclusion. I am especially indebted to Barney Rubin for his deeply informed and wise comments and insider tips. By thanking them here I do not mean to attribute any responsibility to them, however, for what is in this book.

I want to thank my literary agents, Steven Wasserman and Brettne Bloom at Kneerim Williams, for their faith in me and in this project, and for being judicious sounding boards and imaginative counselors as I developed it. I am deeply indebted to Alessandra Bastagli, my editor at Palgrave Macmillan, whose sure hand and humane wisdom was so helpful in helping midwife this book. All the staff at Palgrave Macmillan were a pleasure to work with, and I want to thank Alan Bradshaw and Lauren Dwyer in particular.

I could not have written this book without the love and support of my wife, Shahin, whose key insights invariably provoked me to improve my arguments. My son Arman gave invaluable help with the maps and offered needed moral support.

NOTES

INTRODUCTION

1. On American views, see John L. Esposito and Dalia Mogahed, "Muslim True/False: What You Think You Know About Them Is Likely Wrong—And That's Dangerous," *Los Angeles Times*, April 2, 2008. On British opinions, see Jonathan Wynne-Jones and Patrick Sawer, "Muslims Must Do More to Integrate, Says Poll," *Telegraph* (London) January 14, 2008. On British fear, see Philip Johnston, "Islam Poses a Threat to the West, Say 53 pc in Poll," *Telegraph* (London), August 25, 2006. On French views, see Pew Global Attitudes Project, "The Great Divide: How Westerners and Muslims View Each Other: Europe's Muslims More Moderate," June 22, 2006, at http://pewglobal.org/reports/display.php?PageID=830.
2. World Economic Forum, *Islam and the West: Annual Report on the State of Dialogue*, Geneva, Switzerland, January 2008, at http://www.weforum.org/pdf/C100/Islam_West.pdf.
3. Joseph A. Kechichian, "Condemn Giuliani's War on Islam," *Gulf News*, September 15, 2008, at http://www.gulfnews.com/opinion/columns/world/10245142.html.
4. Claudia Deane and Darryl Fears, "Negative Perception of Islam Increasing: Poll Numbers in U.S. Higher Than in 2001," *Washington Post*, March 9, 2006; Marilyn Elias, "U.S. Muslims Under a Cloud," *USA Today*, August 10, 2006.
5. I say "Middle Eastern" rather than "Muslim" because I've had my run-ins with Maronite Catholic, Jewish, Eastern Orthodox, and Baha'i fundamentalists, too.

CHAPTER 1

1. Michael T. Klare, "The Pentagon v. Peak Oil: How Wars of the Future May Be Fought Just to Run the Machines That Fight Them," Tomdispatch.com, June 14, 2007, at http://www.tomdispatch.com/post/174810/
2. Bob Woodward, "Greenspan: Ouster of Hussein Crucial for Oil Security," *Washington Post*, September 17, 2007.
3. Robert Bryce, *Gusher of Lies: The Dangerous Delusions of "Energy Independence"* (New York: Public Affairs / Perseus, 2008), p. 16.
4. Usamah Bin Laden / Mulla Omar, n.d. [1999?], AFGP–2002–600321, Arabic original, Combating Terrorism Center, West Point, via http://ctc.usma.edu/harmony/harmony_index.asp.

5. Cihan Aksan and Jon Bailes, "Interview with Abdel Bari Atwan," *State of Nature* (Spring 2006), at http://www.stateofnature.org/abdelBariAtwan.html; see also Abdel Bari Atwan, *The Secret History of al-Qaeda*, rev. ed. (Berkeley: University of California Press, 2008).

6. Douglas Little, "Cold War and Covert Action: The United States and Syria, 1945–1958," *Middle East Journal* 44, no. 1 (Winter 1990), pp. 51–75; idem., "Pipeline Politics: America, TAPLINE, and the Arabs," *Business History Review* 64, no. 2 (Summer 1990), pp. 255–85; idem., *American Orientalism* (Chapel Hill, N.C.: University of North Carolina Press, 2004), pp. 53–54. I benefited from reading the seminar paper of Daniel Green, "Blowback in the Middle East: American and Nazi Collaboration in the 1949 Syrian Coup," carried out for my seminar on Modern Middle Eastern History in winter 2008 at the University of Michigan.

7. James Bill, *The Eagle and the Lion: The Tragedy of American-Iranian Relations* (New Haven, Conn.: Yale University Press, 1988), p. 63.

8. Stephen Kinzer, *All the Shah's Men: An American Coup and the Roots of Middle East Terror* (Hoboken, N.J.: John Wiley & Sons, 2003); Mark J. Gasiorowski and Malcolm Byrne, eds., *Mohammad Mosaddeq and the 1953 Coup in Iran* (Syracuse, NY: Syracuse University Press, 2004); and Maziar Behrooz, "Tudeh Factionalism and the 1953 Coup in Iran," *International Journal of Middle East Studies* 33, no. 3 (August 2001), pp. 363–82.

9. Salim Yaqub, *Containing Arab Nationalism: The Eisenhower Doctrine and the Middle East* (Chapel Hill, NC: University of North Carolina Press, 2004), p. 224.

10. "Memorandum of Conference with President Eisenhower," July 20, 1958, quoted in Irene L. Gendzier, "Oil, Politics and U.S. Intervention," in William Roger Louis and Roger Owen, eds., *A Revolutionary Year: The Middle East in 1958* (London: I. B. Tauris, 2002), p. 131.

11. "Memorandum of Discussion at the 406th Meeting of the National Security Council," May 13, 1959, quoted in Roger Owen, "The Dog that Neither Barked nor Bit: The Fear of Oil Shortages," in Louis and Owen, *Revolutionary Year*, p. 287.

12. Tim Weiner, *Legacy of Ashes: The History of the CIA* (New York: Doubleday, 2007), p. 141; David Morgan, "Ex-U.S. Official Says CIA Aided Baathists; CIA Offers No Comment on Iraq Coup Allegations," Reuters, April 20, 2003, via Lexis Nexis or http://www.commondreams.org/headlines03/0420–05.htm.

13. Entrepreneur Calouste Gulbenkian had received the remainder of the shares, about 5 percent.

14. Little, *American Orientalism*, p. 62; Joe Stork, *Middle East Oil and the Energy Crisis* (New York: Monthly Review Press, 1975), pp. 102–8, 189–94.

15. Memorandum from Robert W. Komer of the National Security Council Staff to the President's Special Assistant for National Security Affairs ([McGeorge] Bundy), Washington, December 29, 1961, no. 156, *Foreign Relations of the United States [FRUS], 1961–1963*, vol. 17, *Near East, 1961–1962*, at http://www.state.gov/r/pa/ho/frus/kennedyjf/xvii/17710.htm.

16. Ibid., nos. 153, 157; Kennedy Library, "Secret Memorandum for the President: R. W. Komer to Kennedy," National Security Files, Countries, box no. 117, Iraq 1/63–2/63, quoted in Bill Zeman, "U.S. Covert Intervention in Iraq 1958–1963: The Origins of U.S. Supported Regime Change in Modern Iraq," master's thesis (Pomona: California State Polytechnic University, 2006), pp. 52–53.

17. Weiner, *Legacy of Ashes*, p. 141, and sources cited.

18. Memorandum of a Briefing by Director of Central Intelligence [John] McCone, no. 252, *FRUS*, vol. 34, at http://www.state.gov/www/about_state/history/vol_xxxiv/z.html.

19. Ibid.

20. "OPEC Share of World Crude Oil Reserves (2006)," OPEC Facts and Figures, at http://www.opec.org/home/PowerPoint/eserves/OPEC%20share.htm.

21. The full seriousness of the crisis was borne in on me at the Energy and the Social Sciences Workshop sponsored by the University of Michigan's Institute for Social Research on May 19, 2008, in Ann Arbor, especially the papers of Carl Simon, Irv Salmeen, and Barry Rabe. See http://www.isr.umich.edu/carss/about/workshop-schedule.html.

22. The amount of new oil reserves identified per decade fell from 450 billion barrels in the 1950s to only 150 billion barrels in the 1990s. Michael T. Klare, *Rising Powers, Shrinking Planet* (New York: Metropolitan Books, 2008), pp. 38–39.

23. Michael T. Klare, *Blood and Oil: The Dangers and Consequences of America's Growing Dependency on Imported Petroleum* (New York: Metropolitan Books/Henry Holt & Co., 2004). I share many of Klare's analyses but am not as optimistic as he is that American petroleum independence can be achieved anytime soon, at least in ways that do not exacerbate climate change and ecological degradation (e.g., if we depended on liquefied coal).

24. Klare, *Rising Powers*, chap, 3; Peter Tertzakian, *A Thousand Barrels a Second* (New York: McGraw-Hill, 2006), chap. 4.

25. "China Imports Record 163m Tons of Crude Oil Last Year," *Xinhua*, January 12, 2008

26. "China Vows to Make Positive Contributions to World's Energy Security," People's Daily Online, December 26, 2007, at http://english.people.com.cn/90001/90776/90785/6327630.html.

27. Tom Bergin, "Shell Pulls Out of Iran Gas Deal," Reuters, May 10, 2008.

28. Asian Development Bank, "India," in "Asian Development Outlook 2008" (Manila, 2008).

29. Joseph Dancy, "Energy Sector: Crude Oil Demand from China, India, Rockets Upward," *Market Oracle*, May 19, 2008, at http://www.marketoracle.co.uk/Article4753.html.

30. "India Cos. to Invest $3 Bln on Gas in Iran Block——Source," Reuters, June 13, 2008.

31. Afshan Subohi, "Security Risks to Gas Pipelines," *Dawn* (Karachi), April 21, 2008; Isambard Wilkinson, "Balochistan Peace Bid Runs into Rocky Path," *The National* (Abu Dhabi), June 9, 2008.

32. Dr. Robert J. Wirsing, "Baloch Nationalism and the Geopolitics of Energy Resources: The Changing Context of Separatism in Pakistan" (Carlisle Barracks, PA: Strategic Studies Institute of the US Army War College, 2008), http://www.strategicstudiesinstitute.army.mil/pdffiles/PUB853.pdf

33. "Peace Pipeline Favored Over U.S. Objection," UPI, June 18, 2008.

34. Rob Johnson, *Oil, Islam and Conflict: Central Asia since 1945* (London: Reaktion Books, 2007), chap. 9.

35. Adam Tarock, "The Politics of the Pipeline: The Iran and Afghanistan Conflict," *Third World Quarterly* 20, no. 4 (1999), pp. 801–20; Joe Stephens and David B. Ottaway, "Afghan Roots Keep Adviser Firmly in the Inner Circle," *Washington Post*, November 23, 2001.

36. Mubarak Zeb Khan, "Basic Accord for Turkmen Gas Project Signed," *Dawn* (Karachi), April 24, 2008.

37. Klare, *Rising Powers*, pp. 130–131.

38. M. K. Bhadrakumar, "Russia Takes Control of Turkmen (World?) Gas," *Asia Times*, July 30, 2008.

39. Intergovernmental Panel on Climate Change, "Climate Change 2007: IPCC Fourth Assessment Report," United Nations, November 2007, at http://www.ipcc.ch/#.

40. Seth Borenstein, "NASA Global Warming Scientist: Dump Coal Power and Clean Up Emissions or We're Toast," Associated Press, June 23, 2008; James Hansen, "Global Warming Twenty Years Later: Tipping Points Near," June 23, 2008, at http://www.columbia.edu/~jeh1/2008/TwentyYearsLater_20080623.pdf.

41. Ian Sample, "Scientists Offered Cash to Dispute Climate Study," *Guardian*, February 2, 2007.

42. Robin McKie, "Meltdown in the Arctic Is Speeding Up," *The Observer*, August 10, 2008.

43. In 2008, U.S. consumption was projected to fall to a little over 20 million barrels a day from previous highs nearly 21 mbb/day, because of a slowing economy, high prices, and replacement of small amounts of petroleum by ethanol: "U.S. Oil Consumption Declines," *Oil Voice*, April 5, 2008, at http://www.oilvoice.com/n/US_Oil_Consumption_Declines/ff895835.aspx

44. David Adam, "Alarm Over New Oil-From-Coal Plans," *Guardian*, February 20, 2008. Some speak of sequestering the carbon emissions, but turning carbon into liquids for storage in the ground is extremely expensive. Only a fraction of the new carbon emissions could be avoided in this way, and carbon dioxide leaks from underground storage holds would be lethal to human beings.

45. Mark Clayton, "Carbon Cloud Over a Green Fuel," *Christian Science Monitor*, March 23, 2006. Better candidates for ethanol production, such as switchgrass, can make a contribution to resolving the energy crisis if methods can be found for efficiently breaking down tough membranes such as cellulose; see David Biello, "Grass Makes Better Ethanol than Corn Does," *Scientific American*, January 8, 2008. "Another Inconvenient Truth: How Biofuel Policies Are Deepening Poverty and Accelerating Climate Change," Oxfam, June 2008, at http://www.oxfam.org/en/files/bp114_inconvenient_truth.pdf/; Peter Terzakian, *A Thousand Barrels a Second* (New York: McGraw-Hill, 2006), pp. 205–7.

46. Daniel G. Nocera, "On the Future of Global Energy," *Daedalus* 135, no. 4 (Fall 2006), p. 112.

47. Environmental Iowa, "Redirecting Iowa's Energy," December 20, 2006, at http://www.environmentiowa.org/reports/energy/energy-program-reports/redirecting-iowa39s-energy.

48. Bart Jones and Letta Tayler, "CIA Knew of Plot Against Venezuela's Chavez; Leader Not Warned, Documents Reveal," *Newsday*, November 24, 2004.

49. Carmen Gentile, "Venezuela, China Set to Ink New Oil Deal," UPI, May 7, 2008.

50. Usamah Bin Laden, ""Declaration of War against the Americans Occupying the Land of the Two Holy Places" (1996), Online Newshour, Public Broadcasting Service, at http://www.pbs.org/newshour/terrorism/international/fatwa_1996.html.

51. Thomas L. Friedman, "The Energy to Be Serious," *International Herald Tribune*, May 3, 2008.

52. Dianna Dilworth, "Zero Carbon; Zero Waste in Abu Dhabi: Foster + Partners Is Building an Eco-Friendly Oasis in the Desert," *BusinessWeek*, August 1, 2007, at http://www.businessweek.com/innovate/content/aug2007/id2007081_901739.htm?chan=innovation_architecture_top+stories; Simeon Kerr, "Work Starts on $22bn Carbon-Neutral City in Abu Dhabi," February 12, 2008, at http://www.arabenvironment.net/archive/2008/2/466634.html; Chris Stanton, "Carbon-Neutral City Planned for Jordan," *The National*, May 15, 2008, at

http://www.thenational.ae/article/20080515/BUSINESS/547587520; "Global Warming Could Displace Millions in the Middle East," *AMEInfo* (United Arab Emirates), February 25, 2008, at http://www.ameinfo.com/148002.html.

CHAPTER 2

1. "MSNBC's Republican Presidential Debate," Federal News Service, May 3, 2007, via LexisNexis.
2. Paul Berman, *Terror and Liberalism* (New York: Norton, 2003), pp. 59–60.
3. The tourist industry employs 12 percent of the labor force, amounts to 11.6 percent of the gross national product, and accounts for 20 percent of Egypt's foreign exchange earnings.
4. Alain Navarro, "No Alcohol Means Fewer Stars for Egypt Luxury Hotel," Agence France Presse, June 17, 2008.
5. Lydia Saad, "Americans' Most and Least Favored Nations: Canada and Great Britain Remain the Most Popular Allies," Gallup, March 3, 2008, at http://www.gallup.com/poll/104734/Americans-Most-Least-Favored-Nations.aspx.
6. Ibid.
7. "Muslim Public Opinion on US Policy, Attacks on Civilians and al Qaeda," Worldopinion.org, Program on International Policy Attitudes (PIPA), Center for International and Security Studies at Maryland and the Center on Policy Attitudes, April 24, 2007, at http://www.worldpublicopinion.org/pipa/pdf/apr07/START_Apr07_rpt.pdf.
8. Ibid.
9. Ibid.
10. Esra'a, "American TV in Arab Households," *Mideast Youth,* November 16, 2006, at http://www.mideastyouth.com/2006/11/16/american-tv-in-arab-households/.
11. "Atta's Father Praises London Bombs," CNN, Wednesday, July 20, 2005, at http://www.cnn.com/2005/WORLD/meast/07/19/atta.father.terror/index.html.
12. Juan Cole, *Colonialism and Revolution in the Middle East: Social and Cultural Origins of Egypt's 'Urabi Revolution* (Princeton, N.J.: Princeton University Press, 1983).
13. For al-Banna's statement see Stefan Wild, "National Socialism in the Arab near East between 1933 and 1939," *Die Welt des Islams,* New Series, Bd. 25, Nr. 1/4 (1985), pp. 126–173, this quote on p. 138; for the very limited influence of Nazism see Francis Nicosia, "Arab Nationalism and National Socialist Germany, 1933–1939: Ideological and Strategic Incompatibility," *International Journal of Middle East Studies* 12, no. 3 (November, 1980), pp. 351–372. For the rejection of fascism by mainstream Egyptian liberals, see Israel Gershoni, "Egyptian Liberalism in an Age of 'Crisis of Orientation': Al-Risala's Reaction to Fascism and Nazism, 1933–39," *International Journal of Middle East Studies* 31, no. 4 (November 1999), pp. 551–76.
14. Thomas Mayer, "Egypt and the 1936 Arab Revolt in Palestine," *Journal of Contemporary History* 19, no. 2 (April 1984), pp. 275–87.
15. Sa'id 'Abd al-Rahman Yusuf 'Abdu'llah, *Mahmud Fahmi al-Nuqrashi wa Dawruhu fi al-Siyasah al-Misriyyah wa Hall Jama'at al-Ikhwan al-Muslimin (1888–1948)* (Cairo: Madbouli, 1995), pp. 621–66; Richard P. Mitchell, *The Society of Muslim Brothers* (Oxford: Oxford University Press, 1969, 1993), pp. 62–65; Ziad Munson, "Social Movements Within Islam: Islamic Mobilization: Social Movement Theory and the Egyptian Muslim Brotherhood," *Sociological Quarterly* 42, no. 4 (Autumn 2001), pp. 487–510.

16. Hasan al-Jamal, *Jihad al-Ikhwan al-Muslimin fi al-Qanah wa-Filastin* (Cairo: Dar al-Tawzi' wa-al-Nashr al-Islamiyah, 2000).

17. Avi Shlaim, *The Iron Wall: Israel and the Arab World* (New York: Norton, 2000); Rashid Khalidi, *The Iron Cage: The Story of the Palestinian Struggle for Statehood* (Boston: Beacon Press, 2006); Ilan Pappe, *The Ethnic Cleansing of Palestine* (Oxford: Oneworld, 2006); Benny Morris, *The Birth of the Palestinian Refugee Problem, 1947–1949* (Cambridge: Cambridge University Press, 1987).

18. "Politics in God's Name," *Al-Ahram Weekly* no. 247, November 16–22, 1995, at http://www.ahram.org.eg/weekly/archives/parties/muslimb/polgod.htm.

19. Mitchell, *The Society of Muslim Brothers,* pp. 111, 150–53; Joel Gordon, *Nasser's Blessed Movement: Egypt's Free Officers and the July Revolution* (New York: Oxford University Press, 1992), pp. 180–82.

20. Malika Zeghal, "Religion and Politics in Egypt: The Ulema of al-Azhar, Radical Islam, and the State (1952–94)," *International Journal of Middle East Studies* 31, no. 3 (August 1999), pp. 371–99, 375.

21. Sayyid Qutb, *Ma'alim fi al-Tariq* [Milestones]. Arabic text online, chap. 4 on jihad, at http://www.tawhed.ws/r?i=1522&PHPSESSID=56158f4451acc89873bd 0b70681fb520; William E. Shepard, "Sayyid Qutb's Doctrine of Jahiliyya," *International Journal of Middle East Studies* 35, no. 4 (2003), pp. 521–45.

22. Ibid.

23. 'Abd Allah Imam, *'Abd al-Nasir wa al-Ikhwan al-Muslimun* (Cairo: Dar al-Khayyal, 1997), p. 185.

24. Berman, *Terror,* p. 60.

25. Rachel Scott, "An 'Official' Islamic Response to the Egyptian al-Jihad Movement," *Journal of Political Ideologies* 8, no. 1 (2003), pp. 39–61, this point on p. 51, at http://www.idst.vt.edu/pubs/Scott.pdf.

26. While it is true that Muslim fundamentalists often ridicule figures like the grand imam as lackeys of the secular Egyptian government, many ordinary Sunni Muslims pay attention to al-Azhar fatwas.

27. Pew Global Attitudes, "The Great Divide: How Westerners and Muslims View Each Other," June 22, 2006, at http://pewglobal.org/reports/display.php?Report ID=253.

28. "Muslim Public Opinion on US Policy," PIPA.

29. Dalia Mogahed, "Islam and Democracy," Gallup World Poll, Special Report: Muslim World, February 2008, at http://media.gallup.com/MuslimWestFacts/PDF/ GALLUPMUSLIMSTUDIESIslamandDemocracy030607rev.pdf.

30. Freedom Forum First Amendment Center at Vanderbilt University, "State of the First Amendment Survey," conducted by the Center for Survey Research and Analysis at the University of Connecticut, February 26–March 24, 1999, at http://www.pollingreport.com/civil2.htm. N=1,001 adults nationwide.

31. Nazih N. M. Ayubi, "The Political Revival of Islam: The Case of Egypt," *International Journal of Middle East Studies* 12, no. 4 (December 1980), pp. 481–99, esp. 493–94.

32. Nashwa al-Hufi, "Hawwalat Thalath Shakhsiyyat al-Zawahiri min ibn 'ai'ilah aristuqratiyyah ila al-matlub raqam 2 fi al-'alam," *Al-Sharq al-Awsat,* October 17, 2001; Youssef H. Aboul-Enein, "Ayman al-Zawahiri: Ideologue of Modern Islamic Militancy," *Future War Series* 21 (Maxwell AFB, AL: USAF Counterproliferation Center, 2004), pp. 1–2.

33. "Part Three of New Book by Egyptian Islamic Jihad Leader Ayman al-Zawahiri," *Al-Sharq al-Awsat,* in Arabic, December 4, 2001, p. 6, translated by the

Foreign Broadcast Information Service (FBIS) and distributed by the World News Connection.

34. Denis J. Sullivan and Sana Abed-Kotob, *Islam in Contemporary Egypt: Civil Society vs. the State* (Boulder, CO: L. Rienner, 1999).

35. "Congressmen and Doctor Call for Increased Aid to Afghan Resistance," States News Service, October 15, 1985; the best overview of the Reagan jihad against the Soviet Union in Afghanistan is Steve Coll, *Ghost Wars: The Secret History of the CIA, Afghanistan, and Bin Laden, from the Soviet Invasion to September 10, 2001* (New York: Penguin Press, 2004).

36. "Religious Lobbyist Sees 'Christian-Bashing' in GOP," Associated Press, June 12, 1987.

37. David Reed, "Robertson Calls on Soviets to Leave Afghanistan," Associated Press, October 3, 1987.

38. Personal communication, Flagg Miller, 2005. Miller is going through tapes of al-Qaeda meetings in Afghanistan discovered by David Edwards after the 2001 Afghanistan war.

39. "Sahafi amda sanawat fi Afghanistan ya'rid fi Landan Sharitan Jadidan li Bin Ladin," *al-Sharq al-Awsat,* September 9, 2002.

40. Lawrence Wright, *The Looming Tower* (New York: Alfred A. Knopf, 2006), pp. 224–28; Barnett Rubin, personal communication, September 3, 2008.

41. "Nass bayan al-Jibhah al-Islamiyyah al-'Alamiyyah li Jihad al-Yahud wa al-Salibiyyin," *Al-Quds Al-'Arabi,* February 23, 1998; Federation of American Scientists, transl., "Jihad against Jews and Crusaders: World Islamic Front Statement," February 23, 1998, at http://www.fas.org/irp/world/para/docs/980223-fatwa.htm.

42. "1997 Massacre Changed Egypt's Tourism," Associated Press, November 19, 2007, at http://news.yahoo.com/s/ap_travel/20071119/ap_tr_ge/travel_brief_egypt _luxor_massacre_1.

43. I benefited in understanding this recantation literature from the fine seminar paper of Eric Schewe on this subject, carried out for my seminar, History 749, in Winter 2008 at the University of Michigan.

44. Rory McVeigh, "Structured Ignorance and Organized Racism in the United States," *Social Forces* 82, no. 3. (March 2004), pp. 895–936, this point on p. 898. Four major groups make up the white supremacy movement, including members of the Ku Klux Klan networks, neo-Nazis, skinheads, and believers in Christian Identity theology.

45. Lou Michel and Dan Herbeck, *American Terrorist: Timothy McVeigh and the Oklahoma City Bombing* (New York: Regan Books, 2001), p. 109.

46. Ibid., p. 179.

47. Ibid., p. 166

48. Sandy Shore, "FBI Agent: I Found Nichols' Prints," Associated Press Online, November 14, 1997.

49. Howard Witt, "Lawyer Pursues Links Between Neo-Nazis, Oklahoma City Bombing," *Chicago Tribune,* December 8, 2006.

50. William Chaloupka, "The County Supremacy and Militia Movements: Federalism as an Issue on the Radical Right," *Publius* 26, no. 3 (Summer 1996), pp. 161–75, this information on p. 162, quoting "Distrust of Government," ABC News/Washington Post Poll, May 17, 1995.

51. John L. Esposito and Dalia Mogahed, *Who Speaks for Islam? What a Billion Muslims Really Think* (New York: Gallup Press, 2007), p. 48.

52. Marisol Bello, "FBI: Hate Crimes Escalate 8% in 2006," *USA Today*, November 19, 2007, at http://www.usatoday.com/news/nation/2007–11–19-hate-crime_N.htm.

53. David Holthouse and Mark Potok, "The Year in Hate: Active U.S. Hate Groups Rise to 888 in 2007," at http://www.splcenter.org/intel/intelreport/article.jsp?aid=886.

54. Esposito and Mogahed, *Who Speaks for Islam?* pp. 69–70.

55. Fawaz Gerges, *The Far Enemy: Why Jihad Went Global* (New York: Cambridge University Press, 2005); Wright, *The Looming*, p. 307.

56. "Al-Nass al-kamil li sharit al-fidiyu al-mansub li Bin Ladin," at http://www.uaegoal.com/vb/showthread.php?t=924 (accessed February 8, 2008).

57. Ayellet Yehiav, "Post-Elections Assessment: The Muslim Brotherhood in Egypt's Parliament," *Strategic Assessment* 8, no. 4 (February 2006), at http://www.tau.ac.il/jcss/sa/v8n4p5Yehiav.html.

58. Abd al-Sattar Ibrahim, "'Akif li 'al-Sharq al-Awsat': al-Ikhwan didd istihdaf tanzim al-Qa'ida li al-madaniyyin," *Al-Sharq al-Aws'at*, May 25, 2008, at http://www.asharqalawsat.com/details.asp?section=4&issueno=10771&article=472208&feature=.

59. Marc Lynch, "Assessing the Muslim Brotherhood 'Firewall,'" *Abu Aardvark*, May 12, 2008, at http://abuaardvark.typepad.com/abuaardvark/2008/05/assessing-the-m.html.

CHAPTER 3

1. Wolf Blitzer, "Interview with Prince Turki Al-Faisal," CNN Showdown: Iraq, December 23, 2002, via LexisNexis.

2. "Saudi Arabia Declares al Qaeda Defeated," June 9, 2006, at http://www.strategypage.com/htmw/htterr/articles/20060609.aspx; Roel Meijer, "The 'Cycle of Contention' and the Limits of Terrorism in Saudi Arabia," in Paul Aarst and Gerd Nonneman, eds., *Saudi Arabia in the Balance: Political Economy, Society, Foreign Affairs* (New York: New York University Press, 2005), pp. 271–311.

3. Elizabeth Sirriyeh, "Wahhabis, Unbelievers and the Problems of Exclusivism," *Bulletin of the British Society for Middle Eastern Studies* 16, no. 2 (1989), pp. 123–32; Esther Peskes and Werner Ende, "Wahhabiyya," Encyclopedia of Islam, Brill Online; Guido Steinberg, "The Wahhabi Ulama and the Saudi State, 1745 to the Present," in Aarts and Nonneman, eds., *Saudi Arabia in the Balance*, pp. 11–34.

4. Douglas Little, "Pipeline Politics: America, TAPLINE, and the Arabs." *Business History Review* 64, no. 2 (Summer 1990), pp. 255–85; Robert Vitalis, *America's Kingdom: Mythmaking on the Saudi Oil Frontier* (Stanford, Calif.: Stanford University Press, 2007).

5. Bilal Hashmi, "The Beginnings of U.S.-Pakistan Alliance," *Pakistan Forum* 3, no. 6/7 (March–April 1973), pp. 3–9, 32, this quote on p. 8.

6. "Diary Entry by the President," March 28, 1956, *Foreign Relations of the United States*, 1955–1957, 15: 425, quoted in Matthew F. Jacobs, "The Perils and Promise of Islam: The United States and the Muslim Middle East in the Early Cold War," *Diplomatic History* 30, no. 4 (2006), pp. 705–39, this quote on p. 734.

7. J. Citino, *From Arab Nationalism to OPEC: Eisenhower, King Sa'ud, and the Making of US-Saudi Relations* (Bloomington: University of Indiana Press, 2002), p. 120; see also Salim Yaqub, *Containing Arab Nationalism: The Eisenhower Doctrine and the Middle East* (Chapel Hill: University of North Carolina Press, 2004), p. 103.

8. Citino, *From Arab Nationalism to OPEC*, pp. 126–27.

9. Yaqub, *Containing Arab Nationalism,* pp. 16, 108.
10. Jacobs, "The Perils and Promise of Islam," p. 734.
11. Citino, *From Arab Nationalism to OPEC,* p. 118.
12. Thomas Hegghammer, "Saudis in Iraq: Patterns of Radicalization and Recruitment," *Cultures and Conflicts,* English documents, mis en ligne le 12 juin 2008, at http://www.conflits.org//index10042.html.
13. U.S. State Department, *Country Reports on Terrorism,* released by the Office of the Coordinator for Counterterrorism, April 30, 2008: chapter 5–5.3, "Collaboration with Saudi Arabia," at http://www.state.gov/s/ct/rls/crt/2007/104112.htm. The report adds, "The government announced a project to secure its border with Iraq as part of its larger border modernization program. The project will increase physical barriers and electronic surveillance of the northern border. In the interim, the Ministry of the Interior has deployed additional forces to the border area and has been successful in interdicting illicit movement of persons and equipment across the Saudi-Iraq border. The Saudi government announced the arrest of several hundred individuals who were planning to travel to Iraq or were actually en route, and increased its security cooperation with the Government of Iraq."
14. Ma'd Fayyad, "Muwaffaq al-Ruba'i li 'al-Sharq al-Awsat'," *al-Sharq al-Awsat,* April 23, 2008.
15. U.S. State Department, *Country Reports on Terrorism,* chap. 5–5.3; Ambassador Cofer Black, Coordinator for Counterterrorism, "Saudi Arabia and the Fight Against Terrorist Financing," Testimony before the House Committee on International Relations, Subcommittee on the Middle East and Central Asia, Washington, D.C., March 24, 2004, at http://www.state.gov/s/ct/rls/rm/2004/30740.htm.
16. Robin Wright, "From the Desk of Donald Rumsfeld," *Washington Post,* November 1, 2007.
17. M. A. Ramady, *The Saudi Arabian Economy: Policies, Achievements and Challenges* (New York: Springer, 2005), chap. 12.
18. Roger Hardy, "Unemployment, the New Saudi Challenge," BBC News, October 4, 2006, at http://news.bbc.co.uk/2/hi/business/5406328.stm.
19. Abeer Mishkhas, "How Could Such Things Happen in Saudi Arabia?" *Arab News,* January 31, 2008, at http://arabnews.com/?page=7&section=0&article=106294&d=31&m=1&y=2008.
20. "Who Profits from Gulf Oil Revenue?" Al-Jazeera International, June 21, 2008, at http://www.youtube.com/watch?v=TIJRXb_uzkM&e/.
21. John Kifner, "The World: Ruling Class; Building Modernity on Desert Mirages," *New York Times,* February 7, 1999.
22. United Nations Department of Economic and Social Affairs, Population Division, "World Urbanization Prospects: 2005 Revision," Tables: Population of Urban and Rural Areas at Mid-year and Percentage Urban, 2005, at http://www.un.org/esa/population/publications/WUP2005/2005wup.htm.
23. "Saudi Arabia's Brand-new $34.7-Billion City," *International Construction Review,* June 13, 2008, at http://www.ciobinternational.org/news/view/1349.
24. Mansoor Moaddel, "The Saudi Public Speaks: Religion, Gender and Politics," in Mansoor Moaddel, ed., *Values and Perceptions of the Islamic and Middle Eastern Publics* (New York: Palgrave Macmillan, 2007), pp. 209–46, this point on pp. 218–19.
25. Laza Kekic "The Economist Intelligence Unit's Index of Democracy, 2007" at http://www.economist.com/media/pdf/Democracy_Index_2007_v3.pdf, which lists Saudi Arabia at 159, toward the bottom of the index, whereas numerous

Muslim-majority states have better positions on the list, including Lebanon (85) and Senegal (94) and even Pakistan (113), Jordan (113), and Egypt (115). Pakistan's position on the index should improve considerably with the return to civilian rule in August of 2008.

26. Daniel Pipes, "The Scandal of U.S.-Saudi Relations," *National Interest* (Winter 2002/03).

27. For an argument that the main problem is not the Wahhabi traditions, see Sherifa Zuhur, "Islamic Threat, Political Reform, and the Global War on Terror" (Carlisle, PA: Strategic Studies Institute, U.S. Army War College, 2005), at http://www .strategicstudiesinstitute.army.mil/pdffiles/PUB598.pdf.

28. Kenneth Ballen, "Look Who's Pro-U.S. Now: Saudi Arabia," *Christian Science Monitor,* January 8, 2008; Terror Free Tomorrow, "Results of a New Nationwide Survey of Saudi Public Opinion," December 2007, at http://www.terrorfree-tomorrow.org/upimagestft/TFT%20Saudi%20Arabia%20Survey.pdf.

29. Daniel Johnson, "How Saudi Arabia Spreads Terrorism and Hatred of the West," *Telegraph* (London), July 22, 2003.

30. Robert Pape, *Dying to Win: The Strategic Logic of Suicide Terrorism* (New York: Random House, 2006).

31. Ruddy Doom and Koen Vlassenroot, "Kony's Message: A New Koine? The Lord's Resistance Army in Northern Uganda," *African Affairs* 98, no. 390 (January 1999), pp. 5–36; Kevin Ward, "'The Armies of the Lord': Christianity, Rebels and the State in Northern Uganda, 1986–1999," *Journal of Religion in Africa* 31 (May 2001), pp. 187–221.

32. "Hay'at al-Amr bi al-Ma'ruf wa al-Nahy 'an al-Munkar laisat jihaz Tasallut: Sumuww Wazir al-Dakhiliyyah," *Al-Yawm al-Su'udi,* November 28, 2002, at http://www.alyaum.com/issue/article.php?IN=10758&I=35238 (reprinted from *Al-Siyasah* [Kuwait], November 27, 2002).

33. Quintan Wiktorowicz, "The Salafi Movement in Jordan," *International Journal of Middle East Studies* 32 (2000): 219–40.

34. Israel Shahak and Norton Mezvinsky, *Jewish Fundamentalism in Israel* (London: Pluto Press, 1999); Ian Lustick, *For the Land and the Lord: Jewish Fundamentalism in Israel* (New York: Council on Foreign Relations, 1988)

35. Terror Free Tomorrow, "Results of a New Nationwide Survey of Saudi Public Opinion."

36. Moaddel, "The Saudi Public Speaks: Religion, Gender and Politics," p. 214.

37. David S. Cloud, "U.S. Set to Offer $20 Billion Arms Deal to Saudi Arabia and Other Gulf States," *International Herald Tribune,* July 29, 2007.

38. Juan Cole, "What Michael Moore (and the Neocons) Don't Know About Saudi Arabia," Salon.com, August 5, 2005, at http://dir.salon.com/story/news/feature/ 2005/08/05/fahd/.

39. Steve Coll, *Ghost Wars: The Secret History of the CIA, Afghanistan, and bin Laden, From the Soviet Invasion to September 10, 2001* (New York: Penguin Press, 2004); Rachel Bronson, *Thicker Than Oil: America's Uneasy Partnership with Saudi Arabia* (Oxford: Oxford University Press, 2006), chap. 9.

40. "Al-Su'udiyyah: Al-Shi'ah yaktasihun maqa'id al-Qatif wa al-Ahsa,'" CNN Arabic, April 23, 2005, at http://arabic.cnn.com/2005/saudi.2005/4/21/2nd.elections/ index.html.

41. Terror Free Tomorrow, "Results of a New Nationwide Survey of Saudi Public Opinion."

42. Kevin Whitelaw, "Saudi Arabia Tries to Rehabilitate Its Jihadists," *US News & World Report*, May 1, 2008; Peter Bergen, "Letter from Riyadh: Are We Witnessing a Saudi Glasnost?" National Review Online, February 14, 2005, at http://www.nationalreview.com/comment/bergen200502140750.asp.

43. Joby Warrick, "U.S. Cites Big Gains Against Al-Qaeda: Group Is Facing Setbacks Globally, CIA Chief Says," *Washington Post*, May 30, 2008.

44. Joseph Kostiner, "Coping with Regional Strategies: A Case Study of Crown Prince Abdullah's Peace Initiative," in Aarts and Nonneman, *Saudi*, pp. 352–71.

45. Thomas E. Ricks, "Briefing Depicted Saudis as Enemies: Ultimatum Urged to Pentagon Board," *Washington Post*, August 6, 2002; Steve Simon, "Riyadh Revisions," *American Prospect*, May 20, 2007.

46. Simon, "Riyadh Revisions."

47. Mamoun Fandy, "The Mecca Factor," *Guardian*, March 27, 2007.

48. F. Gregory Gause, "Memo to the President: How to Reform Saudi Arabia without Handing It to Extremists," *Foreign Policy* 144 (September–October 2004), pp. 66–70.

49. Alistair Lyon, "Qatar Pulls Off Mediation Coup in Lebanon Crisis: Tiny Gulf State of Qatar Succeeds in Halting Lebanon Clashes Where UN, Arab League, France Failed," Middle East Online, May 23, 2005, at http://www.middle-east-online.com/English/?id=26064.

50. Marc Lynch, *Voices of the New Arab Public: Iraq, Al Jazeera, and Middle East Politics Today* (New York: Columbia University Press, 2006).

51. Juan Cole, "Clinton and Obama on Aljazeera," Salon.com, May 12, 2008, at http://www.salon.com/opinion/feature/2008/05/12/aljazeera/

52. A similar point is made by Josh Rushing with Sean Elder, *Mission Al Jazeera* (New York: Palgrave Macmillan, 2007), chap. 6.

53. Ian Sample, "Messages of Fear in Hi-tech Invisible Ink," *Guardian*, August 11, 2005.

54. "Reporters without Borders Outraged at Bombing of Al-Jazeera Office in Baghdad," April 8, 2003, at http://www.rsf.org/article.php3?id_article=5945.

55. Juan Cole, "Did Bush Plan to Bomb Al-Jazeera?" Salon.com, November 30, 2005, at http://dir.salon.com/story/opinion/feature/2005/11/30/al_jazeera/.

56. Oxford Analytica, "The Advent of Terrorism in Qatar," Forbes.com, March 25, 2005, at http://www.forbes.com/2005/03/25/cz_0325oxan_qatarattack.html.

57. "Human Rights Watch Memorandum to the Government of Saudi Arabia on Human Rights Priorities in the Kingdom," Human Rights Watch, February 7, 2006, at http://hrw.org/english/docs/2006/02/07/saudia12622.htm.

58. Joseph McMillan, "Saudi Arabia and Iraq: Oil, Religion, and an Enduring Rivalry" (Washington, D.C.: US Institute of Peace, 2006), at http://www.usip.org/pubs/specialreports/sr157.pdf.

CHAPTER 4

1. Roy Maynard, "McCain Played to His Strengths," *Tyler* (Texas) *Morning Telegraph*, February 27, 2008.

2. "U.S. Will Complete Mission in Iraq–Cheney," Reuters, March 18, 2008.

3. Amatzia Baram, "The Ruling Political Elite in Bathi Iraq, 1968–1986: The Changing Features of a Collective Profile," *International Journal of Middle East Studies* 21, no. 4 (November 1989), pp. 447–93.

4. "McCain Mistakenly Says Iran Allowing Al Qaeda Fighters Into Country, Later Corrects Error," Associated Press, March 19, 2008.

5. The literature on the Iraq War is now vast. I list some basic texts for general readers (and apologize to my friends who have authored more specialized studies): Anthony Shadid, *Night Draws Near: Iraq's People in the Shadow of America's War* (New York: Henry Holt, 2004); George Packer; *The Assassins' Gate: America in Iraq* (New York: Farrar, Straus and Giroux, 2005); Thomas E. Ricks, *Fiasco* (New York: Penguin Press, 2006); Rajiv Chandrasekaran, *Imperial Life in the Emerald City* (New York: Alfred A. Knopf, 2006); Ahmed Hashem, *Insurgency and Counter-Insurgency in Iraq* (Ithaca, NY: Cornell University Press, 2006); Nir Rosen, *In the Belly of the Green Bird* (New York: Free Press, 2006); Patrick Cockburn, *Muqtada al-Sadr, the Shia Revival, and the Struggle for Iraq* (New York: Scribner, 2008).

6. "Terror Connection?" *CNN American Morning with Paula Zahn*, December 12, 2002, via LexisNexis.

7. "U.S. General: Al-Zarqawi Leads 90% of Iraq Attacks," Associated Press, April 10, 2006.

8. Malcolm W. Nance, *The Terrorists of Iraq: Inside the Strategy and Tactics of the Iraq Insurgency* (Charleston, S.C. : Booksurge Publishing, 2007); Hashim, *Insurgency and Counter-Insurgency in Iraq.*

9. For ISCI and the Badr Corps, see Juan Cole, "Shia Militias in Iraqi Politics," in Markus Bouillon, David M. Malone, and Ben Rowswell, eds., *Iraq: Preventing a New Generation of Conflict* (Boulder, Co.: Lynne Rienner, 2007), pp. 109–23; for the Sadrists, see Cockburn, *Muqtada,* and Juan Cole, "The United States and Shi'ite Religious Factions in Post-Ba'thist Iraq," *Middle East Journal* 57, no. 4 (Autumn 2003), pp. 543–66.

10. Shibley Telhami, "2008 Annual Arab Public Opinion Poll Survey," Anwar Sadat Chair for Peace and Development at the University of Maryland (with Zogby International), at sadat.umd.edu/surveys/2008%20Arab%20Public%20Opinion%20Survey.ppt.

11. Nicholas D. Kristof, "The Two Israels," *New York Times,* June 22, 2008.

12. Terror Free Tomorrow, "Results of a New Nationwide Survey of Saudi Public Opinion" (December 2007), at http://www.terrorfreetomorrow.org/upimagestft/TFT%20Saudi%20Arabia%20Survey.pdf.

13. "Over Half of Americans Say They Tend Not to Trust the Press," Harris Poll, no. 24, March 6, 2008, at http://www.harrisinteractive.com/harris_poll/index.asp?PID=878.

14. David Barstow, "Behind TV Analysts, Pentagon's Hidden Hand," *New York Times,* April 20, 2008; Glenn Greenwald, "Media's Refusal to Address the NYT's 'Military Analyst' Story Continues," Salon.com, April 22, 2008, at http://www.salon.com/opinion/greenwald/2008/04/22/analysts/; see, for the general failure of the press with regard to the Iraq War, Greg Mitchell, *So Wrong for So Long* (New York: Sterling Press, 2008).

15. Brian Stelter, "Reporters Say Networks Put Wars on Back Burner," *New York Times,* June 23, 2008.

16. Telhami, "2008 Annual Arab Public Opinion Poll Survey" section on "2008 Media Viewership."

17. "Iraq: Government Incentives for IDPs, Refugees to Return," Integrated Regional Information Networks, June 3, 2008, at http://www.unhcr.org/cgi-bin/texis/vtx/refworld/rwmain?docid=4847bb94c.

18. International Organization for Migration, "Iraq: Governorate Profiles Highlight Latest Displacement Trends," June 20, 2008, at http://www.iom.int/jahia/Jahia/pbnAF/cache/offonce?entryId=17638.

19. Jonathan Finer and Jennifer Rikosk, "Stuck in Syria with No Way Home," *Miami Herald,* June 20, 2008, at http://www.miamiherald.com/opinion/inbox/story/575931.html.

20. Ghassan al-Imam, "Ma'rikat Baghdad: Isti'sal al-Sunnah wa al-'Uruba," *Al-Sharq al-Awsat,* January 16, 2007.

21. Interview, Issam Sayed, CARE, Amman, Jordan, August 21, 2008.

22. "In'idam al-khidmat sabab asasi li hijrat al-'Iraqiyyin," *al-Hayat,* August 26, 2008, at http://www.daralhayat.com/arab_news/levant_news/08–2008/Item–200808 25-fafaaad4-c0a8–10ed–01bf-ee3394862845/story.html.

23. Andrew Lam, "Why 'Little Baghdad' Won't Form in the U.S," *National Catholic Reporter* (Kansas City), February 9, 2007; see also Oxford Analytica, "Refugee Policy," *International Herald Tribune,* July 9, 2007.

24. "Tancredo Statement on Gen. Petraeus Iraq Report," September 10, 2007, at http://tancredo.house.gov/PRArticle.aspx?NewsID=1304.

25. Jonathan Steele and Suzanne Goldenberg, "What Is the Real Death Toll in Iraq?" *Guardian,* March 19, 2008.

26. Tom Engelhardt, "Looking Up: Normalizing Air War From Guernica to Arab Jabour," Tomdispatch.com, January 29, 2008, at http://www.tomdispatch.com/post/174887.

27. Ernesto Londoño and Amit R. Paley, "In Iraq, a Surge in U.S. Airstrikes: Military Says Attacks Save Troops' Lives, but Civilian Casualties Elicit Criticism," *Washington Post,* May 23, 2008.

28. "January 2008—Update on Iraqi Casualty Data," Opinion Research Business, at http://www.opinion.co.uk/Newsroom_details.aspx?NewsId=88.

29. Steele and Goldenberg, "What Is the Real Death Toll in Iraq?"

30. "Fuhus Tibbiyyah takshif ta'dhib al-mu'taqalin fi al-sujun al-amrikiyyah," *Al-Islam al-Yawm,* June 19, 2008, with comments, at http://islamtoday.net/albasheer/show_news_content.cfm?id=85256.

31. "Iraqi Politics in Perspective," Briefing Paper Prepared for President Nixon, May 18, 1972, Tab B, *FRUS, 1969–1976,* vol. E–4, Documents on Iran and Iraq, 1969–1972, at http://www.state.gov/r/pa/ho/frus/nixon/e4/65606.htm.

32. Airgram, Department of State A–38, To: Department of State, From: Am Embassy, Beirut, February 2, 1972, *FRUS, 1969–1976,* vol. E–4, Documents on Iran and Iraq, 1969–1972, at http://www.state.gov/r/pa/ho/frus/nixon/e4/65602.htm.

33. "Al-Shurtah al-'Iraqiyyah tartakib majzarah fi Ba'qubah," al-Zaman, November 6, 2006, at http://www.azzaman.com/index.asp?fname=2006\\11\\11–06\\999.htm &storytitle; "'Izzat al-Duri yuhajim bi shiddah ba'thiyyin yukhattitun li tawhid al-qiyadah," *Al-Hayat,* January 19, 2007, at http://www.daralhayat.com/arab _news/levant_news/01–2007/Item–20070118–36c4710b-c0a8–10ed–0090–682e0 ca2a06c/story.html.

34. "Wazir al-Dakhiliiyah al-'Iraqi yuhadhdhir min Hizb al-'Awdah," *Al-Zaman,* January 14, 2007, http://www.azzaman.com/index.asp?fname=2007\01\01–14\998 .htm&storytitle=.

35. "Ba'th Party Issues Statement Warning of Reprisals over Iraq Oil Law Approval," Jihadist Web Sites—Open Source Center Summary, August 10, 2007, via World News Connection: "The Ba'th Party and the Iraqi Armed Resistance Also Warn Western Companies, Especially Norwegian Ones, Against 'Concluding Deals' with the Agent Gangs That Collaborate with the Occupiers in Northern Iraq, Since Northern Iraq Is an Indivisible Part of Iraq . . ."

36. Mansoor Moaddel, "Trends in the Iraqi Political Values Toward Secular Politics and National Identity: Findings from Values Surveys, December 2004, April 2006, October 2006, March 2007, and July 2007 (Presentation Slides)," 2007, *Values Surveys in Islamic Countries: Findings by Mansoor Moaddel,* Population Studies Center, University of Michigan, at http://www.psc.isr.umich.edu/research/tmp/moaddel_trendsIraqiPoliticalValuesSecularPoliticsNationalIdentity_dec04-jul07.pdf.

37. "Arab Attitudes Towards Political and Social Issues, Foreign Policy and the Media," Public Opinion Poll conducted jointly by the Anwar Sadat Chair for Peace and Development at the University of Maryland and Zogby International, 2004, at http://www.bsos.umd.edu/SADAT/pub/Arab%20Attitudes%20Towards%20Political%20and%20Social%20Issues,%20Foreign%20Policy%20and%20the%20Media.htm; this poll's findings on this issue generally accord for Jordan with those of Mansoor Moaddel, "The Impact of 9/11 on Value Orientations of the Islamic Public in Egypt," 2004, at http://www.psc.isr.umich.edu/research/tmp/moaddel_values-egypt.pdf, but Moaddel's figures for Egypt are substantially different from those of Telhami and Zogby.

38. "Hawl ihtimal dukhul ashkhas al-qutr min tanzim al-Qaeda," August 2002, at http://www.theblackvault.com/documents/capturediraq/ISGZ–2004–019920.pdf; this file was captured by the U.S. military in Iraq and originally posted at a Fort Leavenworth site, but was later taken down. It was preserved on the Web at TheBlackVault.com.

39. Ibid.

40. "Iraq Trained al-Qaeda Operatives: Cheney," Agence France Presse, December 2, 2002; for analysis of this phenomenon more generally, see David Altheide and Jennifer Grimes, "War Programming: The Propaganda Project and the Iraq War," *Sociological Quarterly* 46, no. 4 (2005).

41. "Vice President's Remarks at D-Day Museum," July 1, 2004, http://www.whitehouse.gov/news/releases/2004/07/20040701–8.html.

42. On the state of the Ansar al-Islam camp, see, Borzou Daragahi, "No Sign of Poison in Ansar Camp: Kurdish Group Linked to al-Qaida Pleads Innocence to Reporters," *Pittsburgh Post-Gazette,* February 16, 2003. On U.S. decision not to attack camp, see, Jim Miklaszewski, "Avoiding Attacking Suspected Terrorist Mastermind: Abu Musab Zarqawi Blamed for More than 700 Killings in Iraq," NBC News, March 2, 2004 at http://www.msnbc.msn.com/id/4431601/.

43. John J. Mearsheimer and Stephen M. Walt, *The Israel Lobby and U.S. Foreign Policy* (New York : Farrar, Straus and Giroux, 2007), pp. 239–50

44. Douglas Jehl, "Qaeda-Iraq Link U.S. Cited Is Tied to Coercion Claim," *New York Times,* December 9, 2005.

45. Gary McWilliams, "Dick Cheney Ain't Studyin' War No More," *Business Week,* March 2, 1998.

46. Patrick Crow, "U.S. Petroleum Firms Hit Hard by Washington's Unilateral Sanctions," *Oil & Gas Journal,* May 5, 1997.

47. "Former US Defence Secretary Says Iran-Libya Sanctions Act 'Wrong,'" *Malaysia General News,* April 20, 1998, via LexisNexis.

48. John Macleay, "BHP Pipeline Should Not Face US Sanctions, Says Cheney," *Australian,* April 20, 1998.

49. Thomas W. Lippman, "Hill Races White House to Get Tough with Iran; Pro-Israel Lobby Pushes Strict Commerce Ban," *Washington Post,* April 2, 1995;

George Moffett, "Push to Widen Libya Sanctions Riles US Allies," *Christian Science Monitor,* January 24, 1996.

50. Shirl McArthur, "Congress Keeps Pressure on Iran," *Washington Report on Middle East Affairs* 16, no. 5 (February 28, 1998), p. 24.

51. Richard Cheney, "The Gulf War: A First Assessment," Soref Symposium, Washington Institute for Near East Policy, April 29, 1991, at http://web.archive.org/web/2004113 0090045/http://www.washingtoninstitute.org/pubs/soref/cheney.htm.

52. Ron Suskind, *The Price of Loyalty: George W. Bush, the White House and the Education of Paul O'Neill* (New York: Simon and Schuster, 2004), p. 96.

53. Juan Cole, "All the Vice President's Men," Salon.com, October 28, 2005, at http://archive.salon.com/news/feature/2005/10/28/vice_president/index.html.

54. For Cheney's links to the other hawks, see James Mann, *Rise of the Vulcans: The History of Bush's War Cabinet* (New York: Viking, 2004).

55. Mearsheimer and Walt, *The Israel Lobby and U.S. Foreign Policy,* chap. 8.

56. Suskind, *The Price of Loyalty,* pp. 74–75, 85–89.

57. Ron Suskind, "Interview Transcript," The Way of the World Blog, August 7, 2008, at http://www.ronsuskind.com/thewayoftheworld/transcripts/; see also Candace Heckman, "Alleged CIA Forgery: Ron Suskind's Notes," Seattlepi.com, August 8, 2008, at http://blog.seattlepi.nwsource.com/thebigblog/archives/145626.asp?from=blog_last3.

58. Patrick Cockburn, "Oil Giants Return to Iraq: Shell, BP, ExxonMobil and Total Set to Sign Deal with Baghdad," *Independent,* June 20, 2008.

59. Juan Cole, "The Ayatollahs and Democracy in Iraq" (ISIM Papers Series) (Amsterdam: Amsterdam University Press, 2006).

60. Marta Reynal-Querol, "Ethnicity, Political Systems, and Civil Wars," *Journal of Conflict Resolution* 46, no. 1 (February 2002), pp. 29–54; Eyal Baharad and Shmuel Nitzan, "Ameliorating Majority Decisiveness through Expression of Preference Intensity, *American Political Science Review* 96, no. 4 (December 2002), pp. 745–54.

61. Paul Collier, "Rebellion as a Quasi-Criminal Activity," *Journal of Conflict Resolution* 44, no. 6 (December 2000), pp. 839–53; Nicholas Sambanis, "Do Ethnic and Nonethnic Civil Wars Have the Same Causes? A Theoretical and Empirical Inquiry (Part 1)," *Journal of Conflict Resolution* 45, no. 3 (June 2001), pp. 259–82.

62. John McGarry, "Asymmetrical Pluralism and the Federal State," International Conference on Federalism, Brussels, March 3–5, 2005, working draft paper at http://er.uqam.ca/nobel/creceqc/IMG/pdf/Asymmetrical_Federalism_and_the_Pluri-national_State-draft.pdf.

63. Ma'd Fayyad, "Barzani: al-Hukumah al-Markaziyyah la tunaffidh wu'udaha," *Al-Sharq al-Awsat,* August 30, 2008; "Mas'ul fi quwwat al-bishmirkah: Ayy ta'arrud 'askari li quwwatina fi Diyala sayuqabal bi al-mithl," *Al-Sharq al-Awsat,* August 31, 2008

CHAPTER 5

1. "Obama's Comments Hinder Antiterror Efforts: Owais," *Dawn,* August 4, 2007.

2. For the colonial background and partition, see David Gilmartin, *Empire and Islam: Punjab and the Making of Pakistan* (Berkeley: University of California Press, 1988); Ian Talbot, *India and Pakistan* (Oxford: Oxford University Press, 2000); Peter van der Veer, *Religious Nationalism: Hindus and Muslims in India* (Berkeley: University of California Press, 1994).

3. For recent surveys see Mary Anne Weaver, *Pakistan: In the Shadow of Jihad and Afghanistan* (New York: Farrar, Straus and Giroux, 2002), and Stephen Philip Cohen, *The Idea of Pakistan* (Washington, D.C.: Brookings Institution Press, 2004).

4. Ayesha Jalal, *The Sole Spokesman: Jinnah, the Muslim League, and the Demand for Pakistan* (Cambridge: Cambridge University Press, 1985); Stanley Wolpert, *Jinnah of Pakistan* (Oxford: Oxford University Press, 1984).

5. Seyyed Vali Reza Nasr, *Mawdudi and the Making of Islamic Revivalism* (Oxford: Oxford University Press, 1996).

6. "Results of a New Nationwide Public Opinion Survey of Pakistan Before the June 2008 Pakistani By-Elections," Terror Free Tomorrow Center for Public Opinion and New America Foundation, June 2008, at http://www.terrorfreetomorrow. org/upimagestft/PakistanPollReportJune08.pdf.

7. Kimberly Kweder, "Fears Over Afghan Border; Terror War Skirmishes Worry D.C. Conferees," *Washington Times,* June 25, 2008.

8. "'Avamm aur hukumat qaba'ili 'ilaqon par ghair mulki hamle bardasht nahin karenge," *Jang* (Lahore), September 10, 2008.

9. In the summer of 2008 Pakistanis gave Musharraf a 73 percent unfavorability rating, up from 53 percent in the summer of 2007.

10. With the recent advent of a civilian government, however, the prime minister in summer 2008 announced a $47.7 billion defense budget, representing a little over 14 percent of government expenditures (down from 17 percent the previous year), and pledged more transparency on this subject. Ayesha Siddiqa, *Military Inc.: Inside Pakistan's Military Economy* (London: Pluto Press, 2007); Nirupama Subramanian, "Pakistan: Debate on Defence Spending," *The Hindu,* June 17, 2008, at http://www .hindu.com/2008/06/17/stories/2008061755610900.htm; for the historical background of the militarization of Pakistani society, see Ayesha Jalal, *The State of Martial Rule: The Origins of Pakistan's Political Economy of Defence* (Cambridge: Cambridge University Press, 1990), and Stephen P. Cohen, *The Pakistan Army: With a New Foreword and Epilogue* (Karachi : Oxford University Press, 1998).

11. "Results of a New Nationwide Public Opinion Survey of Pakistan Before the June 2008 Pakistani By-Elections."

12. "Asif Ali Zardari: Profile," BBC, September 6, 2008, at http://news.bbc.co.uk/1/ hi/world/south_asia/4032997.stm.

13. Zahid Hussain, "Leader Emerging in Pakistan," *Wall Street Journal,* September 2, 2008.

14. David Rohde, "Pakistani Middle Class, Beneficiary of Musharraf, Begins to Question Rule," *New York Times,* November 25, 2007.

15. David Rohde and Salman Masood, "Cynicism Takes Root in Pakistan; In Rural Punjab, Low Faith in Leaders," *International Herald Tribune,* December 5, 2007.

16. Paul Titus, "Honor the Baloch, Buy the Pushtun: Stereotypes, Social Organization and History in Western Pakistan," *Modern Asian Studies* 32, no. 3 (July 1998), pp. 657–87; Charles Lindholm, "Quandaries of Command in Egalitarian Societies: Examples from Swat and Morocco," in Juan R. I. Cole, ed., *Comparing Muslim Societies* (Ann Arbor: University of Michigan Press, 1992), pp. 63–96.

17. Titus, "Honor the Baloch, Buy the Pushtun," p. 662.

18. Hermann Kreutzmann, "Globalization, Spatial Integration, and Sustainable Development in Northern Pakistan," *Mountain Research and Development* 15, no. 3 (August 1995), pp. 213–27.

19. Barbara Daly Metcalf, *Islamic Revival in British India: Deoband, 1860–1900* (Princeton, N.J.: Princeton University Press, 1982).

20. Dexter Filkins, "Right at the Edge," *New York Times Magazine,* September 7, 2008.

21. C. Christine Fair, Clay Ramsay, and Steven Kull, "Pakistani Public Opinion on Democracy, Islamist Militancy, and Relations with the US," WorldPublicOpinion.org and the United States Institute of Peace, January 7, 2008, at http://www.worldpublicopinion.org/pipa/pdf/jan08/Pakistan_Jan08_rpt.pdf.

22. Mark Mazetti, Helene Cooper, and Carlotta Gall, "U.S. Is Prodding Pakistani Leader to Share Power," *New York Times,* August 15, 2007.

23. "Pakistan: Editorial Urges People to Protest Against 'Aggressive' Remarks of Bush: Editorial: 'Crusader Bush's Strange Logic,'" *Nawa-e Waqt,* December 3, 2007, trans. Open Source Center, via World News Connection.

24. Lydia Saad, "Americans' Most and Least Favored Nations: Canada and Great Britain Remain the Most Popular Allies," Gallup, March 3, 2008, at http://www.gallup.com/poll/104734/Americans-Most-Least-Favored-Nations.aspx.

25. Ibid.

26. The Muslim League split after the 1999 Musharraf coup. Those party members still loyal to Nawaz Sharif called themselves the "Muslim League (N)," with the "N" standing for Nawaz. The branch that supported Musharraf named itself for the honorific of Muhammad Ali Jinnah, the country's founder, called Qa'id-i A'zam or "the Great Leader" in Urdu. It is therefore known as the "Muslim League (Q)."

27. "Bollywood Divas Light Up Billboards Again in NWFP," *Voice of India,* May 1, 2008, at http://voiceofindia.in/index.php?option=com_content&task=view&id=964&Itemid=79.

28. Lydia Saad, "Americans' Most and Least Favored Nations: Canada and Great Britain Remain the Most Popular Allies," Gallup, March 3, 2008, at http://www.gallup.com/poll/104734/Americans-Most-Least-Favored-Nations.aspx.

29. "German Envoy Reported to Be Pessimistic on Afghan Security Situation," Hans-Ulrich Seidt interview in *Die Welt,* BBC Monitoring International Reports, September 29, 2006, via LexisNexis.

30. Barnett R. Rubin, "Saving Afghanistan," *Foreign Affairs,* January/February 2007, at http://www.foreignaffairs.org/20070101faessay86105-p30/barnett-r-rubin/saving-afghanistan.html; idem., private communication, September 3, 2008.

31. For overviews of this earlier period, see David Edwards, *Before Taliban: Genealogies of the Afghan Jihad* (Berkeley: University of California Press, 2002); Barnett Rubin, *The Fragmentation of Afghanistan: State Formation and Collapse in the International System* (New Haven, Conn.: Yale University Press, rev. edn. 2002); Larry P. Goodson, *Afghanistan's Endless War: State Failure, Regional Politics, and the Rise of the Taliban* (Seattle: University of Washington Press, 2001); Juan Cole, "Taliban, Women and the Hegelian Private Sphere," in Robert D. Crewes and Amin Tarzi, eds., *The Taliban and the Crisis of Afghanistan* (Cambridge, Mass.: Harvard University Press, 2008), pp. 118–54; Ahmed Rashid, *Taliban: Militant Islam, Oil, and Fundamentalism in Central Asia* (New Haven, Conn.: Yale University Press, 2001).

32. Barnett R. Rubin and Jake Sherman, "Counter-Narcotics to Stabilize Afghanistan: The False Promise of Crop Eradication" (New York: Center on International Cooperation, New York University, 2008); Senlis Council (Security and Development Policy Group), "US Policy in Afghanistan: Senlis Council Recommendation," February 2008, via http://www.senliscouncil.net/modules/media_centre/press_releases/UShalt.

33. Department of Defense, "Report on Progress toward Security and Stability in Afghanistan," June 2008, at http://www.defenselink.mil/pubs/Report_on_Progress_toward_Security_and_Stability_in_Afghanistan_1230.pdf; Julian Borger, "Failed Afghan Drug Policy Harming Us, Says Iran," *The Guardian,* September 11, 2008; "Iran Says Commitment to Rebuild Afghanistan Key to Return of Refugees," *Tehran Times,* September 7, 2008.

34. For energy competition and bases in Central Asia, see Steve Hargreaves, "Tensions Rise in Energy-Rich Central Asia," CNNMoney.com, April 8, 2008, at http://money.cnn.com/2008/04/07/news/international/asia_gas/?postversion=2008040810. For Uzbekistan base rights, see Robin Wright and Ann Scott Tyson, "U.S. Evicted From Air Base in Uzbekistan," *Washington Post,* July 30, 2005.

35. Norma Greenaway, "Terrorists Will Target Afghan Pipeline, Expert Says," Canwest News Service, June 19, 2008, at http://www.canada.com/topics/news/world/story.html?id=d318d840-e078–4c8f-a1d4-ed65f48be901.

36. "Results of a New Nationwide Public Opinion Survey of Pakistan Before the June 2008 Pakistani By-Elections."

37. Ibid.

38. "Germany Discovers a War in Afghanistan," *Der Spiegel,* September 8, 2008.

39. Rubin and Sherman, "Counter-Narcotics to Stabilize Afghanistan."

40. Ibid.

CHAPTER 6

1. Juan Cole, *Sacred Space and Holy War: The Politics, Culture and History of Shiite Islam* (London: I. B. Tauris, 2002), chap. 10.

2. Juan Cole, "The Danger of Bush's Anti-Iran Fatwa," Salon.com, January 30, 2007, at http://www.salon.com/opinion/feature/2007/01/30/iran_ashura.

3. "Iran," Pollingreport.com, 2006–2007, at http://www.pollingreport.com/iran.htm.

4. Arshin Adib-Moghaddam, *Iran in World Politics: The Question of the Islamic Republic* (New York: Columbia University Press, 2008), pp. 160–61.

5. "Public Opinion in Iran," WorldPublicOpinion.org/Search for Common Ground, April 7, 2008, at http://www.worldpublicopinion.org/pipa/pdf/apr08/Iran_Apr08_rpt.pdf.

6. Statement by Director-General of the OPCW, Organisation for the Prohibition of Chemical Weapons, Office of the Director General, December 8, 2000, at http://www.opcw.org/synthesis/html/s3/DG-IRAN.htm; Markus Binder, "Iran's First-Generation Chemical Weapons Evaporate, as Certainty Declines in U.S. Intelligence Reports," *WMD Insights,* February 2008, at http://www.wmdinsights.com/I22/I22_ME2_Iran1stGenCW.htm; "Chemical Weapons (Iran)," GlobalSecurity.org, 2008, at http://www.globalsecurity.org/wmd/world/iran/cw.htm.

7. Daniel Byman, "Iran, Terrorism, and Weapons of Mass Destruction," *Studies in Conflict and Terrorism* 31 (2008): 169–81, at http://www.brookings.edu/~/media/Files/rc/articles/2008/03_iran_byman/03_iran_byman.pdf.

8. For Abdullah's statement, see "King Abdullah Says US Policy toward Iran Is Nondiplomatic," IRNA [Islamic Republic News Agency], June 11, 2008. On Arab population, see Shibley Telhami, Principal Investigator, "2008 Annual Arab Public Opinion Poll Survey," Anwar Sadat Chair for Peace and Development at the University of Maryland (with Zogby International), at sadat.umd.edu/surveys/2008%20Arab%20Public%20Opinion%20Survey.ppt.

9. Ibid., pp. 243–52.

10. David Remnick, "War Without End?" *New Yorker*, April 21, 2003.

11. Adam Zagorin, "Khatami: American 'Conceit and Pride' Led to Iraq Mess," *Time*, September 8, 2006.

12. "'Holocaust' TV Serial Captivates Iran," Agence France Presse, October 9, 2007.

13. "Mahmud Ahamadinizhad: Isra'il bayad az safhih'-i ruzgar mahv shavad," *Iran Imruz*, October 26, 2005, at http://www.iran-emrooz.net/index.php?/news/more/4898/. This is actually a slight misquotation of Khomeini. Ahmadinejad misremembered the word "arena" as "page" (they are similar in Persian).

14. "Iranian Television Broadcasts President Ahmadinezhad's Interview with French TV," Vision of the Islamic Republic of Iran Network 1, March 25, 2007, trans. FBIS and carried by World News Connection.

15. Zagorin, "Khatami."

16. "Iran's President Ahmadinezhad Holds New York News Conference 21 September," Islamic Republic of Iran News Network Television (IRINN), September 22, 2006, trans. FBIS and carried by World News Connection.

17. "Iranian Television Broadcasts President Ahmadinezhad's Interview with French TV."

18. Many of the latter were forced to flee countries such as Iraq, Yemen, and Tunisia after 1948 because of anti-Jewish riots provoked by the Zionists' expulsion of the Palestinians. Like the Palestinians before them, they suffered ethnic cleansing and an almost complete loss of property. About 200,000 Iranian Jews also went to Israel, mainly for economic reasons.

19. Lucy Ash, "Israel Faces Russian Brain Drain," BBC, November 25, 2004, at http://news.bbc.co.uk/1/hi/programmes/crossing_continents/4038859.stm.

20. Ian S. Lustick, "Abandoning the Iron Wall: Israel and 'the Middle Eastern Muck,'" *Middle East Policy* 15, no. 3 (Fall, 2008), pp. 30–56; Ian S. Lustick, "Recent Trends in Emigration from Israel: The Impact of Palestinian Violence," Association for Israel Studies, Jerusalem, June 14–16, 2004, rev. ed., at http://www.aisisraelstudies.org/2004papers/Lustick_AIS_2004paper_updt.pdf.

21. A Christian Arab originally from Jaffa told me in June 2008 that he had seen Russian congregants at his own church in Tel Aviv.

22. "Video: 60 Minutes Edited Ahmadinejad Interview," *Mathaba*, September 21, 2008, at http://www.mathaba.net/0_index.shtml?x=606794; "Transcript: Interview with Iranian President Mahmoud Ahmadinejad," *Larry King Live*, CNN, September 23, 2008, at http://transcripts.cnn.com/TRANSCRIPTS/0809/23/lkl.01.html.

23. Bernard Lewis, "Does Iran Have Something in Store?" *Wall Street Journal*, August 8, 2006.

24. Kamal Nazer Yasin, "Iran: Theological Controversy in Islamic Republic Could Have Profound Political Ramifications," *Eurasia Insight*, May 30, 2008, at http://www.eurasianet.org/departments/insight/articles/eav053008.shtml.

25. Kamal Nazer Yasin, "Iran: Conservatives Trying to Get President Ahmadinejad to Moderate Behavior," *Eurasia Insight*, June 10, 2008, at http://www.eurasianet.org/departments/insight/articles/eav061008.shtml.

26. Office of the Director of National Intelligence, "Iran: Nuclear Intentions and Capabilities," December 3, 2007, at http://www.dni.gov/press_releases/20071203_release.pdf; Mark Mazzetti, "U.S. Says Iran Ended Atomic Arms Work," *New York Times*, December 3, 2007.

27. Dafna Linzer, "Iran Is Judged 10 Years from Nuclear Bomb: U.S. Intelligence Review Contrasts with Administration Statements," *Washington Post*, August 2, 2005.

28. "Obama Vows to Stop Iran from Having Nuclear Arms," Reuters, June 4, 2008.
29. Yitzhak Benhorin, "McCain to AIPAC: I'm Committed to Making Certain Israel Maintains Military Edge," *Israel News*, June 2, 2008.
30. "Iranian TV: Ayatollah Khamene'i Speaks on Khomeyni's Death Anniversary," Tehran Vision of the Islamic Republic of Iran Network 1, in Persian, June 4, 2006, trans. Open Source Center, and carried by the World News Connection database available at most research libraries.
31. "Public Opinion in Iran," WorldPublicOpinion.org, search for Common Ground, April 7, 2008, at http://www.worldpublicopinion.org/pipa/pdf/apr08/Iran_Apr08_rpt.pdf.
32. "Talash-i Danishmandan . . . bih Ab-i Sangin Dast Yaft," *Kayhan*, August 27, 2006, at http://www.kayhannews.ir/850605/2.htm#other201.
33. "Ahmadinejad: Iran's Nuclear Activities Are 'Completely Peaceful and Transparent,'" United Nations Radio, September 25, 2007, at http://www.un.org/radio/story.asp?NewsID=7823.
34. Jonathan S. Landay, "Bush Erroneously Says Iran Announced Desire for Nuclear Weapons," *McClatchy Newspapers*, March 20, 2008.
35. Dafna Linzer, "Past Arguments Don't Square with Current Iran Policy," *Washington Post*, March 27, 2005.
36. Reese Erlich, "U.S. Tells Iran: Become a Nuclear Power," *Foreign Policy in Focus*, November 28, 2007, at http://www.fpif.org/fpiftxt/4768.
37. Abbas Amanat, "The Persian Complex," *New York Times*, May 25, 2006; Nikki R. Keddie, *Modern Iran: Roots and Results of Revolution*, rev. ed. (New Haven, Conn.: Yale University Press, 2006); Ervand Abrahamian, *Iran between Two Revolutions* (Princeton, N.J. : Princeton University Press, 1982): Ali M. Ansari, *Confronting Iran: The Failure of American Foreign Policy and the Next Great Crisis in the Middle East* (New York: Basic Books, 2006).
38. Office of the Spokesman, United States Department of State, "Update on Iran Democracy Promotion Funding," Washington, DC, June 4, 2007, at http://www.state.gov/r/pa/prs/ps/2007/jun/85971.htm.
39. Armin H. Meyer, "Telegram from the Embassy in Iran to the Department of State," Tehran, October 25, 1966, 1445Z, *Foreign Relations of the United States, 1964–1968*, Volume 34, Energy, Diplomacy, and Global Issues (Washington, D.C.: Department of State), at http://www.state.gov/www/about_state/history/vol_xxxiv/t.html.
40. Memorandum of Conversation, Washington, November 3, 1966, *Foreign Relations of the United States*, ibid.
41. Ansari, *Confronting Iran*, chap. 7; Scott Ritter, *Target Iran: The Truth about the White House's Plans for Regime Change* (New York: Nation Books, 2006), chap. 2.
42. Ewen MacAskill and Robert Tait, "GCHQ Intercepts Helped Alter US Assessment on Iran Threat," *Guardian*, December 6, 2007.
43. "CIA Launched Defection Program for Iran: Report," Agence France Presse, December 10, 2007.
44. "*in rezhim-e eshghalgar-e Qods bayad az sahneh-e ruzgar mahv shavad.*"
45. Charles Kurzman, *The Unthinkable Revolution in Iran* (Cambridge, Mass.: Harvard University Press, 2004).
46. Trita Parsi, *Treacherous Alliance: The Secret Dealings of Israel, Iran, and the US* (New Haven, Conn.: Yale University Press, 2007), pp. 106–26. Iran was so dependent on American military systems that, when it could not get spare parts

after 1979, much of its advanced equipment became useless. The ayatollahs in Tehran were forced to turn to the Israelis and the Vietnamese, neither of them natural ideological allies.

47. For this group, see Augustus Richard Norton, *Hezbollah: A Short History* (Princeton, N.J.: Princeton University Press, 2007).

48. Rana Moussaoui, "Exiles Dream of Returning to Israeli-Occupied Shebaa Farms," *Middle East Times,* June 21, 2008.

49. "Lebanon's Government Adopts Manifesto," Agence France Presse, August 5,2008, at http://www.france24.com/en/20080805-lebanon-government-adopts-manifesto-hezbollah-arms-sleiman.

50. Richard Wike and Juliana Menasce Horowitz, "Lebanon's Muslims: Relatively Secular and Pro-Christian," Global Attitudes Project, Pew Research Center Publications, July 26, 2006, at http://pewresearch.org/pubs/41/lebanons-muslims-relatively-secular-and-pro-christian.

51. Jeffrey Stinson, "Lebanon Relief Effort Raises Houses, Questions," *USA Today,* December 17, 2006.

52. "Khaminih-'i yashabu min Nasri 'llah mas'uliyyatih ka qa'id a'la," *Al-Sharq al-Awsat,* December 13, 2007.

53. "Akthar min milyar dular min al-Su'udiya wa Qatar wa Iran wa Kuwait li Lubnan," *Al-Nahar,* December 2, 2007, mirrored at http://khiyam.com/pages/articles_details.php?articleID=2185.

54. Mohammed Zaatari, "Iranian Group Pledges to Rebuild Eight Bridges in South," *Daily Star* (Beirut), February 22, 2007.

55. Maziar Behrooz, "Leadership and Legitimacy: The Controversy Among the Clergy over Who Should Lead the Islamic State," *Iranian,* January 2, 1997, at http://www.iranian.com/Opinion/Jan98/Behrooz/index.html.

56. Roschanack Shaery-Eisenlohr, "Iran, the Vatican of Shi'ism?" *Middle East Report,* no. 233 (Winter 2004), pp. 40–43, this point on p. 40.

57. "Khaminih-'i yashabu min Nasri 'llah mas'uliyyatih ka qa'id a'la."

58. Richard Sale, "Hamas History Tied to Israel," UPI, June 18, 2002.

59. Sadeq Saba, "Improve Human Rights, EU Urges Iran," BBC, February 4, 2003, at http://news.bbc.co.uk/2/hi/middle_east/2726009.stm.

60. "Olmert: Notion of Greater Israel No Longer Exists," Ynetnews.com, September 14, 2008, at http://www.ynetnews.com/Ext/Comp/ArticleLayout/CdaArticle-PrintPreview/1,2506,L–3596428,00.html.

CONCLUSION

1. "US 'War on Terror' Has Not Weakened al Qaeda, Says Global Poll," World Public Opinion.org, September 28, 2008, at http://www.worldpublicopinion.org/pipa/articles/home_page/547.php?nid=&id=&pnt=547&lb=.

2. "Muslims Believe US Seeks to Undermine Islam," News Center, Common Dreams .org, April 24, 2007, at http://www.commondreams.org/news2007/0424–01.htm.

3. Benjamin Franklin, *The Autobiography of Benjamin Franklin,* Second Edition (New Haven, Conn: Yale University Press, 2003), page 176.

4. "Treaty of Peace and Friendship, Signed at Tripoli November 4, 1796," The Avalon Project: Documents in Law, History and Diplomacy, Lillian Goldman Law Library, Yale Law School, at http://avalon.law.yale.edu/18th_century/bar1796t.asp.

5. See, e.g., my Global Americana Institute, http://www.globam.org/.

6. Ben Lynfield, "The Rise of Avigdor Lieberman," *Nation,* December 14, 2006.

INDEX

al-Imam, Adel, 70
al-Imam, Ghassan, 123–24
India:
    boycott of by Pakistan, 180
    British, 87, 160, 161, 171, 211
    Congress Party of, 161
    democracy of, 80
    economy of, 26–27
    embassy in Kabul, attacks on, 182
    growth of, 26–27
    Hindu majority in, 161
    independence of, 16, 87, 160
    influence on Afghanistan, 185
    Iran and, 26–28
    Islam in, 161–62
    Kashmir and, 162, 166, 203
    oil dependence of, 26–27, 33, 150
    Pakistan and, 160, 162–63, 174, 180, 185,
        187, 203
    Pakistanis' views of, 163
    population of, 26
    poverty of, 27
    railroads in, 212
    regional importance of, 26–27
    Sharif and, 177
    TAPI pipeline and, 28, 187
    ZeeTV of, 168
Indian Oil Company, 26
Indian Oil Corporation, 27
Industrial Revolution, 30
Indyk, Martin, 20, 138
International Atomic Energy Agency (IAEA),
    209, 215–17, 232
Iran:
    Afghanistan and, 186
    alleged ties to terrorism of, 5
    Americans' views of, 47
    Arabs' views of, 119
    Baath's fall and, 149–50, 194
    Baghdad Pact, 88
    Bush on, 210
    demonization of, 231
    diplomacy and, 244
    dual containment and, 20, 136, 138, 149, 151
    European Union and, 233
    Ford administration and, 211
    gas reserves of, 9, 139
    Hamas and, 105, 219, 229, 231, 234
    Hazaras and, 184
    history of, 211–15
    Hizbullah and, 112, 195, 219, 222, 224–26,
        233–34
    influence on Iraq, 154, 194–96
    Iraqi refugees in, 123
    Islam Anxiety and, 193, 196, 197, 208, 217,
        236
    Israel and, 201–207, 218, 233–35
    Lebanon and, 225–27
    Karzai on, 164
    Nixon administration and, 19
    McCain on, 116

    military of, 198
    National Intelligence Estimate on, 207
    nuclear research and programs of, 150, 195,
        197, 205, 208–11, 215–17, 232–33, 235
    oil reserves of, 23, 210
    Pahlevi, 11, 176, 194, 210, 213–15
    Pakistanis' views of, 164
    petroleum industry of, 11, 19, 23, 25–27,
        139–40, 210, 214–15, 227
    political system of, 235–36
    railroads in, 212
    Reagan administration and, 19, 218–19
    revolution in, 66, 100, 194, 201, 215
    Revolutionary Guards Corps, 145, 196, 206
    Saddam Hussein's invasion of, 19
    sanctions on, 137–38, 216, 233, 235
    Saudi Arabia and, 104, 112, 199
    Shiism and, 5, 96, 106, 116, 186, 193, 199,
        213, 216, 218, 220, 224–26, 228–29
    Turkey and, 153
    United States and, 244
    U.S. attempts to isolate, 27–28, 186
    U.S. intelligence on, 198–99
    U.S invasion of Iraq effect and, 34
    women in, 233
    See also Ahmadinejad, Mahmoud; Anglo-
        Iranian Oil Company; Khamenei,
        Mohammad; Khatami, Mohammad;
        Khomeini, Ayatollah; Mosaddegh,
        Mohammad
Iran-Contra scandal, 218
Iran-Iraq War, 130, 150, 194, 198, 210, 218
Iranian Communist Party, 213–14
Iranian Revolutionary Guards Corps (IRGC),
    145, 196, 206
Iranians' views, 197–98, 209, 215, 231, 236
Iraq:
    "al-Qaeda in," 117–18, 132–35, 150
    as "asymmetrical federal" state, 147
    Awakening Councils and, 91, 131, 238
    Baath regime in, 15, 18, 36, 116, 129–35,
        137, 140–42, 145, 149, 194
    Bush on, 117, 196
    Cheney on, 132–33, 137–38
    Da'wa Party in, 220
    dual containment of, 20, 136, 138, 149, 151
    Gulf War and, 9, 20, 69, 75, 84, 101, 104,
        108, 130, 136, 138
    history of, 11–21
    Iranian influence in, 154, 194–96
    Islam Anxiety and, 115–16, 126, 141–42,
        146, 155
    Kurdish question and, 143, 146–49, 152,
        154–55, 203
    McCain on, 115–16
    need for stability in, 151–55, 240, 242–43
    news coverage of, 121–22
    Obama on, 159
    oil reserves of, 23
    petroleum industry of, 11–23, 34, 135–36,
        139–41